Urban Events, Place Branding and Promotion

Urban Events, Place Branding and Promotion explores the phenomenon of place event marketing, examining the ways in which events are used to brand and disseminate information about a place. It provides a novel contribution to the literature, capturing the growing interest in place promotion, and offers in-depth insights on the role of events.

With a focus on urban locations, this book defines the scope and concept of place event marketing. It demonstrates that different kinds of events, for leisure and business, can be used to successfully develop, promote and brand different types of places. Individual chapters written by a variety of leading academics explore how various public and non-governmental institutions that deal with promotion and marketing communications of places can implement event marketing activities and how such institutions organize, co-organize and sponsor different events. The effects of event marketing activities on urban place promotion and branding are thoroughly explored through a variety of international empirical case studies.

This will be of great interest to upper-level students and researchers in events marketing and management, tourism and the broader field of urban geography. The concluding chapter also proposes future research directions.

Waldemar Cudny specializes in urban and tourism geography. He is a graduate of the department of geography at the University of Łódź (Poland), where he received his MA in geography, specialising in spatial economy and spatial urban planning (1999) and his PhD in socio-economic geography (2004). Currently he holds the position of associate professor at the Jan Kochanowski University in Kielce, Poland. Dr Cudny has conducted research on festivals and their impacts on cities, socio-economic transformation of post-socialist cities, urban tourism and car tourism. He has published several books on the role of festivals in the development of cities and 'car tourism.' In recent years, Dr Cudny has been conducting research on city marketing, city promotion and branding. In 2019 his latest book entitled *City Branding and Promotion: The Strategic Approach* (Routledge) was published.

Routledge Contemporary Perspectives on Urban Growth, Innovation and Change

Series edited by Sharmistha Bagchi-Sen, Professor
Department of Geography and Department of Global Gender and Sexuality Studies, State University of New York-Buffalo, Buffalo, NY, USA

Waldemar Cudny, Associate Professor
Working at the The Jan Kochanowski University (JKU) in Kielce, Poland.

Urban transformation affects various aspects of the physical, social, and economic spaces. This series contains monographs and edited collections that provide theoretically informed and interdisciplinary insights on the factors, patterns, processes and outcomes that facilitate or hinder urban development and transformation. Books within the series offer international and comparative perspectives from cities around the world, exploring how 'new life' may be brought to cities, and what the cities of future may look like.

Topics within the series may include: urban immigration and management, gender, sustainability and eco-cities, smart cities, technological developments and the impact on industry and on urban societies, cultural production and consumption in cities (including tourism, events and festivals), the marketing and branding of cities, and the role of various actors and policy makers in the planning and management of changing urban spaces.

If you are interested in submitting a proposal to the series please contact Faye Leerink, Commissioning Editor, faye.leerink@tandf.co.uk.

City Branding and Promotion
The Strategic Approach
Waldemar Cudny

Urban Events, Place Branding and Promotion
Place Event Marketing
Edited by Waldemar Cudny

Urban Events, Place Branding and Promotion

Place Event Marketing

Edited by Waldemar Cudny

LONDON AND NEW YORK

First published 2020
by Routledge
2 Park Square, Milton Park, Abingdon, Oxon OX14 4RN

and by Routledge
52 Vanderbilt Avenue, New York, NY 10017

Routledge is an imprint of the Taylor & Francis Group, an informa business

British Library Cataloguing-in-Publication Data
A catalogue record for this book is available from the British Library

Library of Congress Cataloging-in-Publication Data
Names: Cudny, Waldemar, editor.
Title: Urban events, place branding and promotion : place event marketing / edited by Waldemar Cudny.
Description: Milton Park, Abingdon, Oxon ; New York, NY : Routledge, 2019. | Series: Routledge contemporary perspectives on urban growth | Includes bibliographical references and index.
Identifiers: LCCN 2019028102 (print) | LCCN 2019028103 (ebook)
Subjects: LCSH: City promotion. | Place marketing. | Special events—Marketing.
Classification: LCC HT325 .U74 2019 (print) | LCC HT325 (ebook) | DDC 659.2/930776—dc23
LC record available at https://lccn.loc.gov/2019028102
LC ebook record available at https://lccn.loc.gov/2019028103

ISBN: 978-1-138-35439-5 (hbk)
ISBN: 978-0-429-42484-7 (ebk)

Typeset in Times New Roman
by Apex CoVantage, LLC

MIX
Paper from
responsible sources
FSC
www.fsc.org   FSC® C013985

Printed in the United Kingdom
by Henry Ling Limited

Contents

Figures

Tables

Contributors

Håkan Appelblad, PhD, is a senior lecturer in human geography at the department of geography, Umeå University, Sweden. Appelblad's research interest focuses on tourism, sports tourism and regional development. He teaches regularly on various subfields within geography like tourism, population geography, urban and regional planning and regional development.

Zafeirenia Brokalaki, Dr, is a lecturer in marketing at the University of Leicester, School of Business. She has received a PhD in culture, media and creative industries from King's College London. In the past, she has taught at King's College London in the UK, the University of Arkansas in the USA and the University of Peloponnese in Greece. Zafeirenia is a cultural scholar working at the intersections of consumer research, cultural studies and performance studies. Her broad research areas coalesce around the experiential, symbolic and political dimensions of cultural consumption and the historical transformative dynamics of the arts market. Zafeirenia works on topics that concern the politics of aesthetics with a particular focus on participatory art and non-institutional creativity, the genealogy of the body and embodied/arts-based epistemologies. She has been involved in a range of funded research projects and has served as a consultant for numerous cultural organizations in the United Kingdom, Greece and Cyprus. She is a fellow at the Royal Society of Arts (RSA).

Anne-Marie Broudehoux, PhD, is an associate professor at the School of Design of the University of Quebec at Montreal, Canada, where she has been teaching since 2002. She received her doctoral degree in architecture from the University of California at Berkeley in 2002. She is the author of *Mega-Events and Urban Image Construction: Beijing and Rio de Janeiro*, published by Routledge in 2017. She has given several conference papers and published multiple articles on the socio-spatial impacts of large-scale urban transformations. Her book *The Making and Selling of Post-Mao Beijing*, also at Routledge, was awarded the International Planning History Society book prize in 2006.

Natàlia Cantó-Milà, PhD, is an associate professor and researcher at the Open University of Catalunya in Barcelona, Spain, and has more than ten years' experience in social theory, relational sociology and the sociology of culture.

She holds a PhD in social sciences (2002) from the University of Bielefeld, Germany. Her main research areas are social theory and sociology of culture, of emotions, the future and memory. She has led several research projects related to the sociology of culture, emotions, and the construction of imaginaries of the future financed by the Spanish Ministry of Economy and Competitivity and is editor-in-chief of the journal *Digithum: A relational perspective on culture and society.*

Nancy Chesworth, PhD, is an honourary research associate in the faculty of business at the University of New Brunswick, Saint John, New Brunswick, Canada. Previously, she was associate professor at Mount Saint Vincent University, Halifax, Nova Scotia, Canada. She has also been a visiting professor in Taiwan, China, Vietnam and the Philippines. Over the past 25, years her main focus has been nature-based tourism and sustainable development of tourism is rural areas, including projects in the Caribbean, Vietnam and Nova Scotia. Other research interests include image and branding as a means of creating and growing urban and rural tourism and intercultural communications.

Alba Colombo, PhD, is a senior lecturer and researcher at the Open University of Catalunya in Barcelona, Spain, and has more than ten years' experiences in events research and education. She holds a PhD in social sciences (2012) from the University of Girona. Her main research areas are sociology of culture, cultural industries, the relationship between those industries and festivals, events impacts and their social and cultural effects. She is involved in research projects related to events and their effects, management, policy, economy and social perspectives such as the Euro-Festival Project Arts Festivals and European Public Culture, financed by the Seventh Framework Programme, and the ATLAS Events Monitoring Project.

Roberta Comunian, Dr, is a reader in creative economy at the Department for Culture, Media and Creative Industries at King's College London. She has previously held academic position at the University of Kent, the University of Southampton and the University of Leeds. She holds a European doctorate in network economy and knowledge management from the University of Venice Ca' Foscari (with a bursary from the Italian Ministry of Education). She has in the past conducted research on the relationship between public and private investments in the arts, sponsorship and business investment in the arts. Her PhD work looked at the overlapping dynamics of art and cultural regeneration projects and cultural and creative industries development in the context of Newcastle-Gateshead in the northeast of England. She has also undertaken research on knowledge transfer and creative industries within an AHRC Impact Fellowship Award, School of Performance and Cultural Industries, Faculty of Performance, Visual Arts and Communications, University of Leeds (UK). She has recently researched the role of higher education in the creative economy as part of an AHRC research network grant and has recently explored in various papers the career opportunities and patterns of creative graduates in UK. Dr Comunian is currently working on a new research network grant "Understanding and Supporting Creative Economies In Africa: Education, Networks & Policy" supported by the Arts & Humanities Research Council (AHRC). She also continuing her work on creative graduates, thanks to an ARC funded project in Australia.

Hilary du Cros, PhD, is currently an honorary research fellow of the University of New Brunswick, Canada, and a research associate at the University of Technology, Sydney. She has taught and worked in the Asia Pacific region over the last 34 years and conducted projects for the United Nations World Tourism Organization and UNESCO. These projects include a number in China (Yunnan, Guangdong and Guizhou), India, Hong Kong and Macau. She has an interdisciplinary perspective on cultural heritage management, marketing and sustainable tourism development. She has been an international member of ICOMOS since 1988 and an expert member of the ICOMOS Cultural Tourism Committee since 1999. Her latest books are *Cultural Tourism* (2015), co-authored with Bob McKercher, and *The Arts and Events* (2014) with Lee Jolliffe.

Waldemar Cudny, PhD, is an associate professor in the Institute of Geography in the Jan Kochanowski University in Kielce, Poland. He is a human geographer specializing in urban geography, tourism geography and events. He specializes in the processes of urban development and change as well as in tourism issues, including festival tourism and special interest tourisms i.e. car tourism. He is the author of over 60 research publications including books, edited volumes and articles in peer-reviewed journals. His latest research includes analysis of the role of festivals in the development of urban spaces (*Festivalisation of Urban Spaces*, Springer, 2016) and car tourism (*Car Tourism*, Springer, 2018). Recently, he investigated the issues of place marketing, marketing communications and the branding of cities. He is also the author of a complex monograph entitled *City Branding and Promotion: The Strategic Approach* (Routledge, 2019).

Ronnie Donaldson, PhD, is a professor in the geography and environmental studies department at Stellenbosch University, South Africa. He previously worked at the University of the North, Vista University (Mamelodi Campus) and the University of the Western Cape. He specializes in urban and tourism developmental studies. With over 25 years' experience as a researcher, he has published more than 100 academic journal and chapter articles, four edited books and numerous consultancy and policy reports for various government institutions. His most recent publication is a sole-authored book in 2018 on *Small Town Tourism in South Africa* (Springer). He serves on a number of national academic and research committees reviewing research proposals, academic profiles and standards and also serves on the editorial board of the *Cogent Social Sciences Journal* (Routledge). Over the past ten years, he has been involved in 15 consultancy projects (most as project manager) for local, provincial and national public institutions. The findings of these studies are contributing to the shaping of spatial (e.g. small-town growth potential in the Western Cape study), tourism and urban development policies at various levels of government.

Henry Duckitt is a graduate of the department of geography and environmental studies at Stellenbosch University, South Africa. He obtained his BA honours degree in geography in 2016 and a master's of urban and regional planning in 2018.

Lee Jolliffe, PhD, is a professor of hospitality and tourism in the faculty of business at the University of New Brunswick, Saint John, New Brunswick, Canada. With an academic background in museum studies, Lee is interested in arts events and tourism, heritage tourism and various aspects of niche tourism, including tea tourism and culinary tourism. With Hilary du Cros, she co-authored *The Arts and Events*, published by Routledge in 2014. She has published eight edited or co-edited volumes, four with Channel View Publications and four with Routledge. Recent publications include *Murals and Tourism*, edited with Jonathan Skinner for Routledge in 2017.

Aleksandra Kołtun, PhD, is a researcher and lecturer at the department of philosophy, Maria Curie-Sklodowska University, Lublin, Poland. Her scientific interests concern issues of knowledge production and dissemination; she studies how our physical and social environment influence cognitive performance (e.g. decision making, information processing, understanding, imagination). She is the author of the book *Can Knowledge be a Performative? Performativity in the Studies of Science* (UMCS, 2015) and several articles. She is a coordinator of numerous research projects investigating the practices of knowledge production, the impact of cultural festivals on urban growth and general perceptions of the city, user experience in public spaces, audience development etc.

Xu Ye, PhD, is an assistant professor in the faculty of hospitality and tourism management of Macau University of Science and Technology, Macao, China. She received her PhD in international tourism management and master of business and administration from Macau University of Science and Technology. She received her bachelor's degree in international business English from Nanjing University (China). Her main areas of research expertise include event management, cultural tourism and sustainable tourism management. She specializes in teaching special event management, MICE event and product management, theories and practice of MICE and cultural festival management. Her recent research includes the role of cultural proximity in shaping tourist destination image, the impacts of cultural festivals on residents' subjective well-being, the analysis of the tourism cooperation situation between Jiangsu Province and Portuguese-speaking countries, street art as an alternative attraction: a case of the East Side Gallery, university students' recognition on Xiangshan culture, etc.

Preface

This publication focuses on the phenomenon of place event marketing which is understood as all procedures of branding and promotion of places by means of events. The main focus of the book is cities and towns; therefore, the case studies included in this book represent urban places. The way events are used to brand a selected urban place and disseminate information about it is the subject of study presented in the publication. The volume falls within the range of urban geography, event studies and place marketing. The branding and promotional role of events has not been thoroughly exploited in the contemporary scientific literature; thus, it will come as a novelty in this book. The publication begins with an introductory chapter, wherein the scope, aims and structure of the work are presented. This first chapter also includes the theoretical presentation of the place event marketing concept and activities, as well as outlining their effects on the promotion, marketing communications and branding of different urban spaces (cities and towns). The following chapters present empirical case studies of different events and places around the globe, illustrating the use of events in place event marketing. The book ends with conclusions, where its main outcomes are summarised and further research directions proposed.

1 The concept of place event marketing

Setting the agenda

Waldemar Cudny

Introduction

This publication focuses on the phenomenon of place event marketing, which is understood in this book as all procedures of branding and promotion of places by means of events. The main focus of the book is on cities and towns; therefore the case studies included in this publication represent urban places. In the next part of the chapter, the issues of city branding, promotion and the definition, as well as a division of events, will be given full consideration. However, in the first part of the chapter, a brief presentation of the scope and main aims of the book are necessary. There are several research issues connected with the main topics of this book i.e. branding, promotion and events.

Branding in the case of cities is most often understood as a multidimensional urban development strategy (see Anholt 2008, 2010; Kavaratzis 2018; Cudny 2019). The development of a city brand should lead to the creation of an attractive offer, which is often called a city product. The product should satisfy the city users' demands. On the one hand, the successful brand will be interesting for dwellers and entrepreneurs already residing in the city. On the other hand, it should attract tourists, immigrants and prospective investors. However, branding is a long-term development policy (Lucarelli 2018); it also contains a promotional element (Cudny 2019). City promotion is always about the flow of information between a city and the users of its product (inhabitants, entrepreneurs, tourists). Cities should inform them about new urban products (e.g. new investments, events, recreational areas, tourist assets etc.) because people must know that a new offer exists in order to use it. Moreover, existing elements of the city offer need to be reinforced, and the positive brand image of the whole city should be created. In the latter case, we focus on influencing the recipients' minds with information presenting a city as interesting, offering good living conditions and worth investing in and visiting (Cudny 2019). Both elements—city branding and promotion—can be realized with the use of events.

Events are very diversified (Getz and Page 2016). The event portfolio encompasses festivals and cultural events, sports events, business and political meetings and many other types of gatherings. Events are also diversified in terms of their size (Cudny 2016). There are events of different scales, from local to mega-events of global importance (Hall 1989; Getz 2008, 2010). This large variety of event types and sizes influences the events' impacts on urban localities. These impacts are different and very important in the case of urban areas where most of events are organized. Cudny (2016), on the example of festivals, distinguished the following impacts: spatial, social, cultural, economic, political, environmental and image. It must also be highlighted that events have high media impact. They are widely presented in the traditional media (TV, radio, press) as well as in modern media (i.e. on the internet, including social media) This feature of events is very helpful in the process of brand creation and promotion. In the case of festivals, their impacts are also called functions (Cudny et al. 2012). One of the most important functions of events is that of image creation and promotion. This function is used in order to brand and promote firms (i.e. those that sponsor or organize specific events); however, it is also used in the case of territories, which are branded and promoted with the use of different events. The aforementioned issues are analysed throughout this book and are presented under the umbrella topic of place event marketing.

The way events are used in order to create an urban product (i.e. a wide-ranging urban offer) for inhabitants, tourists and other city users (i.e. branding) and disseminate information about a selected place (i.e. promotion) is the research problem presented in this book. The volume falls within the range of urban geography, event studies, place and city marketing. Except for a few publications (see Broudehoux 2017; Knott and Swart 2018), the branding and promotional role of events has not been thoroughly exploited in the contemporary scientific literature. Thus, the main novelty of this book will be an in-depth presentation of the role of different types of events in the creation of a brand for cities and their promotion.

There are several research aims the book intends to realize:

1   Defining the scope and contents of place event marketing in relation to urban places.
2   Establishing that different kinds of events (festivals, sports events, arts events, business events etc.) could be successfully used in order to develop brands and promote different types of urban places.
3   Analysing how various public and non-governmental institutions that deal with urban development, promotion and marketing communications can implement event marketing activities. Presenting how such institutions organize, co-organize and sponsor different events in order to create promotion and marketing communications, as well as implement place branding.
4   Investigating the effects of event marketing activities on urban place promotion and branding.
5   Presenting a variety of empirical case studies with lessons regarding the use of different events in branding and promotion of urban places around the world.

The research approach used in this book is based on case studies and a multi-method approach. According to Beeton (2005, p. 42) a case study is "a holistic empirical inquiry used to gain an in-depth understanding of a contemporary phenomenon in its real-life context, using multiple sources of evidence". The case studies in this book present different cities from several countries around the globe. They analyse different types and scales of events, including festivals and cultural and sports events. Because research works based on case studies have been criticized among others due to their subjectivity (based on researchers' individual perceptions) and lack of wider comparisons, multiple sources of evidence were introduced in this book in order to investigate the issues in a more rigorous manner (Beeton 2005).

Therefore, in most of the case studies presented in this book, the multi-method approach was adopted. This approach implies the use of several scientific methods in order to analyse a given phenomenon. The approach aims to overcome an individual method's limitations by the simultaneous use of different methods within the same investigation (Brewer and Hunter 1989). The use of combined methods for the study of the same phenomenon allows the most objective results possible (Schutz et al. 2004). Among the individual methods combined in the multi-method approach in this study are qualitative research methods including literature analysis, documents analysis, media coverage analysis, direct observation, in-depth interviews, questionnaires and focus groups. A detailed presentation of the methodology is presented in the introductory parts of individual chapters in the book. However, brief descriptions of the methods used through this volume will be presented in this chapter as well.

The basic qualitative research method used in the book was the analysis of the literature, supplemented with the reports and media analysis. Literature from event studies as well as city marketing underwent analysis. Reports analysis was employed as well. Reports devoted to events let the researchers obtain important information regarding a specific city or an event. The analysis of media materials (from traditional media like press or TV to electronic media e.g. websites and social media) was also important when obtaining information regarding events and their programmes, impacts, media coverage and the peoples' opinions (see Riffe et al. 2014).

One of most important methods used throughout the book was observation. It allows obtaining direct information regarding the observed phenomenon (its structure and dynamics) by examining human interactions in their surroundings (Rhoads and Wilson 2013). We may distinguish between direct observation conducted by the researcher (for example, during the course of an event) and indirect observation, when the researcher uses materials describing other peoples' direct observations. In the case of events, observation may concern the festival programme, the behaviour of its participants etc.

In-depth interviews "involve interaction or dialogue between the researcher or interviewer and the interviewee . . . interviewing is the process of finding, contacting, and meeting with research participants with purpose of asking questions about their experience and knowledge, and then listening – in open and non judgemental ways – to what they say" (Phillips and Johns 2012, p. 145). The in-depth interviews used for the purposes of this book were often realized with the events' organizers as well as with the representatives of cities or destination management organizations.

Another method borrowed from social science is the questionnaire. It is a survey in which respondents answer a set of questions about a given topic. Questionnaire surveys can take two forms: respondent completed and interviewer completed. The questionnaire can be realized in different ways (e. g. household, street, telephone, mail survey etc.) (Veal 2017). Focus groups were used as well. These are group interviews where "a moderator guides the interview while a small group discusses the topics that the interviewer raises. What the participants in the group say during their discussion are the essential data in focus groups" (Morgan 1997, p. 1).

Regarding the structure of the book, the introductory chapter is followed by chapters presenting empirical case studies of different events and places around the globe. The case studies are presented in regional layout. The book ends with conclusions, in which its main outcomes are summarised and further research directions proposed. Regarding the empirical chapters, they present cities from five continents: Europe, Africa, North and South America and Asia (Figure 1.1). The broad portfolio of event types is characterized as well, including sports events, festivals and events connected with the development of the business projects.

The first empirical chapter, written by Håkan Appelblad, explores the role of one-year long event programme of the Umeå2014 – European Capital of Culture. The author presents how a broad portfolio of cultural events organized under the auspices of the European Union supported development and promotion of the peripherally located Swedish city of Umea. The author describes how a regional sub-polar setting and indigenous local culture might be used in order to brand and promote the city. This chapter is based on direct observations and intensive document and media analysis. The third chapter, by Alba Colombo and Natàlia

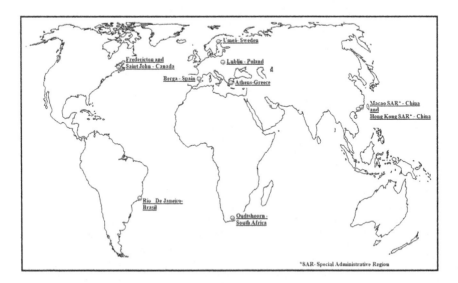

Figure 1.1 Location of case studies areas

Source: Author elaboration

Cantó-Milà, describes a different example of a traditional cultural festival called La Patum de Berga and organized in the city of Berga in Catalonia, Spain. This event draws from Christian tradition of Corpus Christi celebrations. With time it became a part of local tradition and was included in the UNESCO World Intangible Cultural Heritage. The authors investigated how such an event might support city branding and to what extent this festival can be used as a tourist attraction without destroying its authenticity and value for the local community. The next chapter is about participatory art events in Athens, Greece. Both authors, Zafeirenia Brokalaki and Roberta Comunian, discover how bottom-up-created events can change peoples' image of the city and how visitors, creative people and inhabitants may discover the city through art festivals. These chapters are based on qualitative research methods such as observation and interviews with events' organizers and participants as well as on focus groups.

Chapter 5 was written by Aleksandra Kołtun and presents another European example. However, this case study is different because it characterizes the post-socialist Polish city of Lublin. Despite the fact that Poland only entered the European Union in 2004, in many cities through the country, events are successfully used to develop the city and create its brand. In Lublin the city council, together with NGOs, created a cultural development plan, which centres on the events sector. Cultural festivals drawing from local tradition and heritage are the most important part of it. The author describes the branding and promotional outcomes of the organization of festivals on a basis of a comprehensive empirical study. It encompassed the analysis of documents, reports and qualitative research including a survey with 1,562 questionnaires distributed during festivals.

Lee Jolliffe and Nancy Chesworth wrote the sixth chapter, presenting the role of art events in brand creation in the cities of Fredericton and Saint John, located in the New Brunswick province of Canada. The chapter analyzes the role of destination marketing organizations in brand creation with the use of culture and arts events. The authors base their research on intensive material and reports analysis and on in-depth interviews with destination managers. The broad portfolio of art events from both locations is investigated and their connection with strategic brand pillars of both cities is analyzed.

The Canadian case study is followed by the one from South America delivered by Anne-Marie Broudehoux. Chapter 7 discovers the influence of mega events on place brand using the example of large-scale sports events. The 2014 World Cup and the 2016 Olympic Games organized in Rio de Janeiro are studied in the chapter. Repeated observation, ethnography, documents and media reports analysis and other methods were used in order to present both sides of the coin of the branding-through-events process. On the one hand, the official endeavours leading to the creation of an attractive place brand are presented. On the other hand, the community's reactions are analyzed. The results show the contradiction between the official top-down approach to branding and peoples' reactions, followed by bottom-up critics and the community's responses to the government policies.

In Chapter 8, Ronnie Donaldson and Henry Duckitt present the influence of music festivals on the place brand of small towns in South Africa. The chapter draws from the geographical background of the authors. First, it analyses the spatio-temporality of three categories of music festivals in the Western Cape province. Later, the in-depth case study of a classic music festival and its influence on the place brand of the town of Oudtshoorn is characterized. This chapter uses the multi-method approach. Mapping of festivals, media coverage analysis and documents analysis as well as interviews were the sources of information.

Chapters 9 and 10 present case studies of cities in Asia. The former was written by Xu Ye and describes the role of Lusofonia Festival, organized in Macao Special Administrative Region (China), in tourist brand creation. The Lusofonia Festival is organized to honour the Portuguese-speaking community residents in Macao and their contribution to city's development. The analysis is based on the mixed-method approach involving the repertory-grid technique and questionnaires completed by tourists visiting Macao. The results show that the event is an important tourist attraction and an interesting leisure opportunity. For the city, the event is a kind of brand label, displaying its versatile culture and satisfying tourists' diverse needs. Festivals like Lusofonia help diversify the city brand and increase tourist attractiveness beyond Macao's well-known image as the gambling capital of the world.

Chapter 10 is the last factual chapter of the book. It was written by Hilary du Cros and Lee Jolliffe, who present the role of Hong Kong art events in the development of the Chinese Belt and Road Initiative (BRI). The art events presented in this chapter are contributing to the development of Hong Kong's brand, but they also aim to support a large-scale Chinese investment plan i.e. the BRI. Data were obtained through media and document analysis and interviews with key cultural stakeholders involved in tourism and events development. The chapter shows that the Hong Kong Trade Development Council (HKTDC), together with art auction houses located in Hong Kong, brand the city as the central art hub for the BRI. This strategy is justified by the fact that Hong Kong is an important art centre, and it is also an important BRI logistics hub. The development of the art scene in the city, including the organizing of art events, is a good opportunity for China's soft power creation. The existing art scene in Hong Kong is already well established; however, the intensive use of art events in the city for BRI branding is rather an opportunity for the future.

In the concluding chapter, the main scientific outcomes of the whole publication are summarised. The reader will also find an insightful model of the functioning of the event marketing process in an urban context there. The model draws from the results of the analysis presented in the empirical chapters throughout the book.

Place event marketing: an emerging practical and theoretical field

The notion and diversity of events

This part of the chapter will give the readers insight into event marketing. It combines two basic terms: *event* and *marketing*. Therefore, events, their definition and division must be presented, and the notion of marketing and its elements should be characterized. Tara Lunga (2012) stated that the word event is of Latin origin and refers to, among other things, happening or manifestation. According to the *Oxford Wordpower Dictionary* (2002, p. 264), an event is: "1. Something that happens, especially something important or unusual: a historic event; 2. a planned public or social occasion: a fund rising event; 3. one of the races, competitions, etc., in a sports programme: the next event is the 800 metre race". Scientific definitions of events may be found in works by Ritchie (1984), Hall (1989), Goldblatt (1990) and Getz (1991, 2008). Events can be unplanned (e.g. spontaneous gatherings of people, like riots, unscheduled manifestations etc.) or planned (Getz and Page 2016). According to Getz and Page (2016, p. 44), planned events "by definition, have a beginning and an end. They are temporal phenomena, and with planned events the event programme or schedule is generally planned in detail and well publicized in advance. Planned events are also usually confined to particular places, although the space involved might be a specific facility, a very large open space, or many locations simultaneously or in sequence". According to Getz (2008, p. 407), planned events can be divided, according to their scale and rank, into the following:

- occasional mega-events: high tourist demand and high value,
- periodic hallmark events: high tourist demand and high value,
- regional events (periodic and one-time): medium tourist demand,
- local events (periodic and one-time): low demand and low value.

Getz (2008, p. 404) also established a typology of planned events according to their type, which encompasses eight groups:

1   cultural celebrations: festivals, carnivals, commemorations, religious events;
2   political and state: summits, royal occasions, political events, VIP visits;
3   arts and entertainment: concerts, award ceremonies;
4   business and trade: meetings, conventions, consumer and trade shows, fairs, markets;
5   educational and scientific: conferences, seminars, clinics;
6   sport competitions: amateur/professional, spectator/participant;
7   recreational: sport or games for fun;
8   private: weddings, parties.

   Another division of events may be found in the book by Cieślikowski (2016, pp. 21–22). He divided events into several types according to the following criteria:

- place of realization: travelling, stationary;
- duration: one-day, multi-day, staged;
- repeatability: one-off, several-time, cyclical;
- the group of recipients: internal, external;
- accessibility for event goers: closed, open;

- range: small scale, group, mass events;
- goals: image (brand policy related), pro-sales, non-profit, for-profit etc.;
- area of operation: online/multimedia, offline;
- interaction with participants: active, passive;
- goers' attachment to the event: permanent, accidental;
- publicity: media events, events focused on direct viewers;
- company's commitment: own, sponsored;
- benefits for participants: artistic experience, contact with celebrities, entertainment, competitions etc.;
- types/forms of events: music, sports, recreation, picnic, spectacular, extreme, visual, multimedia, for children, trade fairs, festivals, galas, thematic, company, games, happenings etc.

Events are studied in several sciences, including anthropology, sociology, psychology and religious studies but also economics, management, geography and history. The importance of events, due to their multidimensional impacts, is so high that a separate field of studies was established to investigate them i.e. event studies (Getz and Page 2016). All planned events have multidimensional economic and social impacts on host communities, which can be positive or negative. According to Hall (1989), hallmark events may result in corporate investments and economic benefits while large-scale special and mega-events can create international corporate investments in events and facilities, urban redevelopment and tourism promotion. Getz and Page (2016) distinguished the following events' impacts:

- personal: positive (satisfaction, happiness, meet expectations) or negative (waste of time, lack of value, harmfulness);
- social, cultural and political: positive (job creation, development of skills and networks, entertainment) or negative (costs, congestion, conflicts, pollution, diseases);
- economic: positive (revenues from event tourism, entrepreneurship development, local development thanks to investments and revenues) or negative (organization costs, inflation, lack of revenues);
- media: this impact encompasses presentation of events and host locations in traditional and electronic media. The media coverage may be positive (highlighting positive impacts of an event) but may also be negative. The latter may be due to conflicts between inhabitants and tourists, high costs of events organization or negative environmental impacts presented in the media.

On the example of festivals distinguished as positive (defined as functions) and negative (defined as dysfunctions), Cudny et al. (2012, p. 710) divides events' impacts into the following categories:

- economic: income and jobs creation, promotion of cities and regions, economic restructuring through development of services, culture and entertainment, as well as negatives like high organization costs, traffic jams, inflation;

- political: supporting the democratization of life, fighting xenophobia and intolerance (e.g. through multicultural festivals), promoting political parties and negatives such as conflicts between local inhabitants and tourists, lack of acceptance of some festivals, excluding social groups from festival spaces, violence, risky sexual behaviours, use of drugs and alcohol;
- environmental: promotion of environment-friendly policies, development of communal infrastructure and mass transport services and negatives like increases in pollution due to mass event tourism.

On the basis of aforementioned impacts of events, it may be said that they have important impacts on host localities including cities. Events are forms of intangible and temporal products which enrich a city. These products are an offer for consumers like tourists and local inhabitants. Moreover, events cause economic development through income from event tourism and job creation in event sector, and thus, they may be used as investment and redevelopment generators. Events are presented in the media because lots of them are extraordinary experiences. Some of them involve famous people like sportsmen, film people, singers etc. Therefore, they are very interesting for the media and for diversified audiences. When events are covered in the media, the host cities are simultaneously presented and promoted (Cudny 2016). Having these facts in mind, we should remember that the organization of events enriches the city product and is a part of many urban socio-economic development plans as well as branding and promotional strategies (Cudny 2019).

City marketing branding and promotion

Other topics that need to be addressed here are the issues of city marketing, city branding and promotion. Marketing is a typical activity for commercial companies (Kotler and Armstrong 2010); however, in last decades, it has been successfully used by non-commercial entities such as universities, museums and foundations (Tobelem 1997), as well as territories such as countries, regions and cities. In the latter case, it is referred to as city marketing (Florek 2013). Marketing is currently understood differently than it was 30 or 40 years ago. Traditionally, marketing activities were identified with informing people about products and selling them (the telling and selling approach) (Kotler and Armstrong 2010). In this traditional approach, marketers were working on what had been designed and manufactured by industry and services. In that case, we were dealing with a top-down approach. It was the manufacturers who designed and offered specific products to customers. Customers had to be convinced to buy them through marketing activities.

Currently, marketing is based on the reverse approach, which can be described as a bottom-up approach. It starts with an in-depth knowledge of the clients' needs and is followed by products' design and manufacturing. This kind of approach is called sense and respond philosophy (Kotler and Armstrong 2010). According to Kotler and Armstrong (2010, p. 28) currently "Marketing is managing profitable customer relationships. The twofold goal of marketing is to attract new customers by promising superior value and to keep and grow current customers by delivering satisfaction".

According to the marketing approach, a product must not only be properly prepared. It also needs proper promotion. This means that customers have to know
about the product, and they need to perceive it in a positive way (the product mast
have an attractive brand). The product also has to be delivered to the consumers
through correctly selected distribution channels. Moreover, a product needs to
be sold for a certain price, which is treated as another element of marketing. The
right price affects the sales volume and reflects the quality and value of the product. All these activities are conducted by people who work in a given institution
i.e. the staff. These parts form the so-called marketing mix, often referred to as the
5 Ps marketing approach (Kotler et al. 2009).

As already mentioned, marketing activities are conducted not only by commercial companies but also by non-profit organizations. The non-commercial institutions also have their goals, which include fundraising, dissemination, protection
of culture and knowledge, creation of dynamic social and economic development
(in the case of territories) etc. In order to achieve these goals, they need to raise
funds, create a brand, inform consumers about their products, and attract people;
hence, they must conduct complex marketing activities. However, in their case,
these activities do not directly lead to profit; possible profit is only a means to the
realization of other more important goals (Tobelem 1997).

The 1980s and 1990s were the beginning of the neoliberal era. According to
the neoliberal approach, anything can be treated as a product and can be sold
on a free market. This approach is very popular in urban development strategies
implemented in the Western world in recent decades. As part of such development activities, modern cities apply strategies based on marketing assumptions
drawn from corporations. Activities in which the city is treated as a product created by a certain group of people (e.g. city planners and managers), distributed,
promoted and sold for a specific price is referred to as city marketing (Cudny
2019). There are a fast-growing number of cities worldwide, and what they have
to offer becomes more and more similar. Therefore, cities have to compete with
each other for resources such as investors, tourists and immigrants. In order to
win this competition, many cities apply marketing procedures involving product
development, branding and promotion. According to Asnawi (2016), there are
many definitions of city marketing. The author quoted, among others, the following definitions of the phenomenon:

- According to Paddison (1993) city marketing is "more than the promotion of
  place, being used in some cities to rebuild and redefine their image, allied to
  which has been a strategy of targeting specific types of activity which both
  reflect and bolster the image".
- According to Kotler et al. (1999) city marketing is "a method to attract residents and firms. In many municipalities, it is common practice to explore
  these issues with the help of marketing insights".
- According to the Gyeonggi Research Institute (2007), city marketing may
  be defined as "a commercial marketing activity that sells and exchanges city
  spaces for capital, and seeks to attract both visitors and residents. In other

words, city marketing is a strategy to deal with residents, enterprise and visitors as the target market and attract them through promotion combined with values of sales and a city environment" (Asnawi 2016, pp. 3–5).

According to Kotler et al. (1999) there are four main elements used in city marketing strategies in order to gain advantage over competing cities: "design (place as character), infrastructure (place as fixed environment), basic services (place as service provider), attractions (places as entertainment and recreation)". According to Hubbard and Hall (1998) such strategies should encompass "advertising and promotion, large-scale physical redevelopment, public art and civic statuary, mega-events, cultural regeneration, public-private partnerships" (Kavaratzis 2004, p. 61). As stated by Asnawi (2016, p. 5) "City marketing have four goals: 1) the improvement of the urban products, those being the city and everything in contains; 2) the improvement of the incentives for consumers to make use of the city's products; 3) the improvement of infrastructure and institutions that provide or improve access to the city's product and; 4) the communication of the city, making potential customers aware of the products the city has to offer."

As mentioned earlier, the organization of different types of events (as a part of city attractions, mega-events or cultural regeneration) is crucial part of city marketing endeavours. There is a broad portfolio of books dedicated to events and their role in the development of different places including cities and towns (see Smith 2012; Cudny 2016; Getz and Page 2016; Donaldson 2018). In these publications, the focus is put on the importance of sports events and festivals for the socio-economic development of places. However, not many publications emphasize the branding and communicational roles of events (see Broudehoux 2017; Knott and Swart 2018). The latter issue in regard to cities is presented throughout this book and is referred to as place event marketing.

Place event marketing

First, it is important to present the existing definitions of event marketing as the background for the formulation of a place event marketing definition. According to the Cambridge Dictionary (https://dictionary.cambridge.org/dictionary/english/event-marketing), event marketing encompasses two elements:

> the job of advertising products by selling or providing them at events in order to gain new customers; the job of advertising different events so that people will go to them.

Event marketing is defined by American business dictionaries as:

> The activity of designing or developing a themed activity, occasion, display, or exhibit (such as a sporting event, music festival, fair, or concert) to promote a product, cause, or organization. Also called event creation.
> (www.businessdictionary.com/definition/event-marketing.html)

As stated by Jaworowicz and Jaworowicz (2016), there are many definitions of event marketing established in science. The cited authors mentioned several definitions from Germany, the UK, the USA and other countries. According to Nufer (2015) cited in Jaworowicz and Jaworowicz (2016, p. 100), event marketing is "an interactive and experience-oriented communication tool that serves objectives related to specific target groups with the use of events – their planning, implementation and, control within the framework of integrated communication of the company". Šindler (2003, p. 23) defined event marketing simply as "event + marketing". According to Raj et al. (2013, p. 210, cited in Jaworowicz and Jaworowicz 2016, p. 103) "Event marketing is a management process to achieve objectives of an organization through identifying and meetings the needs of consumers who attend the event". Wohlfeil and Whelan (2006, cited in Jaworowicz and Jaworowicz 2016, p. 103) defined the phenomenon as "Creation of 3-dimensional, interactive brand related hyperrealities for consumers by staging marketing events which would result in an emotional attachment to the brand". Finally, Jaworowicz and Jaworowicz (2016, p. 108) gave their own definition of the phenomenon as "one of the tools of integrated marketing communication, based on the use of various types of events to achieve the company's goals in the external and internal environment in the course of direct contact with event participants or through the media".

As stated earlier, on the one hand, the concept of event marketing is referred to as successful strategies of marketing events in order to brand and sell them (Hoyle 2002). On the other hand, event marketing is understood as the use of events in the marketing of products. In the latter sense, the companies' and products' merits are communicated to the wider audience and branded with the use of events, including sports events, festivals, business events etc. (Kotler and Armstrong 2010). Such events are sponsored by the companies, which organize and co-organize them. Products and firms are presented through commercials and public relations activities associated with such events. Companies are often the sole organizer or co-organizer of an event. In this case, a festival or a sports event might be organized in relation to the company and associated with one theme connected with the company's products.

Regarding event marketing as a business strategy, it is important to remember that the event must be a memorable happening which attracts visitors and makes a great impression on them. Without this, the event will not fulfill its aims e.g. will not sell effectively or will not promote products efficiently. As Hoyle (2002, pp. 2–3) stated, in order to create memorable events, they need to encompass 3 Es of event marketing:

- Entertainment: an event must provide unique and attractive entertainment because otherwise people will not be drawn away from their homes to attend an event.
- Excitement: is what makes event memorable. According to Hoyle (2002, p. 2):

Excitement can be part of a tribute to an industry leader, a new corporate logo introduced at a sales conference, or a celebration of an association's anniversary. The point is that it should always be considered as part of an effective marketing plan. For example, the greatest excitement for an attendee may be the eye-opening revelations of that special educational programme that advances knowledge and career opportunities and changes lives forever. Or it may be the impact of that keynote speaker whose motivational message will become a lasting asset, and cherished memory, for the listener.

- Enterprises: may be defined as a readiness to take a risk and a will to try something new. People want to find themselves in uncommon situations and they like to learn from such experiences. Therefore, it is a key of event marketing to offer the unique, new, unexpected situations and experiences they may participate in during an event.

As stated by Wohlfeil and Whelan (2006, pp. 645–646) event marketing's communicative innovation is based on four pillars:

1   Experience-orientation: events are an opportunity to take part in interesting and extraordinary organized life experiences. This gives events an advantage over other forms of communication, e.g. through traditional media or the internet, and causes their high attractiveness in the eyes of the events audience.
2   Interactivity: events give the possibility of mutual interactive dialogue between the senders and recipients of marketing messages. This makes events highly attractive to broadcasters of marketing information (managers, people responsible for marketing communication).
3   Self-initiation: the organization and course of events is under the control of the organizers (marketers), which gives them full control of the way in which brand experiences are anchored in the world of consumer feelings and experiences.
4   Dramaturgy: events offer unique and creative dramaturgy, different from the everyday life of consumers. It is similar to drama during a theatrical play and offers close and exciting contact with the promoted brand. This results in high attractiveness of event marketing for message recipients.

As there are the 5 Ps of marketing (see Kotler et al. 1999), there are also the 5 Ps of event marketing. According to Hoyle (2002, p. 12), they encompass:

1   Product: is an event itself, its programme and the offer which successfully fulfills the needs of event goers. The offer might be entertainment and contact with culture (during a concert or a cultural festival), education (during science festival), business contacts (during fairs), sports experience (during the Olympics) etc.
2   Price: is the cost of participation in an event. Admission may be free (non-ticketed events) or tickets may be sold for a specified price based, among

other things, on the market's ability to pay, the price of competitive events and organizational costs.

3   Place: is the venue or location, i.e. the place where the event is organized. In many situations, the event location is a key factor of event success. It is especially important in the case of place-specific events which are rooted in a host city attraction or heritage. An example could be a film festival based in a city with a rich film heritage and history or a multicultural festival realized in a city with multicultural heritage.

4   Public relations (PR): is most important in terms of the promotion of an event. It is about maintaining relations with the widely understood social environment of an event. As Kotler and Armstrong wrote (2010, p. 452), PR, a part of so-called promotion mix tools, "involves building good relations with various company publics-from consumers and the general public to the media, investor, and government publics". In order to organize and sell events with success, their organizers must sustain positive relations not only with visitors but also with contractors (co-organizing the event), media (transmitting and presenting the event), local authorities (supporting the event) etc.

5   Positioning: is the fifth P of event marketing and should be understood as

the strategy of determining, through intuition, research, and evaluation, those areas of consumer need that your event can fulfill. What types of events is the competition offering? What level of investment are they requiring of their attendees? Who is attending, and who is not? In other words: What niche are we trying to fill? What makes us different and how can we seize upon our unique qualities to market our events? And what markets will be receptive to our event concept?

Summarizing positioning encompasses the recognition of consumers' (event goers') needs and expectations and constructing an event offer which will fulfill the needs of the group of selected visitors so that the event will have the best market position in relation to its expected consumers. This procedure is a key element of modern marketing which is about successful and profitable managing of consumers' needs (see Kotler and Armstrong 2010).

Event marketing, when applied to cities, should be included in city marketing and city branding activities. As stated by Cudny (2019, p. 15), city marketing involves urban socio-economic development and promotion. The main aim of promotion is to create communication between an institution and the end users of its offer (customers). Among the basic means of promotion which form the so-called promotional mix there are advertising, sales promotion, public relations, personal selling and direct marketing (Kotler and Armstrong 2010). In the last decades, cities uses promotion as well (Gold and Ward 1994; Markowski 1999; Czornik 2005; Szromnik 2012), caused by an intensive competition between urban centres across the world. In order to sustain present inhabitants and gain tourists, new investments and immigrants (including creative class members), cities need to communicate with and persuade different groups of people and institutions. Therefore, they introduce different promotional actions into their development strategies (Cudny 2019).

Promotion is an element often included in city branding endeavours (Kavaratzis and Ashworth 2005, 2008). However, branding itself is much wider procedure than only promotion and marketing communication (Anholt 2008, 2010; Ashworth and Kavaratzis 2009; Zenker and Beckmann 2013). Lucarelli (2018) presented place branding in an urban context as a complex and multidimensional hybrid policy which involves commercial and public endeavours resulting from amalgamated influence of different stakeholders and resulting in spatial layout and settings. Branding leads to brand creation. A brand is a "name, term, sign, symbol, or design, or a combination of these that identifies the goods or services of one seller or group of sellers and differentiates them from competitors" (Kotler and Armstrong 2010, p. 255). The aforementioned marketing definition of a brand can be applied to cities. In such a case, we can state that a city brand is created as a result of branding policy and related promotional activities. As a result, the name of the city, often supplemented with a slogan and logo, becomes a symbol of specific benefits and values that the city offers to consumers, i.e. recipients of its product (tourist product, residential, entertainment, cultural, investment product etc.). Behind each brand, there is a specific brand entity which is based on the usefulness of the product, its posting (image) and the advantage over competitors – in our case, over competing cities.

Activities related to previously defined event marketing, understood as both a concept consisting of activities aimed at the effective sale of events and the marketing of products through them, are closely related to activities related to urban branding, which is related to urban marketing. The combination of these approaches can be defined as place event marketing. It may refer to various places (e.g. countries, regions), but the best reference is in the case of cities. Place event marketing of cities is a procedure encompassing the following aspects:

1   Creating a city development policy through the implementation of events. In this case, we are dealing with the convergence of event marketing with city branding, understood as a comprehensive policy of urban development. Events generate broadly understood socio-economic development and are often an element directly included in urban development strategies. The policy of urban development through the organization of events results from the following functions of events:

    a   Creating events as urban products which find buyers i.e. event goers (inhabitants, tourists).
    b   Creating events induces infrastructural investments including objects hosting events (stadiums, spectator halls, exhibition centres) and widely understood technical infrastructure (roads, parking, stations etc.).
    c   Events generate income for local firms offering services for event goers. They also generate employment in the event sector and in related services

(hotels, restaurants, transportation etc.). Therefore, events organization is a factor developing local economy.

2   Events are an excellent means of city promotion because they disseminate information about the cities in which they take place. Thus, they shape the image and brand of a city as a destination full of interesting events, a cultural (in the case of festivals) or sports centre (in the case of sports competitions). Places filled with interesting events are usually positively considered interesting and full of life. Here, we have a convergence between event marketing as a procedure for the promotion of events and event marketing as a procedure for products promotion. In the first case, cities are promoted simultaneously with the promotion of events. In the second case, we can say that the host cities are products promoted by events organized in them. The promotion takes place in several aspects:

a   The events are reported on television and, simultaneously, the host city is presented. One can specify a concrete value that a given city would have to spend to get a comparable media presentation. This is called the advertising equivalent value.
b   Events are promoted by their organizers which are not only cities but also sports or business organizations or cultural institutions. Advertising campaigns (including commercials and PR) for events are used to sell them and are in the organizers' interest because they increase the number of event goers. However, the aforementioned endeavours also promote the destination i.e. the host city.
c   Events attract media attention thanks to the presence of celebrities participating in them. It's about stars of culture (music, film etc.) or sport. Thanks to their presence, the media are interested in the event and they also show the destination where the event takes place.

It should be emphasized that the aforementioned elements (i.e. 5 Ps and 3 Es of event marketing), decisive for the success of given events, are also crucial for the success of cities in which the events are organized. An event which is a good and well-planned product, has a well-chosen price, is organized in an interesting place, has good PR a and well-selected audience (positioning) will succeed. This success will be transferred to the success of the host city. It will lead to its socioeconomic growth, development of infrastructure and promotional benefits. The situation is similar when looking at the aforementioned 3 Es of event marketing (i.e. entertainment, excitement and enterprises). If the event has these 3 Es, it will be successful, and its success will positively affect the development and promotional success of a host city.

Eventually, we may define place event marketing in relation to cities as all activities aimed at enriching the product of a given city by offering its consumers a well-chosen, interesting and diverse portfolio of events. This activity also includes the promotion of a city through the events. This, in turn, enables marketing communication with the recipients of urban products and shapes the positive

Figure 1.2 The structure of place event marketing in cities

Source: Author's elaboration

image and brand of a city. Event marketing is, therefore, a comprehensive group of activities related to city branding and city promotion and can be part of long-term urban development and promotional strategies. Place event marketing in cities includes planning, organizing and promoting urban events, but its goal should be the realization of broadly defined host city development goals and the needs of the urban products' consumers (Figure 1.2).

Place event marketing: several examples

There is a notion of the Barcelona model presented in the scientific literature. The model encompasses significant, multi-aspect, socio-economic changes occurring in localities where long-term development projects were introduced which included the organization of large-scale events (e.g. Olympics, World or European Football Championships). However, other types of events such as large festivals, religious events or fairs can be considered as elements triggering positive outcomes in host localities too (Borzyszkowski 2011, 2014; Marczak 2014).

The name *Barcelona model* comes from the Spanish city of Barcelona, the capital of the Catalonia region, located on the Mediterranean coast. After the Second World War, Barcelona was an industrial and port city. In the 1970s, as a result of the economic crisis and nonfunctional structure based on traditional industry, the city was considered rather negatively as a neglected industrial centre. However, after the death of Francisco Franco in 1975 and the democratization of the political and economic system, Barcelona underwent a series of socio-economic and image changes. Already, at the turn of the 1970s and 1980s, a new social and economic development plan was introduced to induce new functions and improve the city's infrastructure and image. In the 1980s, permission was obtained for the organization of the Olympic Games in Barcelona that took place in 1992.

The Olympic Games were the most important factor that led to the change of the socio-economic structure and image of the city (González 2011).

The first plans for the socio-economic transformation of Barcelona were already established in the second half of the 1970s. In the 1980s, new functions (mainly service oriented) began to be gradually introduced to replace the traditional and ineffective maritime industry. These strategies also involved civic participation, the democratization of life after the Franco era. The strategic plans aimed for infrastructure development, development of social housing, activities aimed at equalizing opportunities and living standards in various areas of the city. In 1986, Barcelona won the competition for the organization of the Summer Olympic Games. This allowed the city to obtain additional government and regional funds for the development of large-scale public projects. Until this time, the city was the centre of the maritime industry and a large port with poorly developed services. In terms of tourism, it was only a hinterland for tourists heading for other towns on the Mediterranean coast. The new development strategy was to make tourists stay in Barcelona as a host destination for the long term (Degen and García 2012).

Therefore, the construction of hotels, sports and recreation centres, museums and cultural and entertainment centres as well as transport infrastructure was sub-sidized and supported. It was possible thanks to the financial resources obtained for the preparation of the Olympic Games. However, the whole programme of preparation for the mega-event was not short term. It was designed with long-term effects in mind, which should occur years after the event. The development strategy was about expanding the city's infrastructure and tourist offer in order to be able to transform it into the centre of tourism, culture, sport and business and make the Barcelona metropolitan ambitions possible (Degen and García 2012).

The aforementioned endeavours should be treated as a long-term city brand-ing strategy, in which the mega-event was an excellent opportunity to implement investment and development projects. These activities were continued after the Olympic Games took place in 1992. They were additionally supplemented by decentralization of city management and the introduction of private capital and public-private projects. The city's brand developed thanks to the Olympics as well. The mega-event was used to change Barcelona's image from a grey and uninteresting industrial urban centre to an interesting city of experiences. The result of the intensive development of services was the replacement of an econ-omy based on an outdated industry with a modern service-oriented structure based on tourism and the knowledge economy (Degen and García 2012).

Change in the image of Barcelona and the transformation of its brand was possible thanks to the introduction of intense promotional campaigns (Luna-Garcia 2008). According to Hospers (2009, p. 231), currently "Barcelona is one of Europe's most popular cities. Even more, it is the city with the seventh best city brand in the world (CBI, 2007). Since the early 1990s, the city has pursued an effective re-imaging strategy, starting with the 1992 Olympic Games". Smith (2012) claims that Barcelona has developed a new image thanks to its strategic social and economic activities and the accompanying promotional campaigns. Thanks to these endeavours, Barcelona cut off its association with traditional industry, political unrest, deprivation and depravation. Therefore the city is currently perceived as a global metropolis with a high standard of living, an interesting tourist offer and an interesting place to live. One of the catalysts of the image was the summer Olympic Games organized in 1992. However, it must not be forgotten that it would not have been possible without the previous introduction of long-term development projects. It should also be said that the aforementioned Barcelona model includes, apart from development projects, also promotional activities aimed at developing a positive image of the city.

According to Borzyszkowski (2014, p. 2), the Barcelona effect includes various social and economic results that occur before and after an event. Among the most important results, there are:

- a short-term increase in income from tourism during the event,
- increasing investment in tourist and sports infrastructure visible already several years before the event,
- a short-term increase in expenditures related to the organization of the event,
- rising tourist attractiveness of the host city as well as a long-term increase in the number of tourists,
- increasing productivity of the local economy as a result of infrastructure improvement,
- rising domestic and foreign investments e.g. in accommodation or sports and recreation facilities.

The Barcelona model is most effective when long-term positive socio-economic and image-related effects are noticeable. In the case of the Barcelona Summer Olympics in 1992, such effects occurred. Therefore, this example can be considered an effective project related to broadly understood event marketing. According to Borzyszkowski (2014, p. 6), the number of hotels in Barcelona increased from 118 (1990) to 187 (2000) and to 223 (2002). The number of tourists increased from 1.7 million (1990) to 3.1 million (2000) and to 3.3 million (2001). The number of tourist overnight stays increased from 3.7 million (1990) to 7.7 million (2000) and to 7.9 million (2001). The quoted data confirmed that the Olympic Games triggered the long-term development of the tourism sector in the host city. As presented by Borzyszkowski (2014), the Barcelona model affects not only tourism. It also affects the attractiveness of the host city for investors, as well as affecting residents and immigrants. Thanks to the event the cultural, entertainment, recreational and sports offer of a host city is strengthened, and the residents' quality of life increases. Other important effects of the Barcelona model are its promotional outcomes. Thanks to the event, a positive image of the destination is shaped, and the knowledge about it is disseminated.

Różycka (2013), quoting a similar example of the European Football Championship UEFA EURO 2012 hosted in Poland and Ukraine, underlines the positive impact of this mega-event on place marketing in the context of countries and cities. She believes that a particularly important result of the organization of major events is the improvement of the image of the host destination (the country or the city). A well-organized event or a series of events may lead to a favourable perception of the destination (see also: Hall 1992; Wilson 2004). According to Różycka, the UEFA Euro 2012 was reported by 10,000 officially registered foreign journalists. Poland as a host country was promoted on such international channels as Skye Sports, BBC One, BBC News, Eurosport, BSkyeB, RTL, SAT 1, Vox, France 3, France 5 and France 2. According to the research conducted among football fans visiting Poland during the event, 80 percent of them would like to return to Poland in the future. About 92 percent declared that they would recommend Poland as a country worth visiting. The EURO 2012 was hosted in the following Polish cities: Gdańsk (hosting 322,000 fans), Poznań (hosting 675,000 fans), Warsaw (hosting 1,282,000 fans) and, Wrocław (hosting 596,000 fans). In Warsaw, the EURO 2012 championship was reported by 2,000 journalists, including 430 foreign journalists from 34 countries. It is estimated that the city would have to spend 35 million Euro to achieve a similar promotional effect. In Gdańsk, about 1,600 journalists worked during the EURO 2012 in the city. The value of the city's promotion in foreign media was estimated at EUR 24 million (Różycka 2013, pp. 26–27).

It should be emphasized that positive socio-economic and promotional effects are not limited to sports events only. According to Cudny and Przybylska (2018, pp. 213–214), the Gdynia Film Festival hosted in the coastal city of Gdynia (Poland) also brought large-scale socio-economic and promotional effects. In the last years (2015–2016), the Gdynia Film Festival was visited by between 50,000 and 60,000 spectators. In 2015 a specially designed festival centre was built for the purposes of festival organization. The mayor of Gdynia admitted that the festival is supported by the city council and that it became an important urban product and a visiting card of the city. Thanks to the festival, Gdynia is changing its image from a port city to a modern urban centre, with culture as an important element of the urban brand. For example, during the 2015 Gdynia Film Festival, the information regarding the event was broadcast in 100 media broadcasts on large Polish public television channels. Additionally, 30 news spots were broadcast in private television, 137 broadcasts on Polish radio and 150 on a regional radio were presented as well. The importance of festivals for the socio-economic development and promotion of host cities was also confirmed in the publication by Cudny (2016). The author analyzed the influences of the organization of festivals on host locations on the example of Lodz –large Polish post-industrial and post-socialist city.

The organization of big events does not always end with such positive effects as those mentioned. For example, many destinations copying the Barcelona model did not achieve similar long-term effects. The UEFA European Football Championship 2004 in Portugal could be an example. The event brought a decline in tourist traffic during the host year and the years afterward. It was similar in the case of the Olympic Games in Greece (2004). Only a slight increase in tourist traffic was recorded in the year of the FIFA 2002 World Cup in South Korea. In addition, the event was accompanied by a decrease in the number of tourists during the following year. In addition, the high costs of events organization, the costs of further maintaining sports facilities, poor event organization, corruption, poorly managed promotional campaigns (Borzyszkowski 2014) are also important problems occurring during and after some large events. Moreover, some tourists (e.g. cultural tourists or leisure tourists) can avoid a trip to a city that organizes a large event because of fear of overcrowding, traffic jams, crimes etc. It should also be pointed out that even the best-organized events are not a sufficient factor leading to the development of a Barcelona model. To achieve the Barcelona model effects, it is necessary to create and implement long-term development and promotional strategies with the event as a core (but not sole) attraction.

The Barcelona model analysis shows the presence of two elements being an integral part of the place event marketing idea. First of all, event marketing includes the creation of social and economic development programmes based on the organization of events. Secondly, it includes the promotion of cities using promotional campaigns organized around the event or a group of events organized in the host city. In this context, endeavours carried out in Barcelona on the occasion of the 1992 Olympic Games may be included in city place event marketing actions. It is, of course, important that these activities had a broader character (as long-term multidimensional strategies) and did not only cover the event itself and the period just before and after it.

References

Anholt, S. (2008). Place branding: Is it marketing, or isn't it? *Place Brand Public Diplomacy*, 4(1), 1–6.

Anholt, S. (2010). *Places: Identity, Image and Reputation*. London and New York, Palgrave Macmillan.

Ashworth, G., & Kavaratzis, M. (2009). Beyond the logo: Brand management for cities. *Journal of Brand Management*, 16(8), 520–531.

Asnawi, A. (2016). *City Marketing: Chronological Definitions* – electronic document. Available at: https://papers.ssrn.com/sol3/papers.cfm?abstract_id=2832540

Beeton, S. (2005). The case study in tourism research: A multi-method case study approach. *Tourism Research Methods: Integrating Theory with Practice*, 37–48.

Borzyszkowski, J. (2011). Wpływ eventu na rynek turystyczny – przykład ślubu księcia Williama i Kate Middleton. *Turystyka Kulturowa*, 6, 4–16.

Borzyszkowski, J. (2014). Efekt barceloński w turystyce: Efekt wpływu wybranych wielkich wydarzeń sportowych na ruch turystyczny w destynacjach-organizatorach. *Roczniki Naukowe Wyższej Szkoły Bankowej w Toruniu*, 13, 479–497.

Brewer, J., & Hunter, A. (1989). Sage Library of Social Research. *Multimethod Research: A Synthesis of Styles* (Vol. 175). Thousand Oaks, CA: Sage Publications, Inc.

Broudehoux, A. M. (2017). *Mega-events and Urban Image Construction: Beijing and Rio de Janeiro*. London and New York: Routledge.

CBI. (2007). *The Anholt City Brands Index (CBI): How the World Views Its Cities*. Available at: http://www.simonanholt.com/? gclid=CIL9sr7l9ZoCFYuB3godkFLpdw

Cieślikowski, K. (2016). *Event marketing, Podstawy teoretyczne i rozwiązania praktyczne*. Katowice: Akademia Wychowania Fizycznego im Jerzego Kukuczki w Katowicach.

Cudny, W. (2014). Festivals as a subject for geographical research, Geografisk Tidsskrift-Danish. *Journal of Geography*, 114(2), 132–142.

Cudny, W. (2016). *Festivalisation of Urban Spaces: Factors, Processes and Effects*. Springer: Cham.

Cudny, W. (2019). *City Branding and Promotion: The Strategic Approach*. London and New York: Routledge.

Cudny, W., Korec, P., & Rouba, R. (2012). Resident's perception of festivals – A case study of Łódź. *Sociológia*, 44(6), 704–728.

Cudny, W., & Przybylska, L. (2018). The urban and cultural functions of the Gdynia film festival. In T. Jenkins (ed). *International Film Festivals: Contemporary Cultures and History Beyond Venice and Cannes* (pp. 197–222). London and New York: I.B. Tauris.

Czornik, M. (2005). *Promocja Miasta*. Katowice: Wydawnictwo Akademii Ekonomicznej w Katowicach.

Degen, M., & García, M. (2012). The transformation of the 'Barcelona model': An analysis of culture, urban regeneration and governance. *International Journal of Urban and Regional Research*, 36(5), 1022–1038.

Donaldson, R. (2018). *Small Town Tourism in South Africa*. Cham: Springer.

Florek, M. (2013). *Podstawy Marketingu Terytorialnego*. Poznań: Wydawnictwo Uniwersytetu Ekonomicznego w Poznaniu.

Getz, D. (1991). *Festivals, Special Events, and Tourism*. New York: Van Nostrand Reinhold.

Getz, D. (2008). Event tourism: Definition, evolution, and research. *Tourism Management*, 29(3), 403–428.

Getz, D. (2010). The nature and scope of festival studies research. *International Journal Event Management Research*, 5(1), 1–47

Getz, D., & Page, S. J. (2016). *Event Studies: Theory, Research and Policy for Planned Events*. London and New York: Routledge.

Gold, J. R., & Ward, S. V. (eds). (1994). *Place Promotion: The Use of Publicity and Marketing to Sell Towns and Regions*. Chichester: John Wiley & Sons.

Goldblatt, J. (1990). *Special Events: The Art and Science of Celebration*. Hoboken: Wiley.

González, S. (2011). Bilbao and Barcelona 'in motion': How urban regeneration 'models' travel and mutate in the global flows of policy tourism. *Urban Studies*, 48(7), 1397–1418.

Gyeonggi Research Institute. (2007). *A Study on the Methodology of Developing City Brand Identity: Cases of Cities in Gyeonggi Province*. Available at: http://www.dbpia.co.kr/journal/articleDetail?nodeId=NODE01438367

Hall, C. M. (1989). The definition and analysis of hallmark tourist events. *GeoJournal*, 19(3), 263–268

Hall, C. M. (1992). *Hallmark Tourist Events: Impacts, Management and Planning*. London: Belhaven Press.

Hospers, G. J. (2009). Lynch, Urry and city marketing: Taking advantage of the city as a built and graphic image. *Place Branding and Public Diplomacy*, 5(3), 226–233.

Hoyle, L. H. (2002). *Event Marketing: How to Successfully Promote Events, Festivals, Conventions, and Expositions*. New York: John Wiley & Sons.

Hubbard, P., & Hall, T. (1998). The entrepreneurial city and the new urban politics. In T. Hall and P. Hubbard (eds). *The Entrepreneurial City: Geographies of Politics, Regime and Representation* (pp. 1–23). Chichester: John Wiley & Sons.

Jaworowicz, M., & Jaworowicz, P. (2016). *Event marketing w zintegrowanej komunikacji marketingowej*. Warszawa, SA: Difin.

Kavaratzis, M. (2004). From city marketing to city branding: Towards a theoretical framework for developing city brands. *Place Branding*, 1(1), 58–73.

Kavaratzis, M. (2018). Place branding: Are we any wiser? *Cities*, 80, 61–63.

Kavaratzis, M., & Ashworth, G. (2005). City branding: An effective assertion or a transitory marketing trick. *Tijdschrift voor Economische en Sociale Geografi e*, 96(5), 506–514.

Kavaratzis, M., & Ashworth, G. (2008). Place marketing: How did we get here and how are we going? *Journal of Place Management and Development*, 1(2), 150–165.

Knott, B., & Swart, K. (2018). Mega-events and place branding legacy for emerging economies. In I. Brittain, J. Bocarro, T. Byers and Swart, K. (eds). *Legacies and Mega Events: Facts or Fairytales* (pp. 159–171). New York and London: Routledge.

Kotler, P., & Armstrong, G. (2010). *Principles of Marketing*. Upper Saddle River: Pearson, Prentice Hall.

Kotler, P., Asplund, C., Rein, I., & Heider, D. (1999). *Marketing Places Europe: Attracting Investments, Industries, Residents and Visitors to European Cities, Communities, Regions and Nations*. London: Pearson Education.

Kotler, P., Keller, K., Brady, M., Goodman, M., & Hansen, T. (2009). *Marketing Management*. Harlow: Pearson Education Limited.

Lucarelli, A. (2018). Place branding as urban policy: The (im) political place branding. *Cities*, 80, 12–21.

Luna-Garcia, A. (2008). Just another coffee! Milking the Barcelona model, marketing a global image, and the resistance of local identities. In A. Cronin and K. Hetherington (eds). *Consuming the Entrepreneurial City* (pp. 143–160). New York: Routledge.

Marczak, M. (2014). Wpływ organizacji wielkich eventów piłkarskich na rozwój turystyki na przykładzie wybranych destynacji. *Turystyka Kulturowa*, 12, 54–67.

Markowski, T. (1999). *Zarządzanie Rozwojem Miast*. Warszawa: PWN.

Morgan, D. L. (1997). *The Focus Group Guidebook*. London: Sage publications.

Nufer, G. (2015). *Event Marketing in Sport und Kultur*. Bergisch: Erich Verlag Schmidt, Gladbach.

Oxford Wordpower Dictionary. (2002). *Słownik angielsko-polski z indeksem polsko-angielskim*. Oxford: Oxford University Press.

Paddison, R. (1993). City marketing, image reconstruction and urban regeneration. *Urban Studies*, 30(2), 339.

Phillips, R., & Johns, J. (2012). *Fieldwork for Human Geography*. London: Sage.

Raj, R., Walters, P., & Rashid, T. (2013). *Events Management: Principles and Practice*. London: Sage.

Rhoads, B. L., & Wilson, D. (2013). Observing our world. In B. Gomez and J. P. Jones III (eds). *Research Methods in Geography: A Critical Introduction* (pp. 26–40). Malden: Wiley-Blackwell.

Riffe, D., Lacy, S., & Fico, F. (2014). *Analyzing Media Messages: Using Quantitative Content Analysis in Research*. New York and London: Routledge.

Ritchie, J. R. B. (1984). Assessing the impacts of hallmark events: Conceptual and research issues. *Journal of Travel Research*, 23(1), 2–11.

Różycka, M. (2013). Marketing miejsca – turystyka eventowa „Efekt UEFA Euro 2012". *Zeszyty Naukowe 3/2013, Wyższa Szkoła Turystyki i Ekologii, Sucha Beskidzka*, 126.

Schutz, P. A., Chambless, C. B., & DeCuir, J. T. (2004). Multimethods research. In K. B. deMarrais and S. D. Lapan (eds). *Foundations for Research Methods of Inquiry in Education and the Social Sciences* (pp. 267–281). Mahwah and London: Lawrence Erlbaum Associates Publishers.

Šindler, P. (2003). *Event Marketing: Jak využít emoce v marketingové komunikaci*. Prague: Grada.

Smith, A. (2012). *Events and Urban Regeneration: The Strategic Use of Events to Revitalise Cities*. London and New York: Routledge.

Szromnik, A. (2012). *Marketing terytorialny. Miasto i region na rynku*. Warszawa: Oficyna Wolters Kluwer business.

Ward, S. (1998). *Selling Places: The Marketing and Promotion of Towns and Cities*, 1850–2000. London: Routledge.

Tara Lunga, M. (2012). Major special events: An interpretative literature review. *Management & Marketing Challenges for the Knowledge Society*, 7(4), 759–776.

Tobelem, J. M. (1997). The marketing approach in museums. In R. Sandell and R. R. Janes (eds). *Museum Management and Curatorship* (pp. 294–312). London and New York: Routledge.

Veal, A. J. (2017). *Research Methods for Leisure and Tourism*. Harlow, UK: Pearson.

Wilson, R. (2004). The impact of cultural events on city image: Rotterdam, cultural capital of Europe 2001. *Urban Studies*, 41(10), 1993.

Wohlfeil, M., & Whelan, S. (2006). Consumer motivations to participate in marketing events: The role of predispositional involvement, association for consumer research, Duluth 2006- Available at: www.acrwebsite.org/volumes/eacr/vol7/EuropeanVolume7_16.pdf

Wohlfeil, M., & Whelan, S. (2006). Consumer motivations to participate in event-marketing strategies. *Journal of Marketing Management*, 22(5–6), 643–669.

Zenker, S., & Beckmann, S. (2013). Measuring brand image effects of flagship projects for place brands: The case of Hamburg. *Journal of Brand Management*, 20(8), 642–655.

Online sources

https://ueaeprints.uea.ac.uk/25883/1/Consumer_Motivations_to_Participate_in_Event_Marketing_Strategies.pdf

https://dictionary.cambridge.org/dictionary/english/event-marketing

www.businessdictionary.com/definition/event-marketing.html

https://dictionary.cambridge.org/dictionary/english/event-marketing

www.businessdictionary.com/definition/event-marketing.html

2 Cultural promotion of place as 'northern' space

The case of the Umeå2014 – European Capital of Culture event

Håkan Appelblad

Introduction

At 5:00 on the evening of Saturday, February 1, 2014, tens of thousands of people gathered along the banks of the Ume River in the city centre of Umeå in northern Sweden. They were there to witness the official inauguration ceremony for Umeå2014 – the European Capital of Culture (ECoC) year, awarded to the city five years earlier. The other EU city awarded the ECoC for 2014 was the Latvian capital, Riga. The winter setting was a natural background for the hour-long cultural performance **Burning Snow** (Figure 2.1). The outdoor show included a mixture of high-tech lighting, drones, artists, snowmobiles and reindeer, featured on or above the ice-covered river. Present at the ceremony was also HRH Crown Princess Victoria, who gave a short opening speech.

Presumably, this inauguration ceremony captured some of the images the Umeå municipality and the organizers behind Umeå2014 wanted to show the outside world, including the rest of Europe. As concisely presented in the *Rough City Guide* that very year, it seemed that the intended message was received:

> Population-wise, Umeå doesn't even make it into Sweden's top ten. But culturally, this remote northern city punches well above its weight. Here, opera and death metal are admired with equal gusto. Bitterly cold winters are not avoided, but embraced in the great outdoors – albeit with gloved hands. And the city's 36,000-odd students, many of them artists, keep things looking fresh. Umeå is this year's European Capital of Culture (along with Riga), and the year-long schedule of happenings should tempt adventurous travelers to make the long journey north.
>
> (*Rough Guide*'s Top Ten Cities 2014)

By European standards, Umeå is a relatively small city (with fewer than 90,000 inhabitants), geographically remote from European as well as Swedish core areas, and at that time was the most northern Capital of Culture ever (Figure 2.2.). A Capital of Culture year is intended to have a positive impact on the host city's cultural sector. As presented by the European Commission, the idea is to put cities at the heart of cultural life. Culture and art can improve the quality of life and

Figure 2.1 The opening ceremony of Umeå2014 – ***Burning Snow***

Source: Umeå2014 (Photo: Fredrik Larsson)

Figure 2.2 Umeå2014 web map with the "Northern Room" and Sápmi

Source: Umeå2014

(Note: Umeå is depicted with the Umeå2014 logo, the smiling heart.)

strengthen the sense of community in the cities awarded the ECoC title (European Commission 2018a).

Seen as an event, the European Capital of Culture year perhaps stretches conventional definitions of events. Planned events are spatial-temporal phenomena and, depending on the setting, those who attend and the content of the programme, each event is unique, implying that you have to 'be there' to fully enjoy it (Getz 2008, p. 404). Hence, events are generally defined through the dimensions of *content, temporalities*, and *spatialities*. From the content dimension, it can be discussed whether an ECoC event can be recognized as a single event or as a collection of single events occurring within a certain period and geographical setting. Temporalities can also be questioned in the case of a programme lasting a full year, thus overbridging the seasonality that occurs over this period. Finally, and of special focus in this chapter, the spatialities are of interest for several reasons. An ECoC event can include regional partners and activities and, hence, transcend the borders of the host city. Further on, the cultural programme can represent geographies beyond the city itself and embrace different notions and aspects of space. The implementation of the ECoC programme also provides various examples of how cities across the continent proactively associate the term 'European' with their particular places and territories (Sykes 2011). The promotion images of Umeå and the ECoC year Umeå2014 included themes referring not only to the city itself but also to other geographies and spaces and certainly also the notion of 'Europe'. Studies on the promotion and images of space may also be seen as an act of place branding. Branding associated with spaces and places is, in essence, a geographical issue and appears to be an emerging research field within geography (Andersson 2014).

An ECoC event is widely recognized as an opportunity to revitalize not only culture but also a city itself. Regenerating cities is a strong theme in the analysis of the effects of ECoC (García 2005). Moreover, cities' urban development plans are often elements of their broadly planned branding programmes. Hence, branding not only consists of promotional endeavours but also encompasses development programmes including, among other things, the organization of events (see Anholt 2010). The most visible example of this deals with large, former industrial cities adapting to a post-industrial setting in which culture becomes a key factor (see Gdaniec 2000). However, what about a different setting – for instance, a small, remote city in the north that is not primarily characterized as an industrial city or that at least has not faced a substantial decline in its industrial sector?

The main aim of this chapter is to examine whether the organization of Umeå2014 – the European Capital of Culture (ECoC) in Umeå in 2014 – influenced the city's socio-economic situation, promotion, and brand. The study is thus also an attempt to contribute to the discussion on events with regard to their dimensions as suggested by Getz (2008): *content, temporalities*, and *spatialities*.

The programme for Umeå2014 included more than 1,000 single cultural events and artistic performances. The main empirical sources used for the analysis presented in this chapter encompass the programme for Umeå2014 and various promotional materials connected with the event. Regarding the empirical sources, the websites of Umeå2014 and the Umeå municipality, as well as evaluation documents, including an evaluation of Umeå2014 by the European Commission, are prime sources. Another important source is the case study by Wåhlin et al. (2016) of Umeå2014 and the participatory process of co-creation and strategies for urban and cultural development. The aforementioned sources were supplemented with the author's direct observations while participating in events selected from the event calendar of the yearlong Umeå2014.

The analysis presented in the study is mainly qualitative, with the adoption of thematic analysis driven by the relational conception of space, as suggested by Thrift (2009). Thus, the focus of the study is to explore the spatialities in the promotion of Umeå and Umeå2014, as well as in single events included in the ECoC year. This means finding references to geography in any form, including more imaginal representations of geographical space. The intent is to discover the most important themes in the Umeå2014 event.

Theoretical approach

All shapes and forms of culture are important assets among the arsenal of possible means of place development and promotion. The interest in culture as an economic asset in urban development has turned out to be a policy field in its own right. Labelled 'culture-led urban regeneration', it has developed as a core strategy in cities throughout the world (García 2005). The launch of the ECoC programme has given European cities awarded the title the opportunity to boost such a culture-led strategy. The economic benefit is also recognized by the European Commission, which highlights that the ECoC event has also become an opportunity for 'regenerating cities, raising the international profile of cities, enhancing the image of cities in the eyes of their own inhabitants, breathing new life into a city's culture, and boosting tourism' (European Commission 2018a). The first visible example of a conscious strategy for making use of an awarded ECoC title can be found in Glasgow in 1990. García (2005) mentions that Glasgow was the first city to:

- win the title after an open national competition,
- have more than three years to plan the event,
- gather public and private support to fund initiatives, and
- understand the potential of using ECoC as a tool for urban regeneration.

Glasgow, and later Liverpool, are perceived as successful in event-led cultural regeneration and in using the ECoC title to transform their city image. The image change has also endured over time (García 2017). Culture has frequently been cited as a key element of the urban tourism function in many European countries. Besides the cities mentioned earlier, Dublin and Barcelona are other visible examples of serious attempts at regenerating former industrial cities through culture (Liu 2015). With Liverpool as an example, Liu concludes that cultural events constitute a boost for cultural tourism in a number of ways: realizing the experience economy, enhancing city image, facilitating urban regeneration, fertilizing cultural provision, and establishing partnerships (Liu 2015, p. 36). Whatever the justifications are for ECoC events, 'culture is being groomed to become "big business"' (Wåhlin et al. 2016, p. 3).

When it comes to the bid for the Swedish ECoC title, Åkerlund and Müller (2012) discovered that Umeå's strategic planners adhered to the 'competitive discourse'. It was hoped that different stakeholders in the city would come together and contribute to its image as a creative and ebullient place, filled with possibilities. While the 'official' discourse, mainly supported by the public sector that strongly supported the bid, promoted positive expectations for the effects of the ECoC event, challenging discourses were also visible during the preparation for both the bid and, later, the ECoC year itself.

A north-south dimension is apparent in Sweden, including when it comes to the degree of peripherality. Northern areas are linked to images frequently used in tourism communication (Müller and Jansson 2007): for instance the Arctic Circle, the indigenous Sami people, great seasonal variation in daylight, the aurora borealis, and the perceived wilderness, promoting such positive notions as solitude, escapism, challenges, and even religion. Consequently, the north is of interest to those seeking experiences that are different from their everyday life and mass tourism destinations (see Schulze 2005).

The city of Umeå represents a sharp contrast and an exception in the area, which is labelled a northern sparsely populated area (NSPA). The designation of NSPA highlights geographical and development aspects related to remoteness that are absent, or less common, in other European regions. These aspects include low population numbers, a harsh climate, and an overall lack of agglomeration benefits (OECD 2017). Despite its regional setting, according to Eriksson (2010), Umeå is promoted as a young, growing, cultural city with successful businesses. Thus, it is a paradox that in order to win the bid to become ECoC, Umeå had to present itself as northern, 'alternative', unusual, and exotic. At the same time, it was struggling to create an image of a modern and creative city, emphasizing culture as a contrast to the promotion of nature through its rural municipalities. But in order to win the race for the Swedish ECoC year 2014, Umeå had to play the indigenous card (Eriksson 2010).

When discussing spatial forms of images or the promotion of cities, a multifaceted or relational view of the spatialities is necessary. Thrift (2009) advocates a relational view on space simplified into four conceptions of it. First, *empirical constructions*: physically visible and measurable elements that form the fabric of our daily lives. Second, *unblocking space*: all kinds of connections in the world. Third, *image space*: images of all shapes and sizes, likely more pervasive than ever before due to the magnitude of images in current society, potentially as important as the things (empirical entities) they depict. Fourth, *place space*: a space understood as a specific place, containing a particular set of qualities while at the same time also providing keys to memory and behaviour. This fourth type is likely the most contested conception of space.

The European capital of culture

The EU itself recognizes the European Capitals of Culture initiative as Europe's most ambitious cultural project in both scope and scale. The former president of the European Commission, José Manuel Barroso, presented it as a flagship cultural initiative, possibly the best known and most appreciated by European citizens (European Communities 2009). As the European Commission (European Commission 2018a) has stated, the ECoC initiative is designed to:

- highlight the richness and diversity of cultures in Europe,
- celebrate the cultural features Europeans share,
- increase European citizens' sense of belonging to a common cultural area, and
- foster the contribution of culture to the development of cities.

The first idea to establish the ECoC, appearing in the early 1980s, originated with Melina Mercouri, former Greek minister of culture. This happened at a time when the European Community had no legislative basis for any cultural policy. Nevertheless, the creation of a yearly cultural festival focusing on cities around Europe was seen as a way to promote European identity and encourage a positive image of the European community in the eyes of its inhabitants (European Parliament 2013). For the first 12 years, capital cities and cities with a renowned cultural profile were awarded the Capital of Culture title. Athens was the first host city (1985), followed by Florence, Amsterdam, and Berlin, and then other major cities from the member states.

In the early 1990s, culture was included for the first time in the legal framework for the European Community. In the Maastricht Treaty of 1992, Article 128, it was stated in the first paragraph: 'The Community shall contribute to the flowering of the cultures of the Member States, while respecting their national and regional diversity and at the same time bringing the common cultural heritage to the fore' (EUR Lex 11997E151). The Treaty provided a way to establish a legal basis for the ECoC programme. Hence, the scope of the programme and its selection criteria changed. The increasing number of EU member states has also widened the geographical field of possible host cities. Until 2004, the appointed cultural cities were designated by national governments. Since then, more specific selection criteria, selection procedures, and rules for nomination have been applied (European Parliament 2013).

Today, two EU cities in different countries are awarded the ECoC title every year. Every third year, an additional city from a country belonging to the European Economic Area (EFTA/EEA) or a potential candidate for EU membership is also selected. The formal call for ECoC bids in the countries entitled to make a proposal opens about six years ahead of the title year. The cities bidding for the title year are required to complete a proposal that refers to the criteria deemed necessary in order to ensure a successful ECoC. In the guide (European

Commission 2018b) for cities preparing a bid for 2020 to 2033, the following six criteria are listed:

a   contribution to the long-term cultural strategy,
b   cultural and artistic content,
c   European dimension,
d   outreach,
e   management,
f   capacity to deliver.

With direct reference to Umeå2014, the guide exemplifies what the European dimension might entail: 'Umeå2014 have built their entire programme around the calendar of the Sami people, the indigenous people of northern Scandinavia' (European Commission 2018b, p. 19).

The geographical setting

Umeå is located in northern Sweden on the Ume River, close to the Gulf of Bothnia about 500 kilometres north of Sweden's capital, Stockholm, and some 300 kilometres south of the Arctic Circle. Umeå is the largest and fastest-growing city in the northernmost province of Norrland, which covers roughly two thirds of the country. Umeå is the most significant urban centre north of the Stockholm-Uppsala region and, at the same time, is relatively remote from the major urban areas in the southern part of Sweden. Umeå municipality is the eleventh largest in the country, with 125,000 inhabitants (2017), of whom 86,000 live in the city (Statistics Sweden). Since the establishment in 1965 of Umeå University, which has become a major landmark in the city, its population has had an average yearly increase of about 1,200. The university has about 33,000 enrolled students and 4,000 employees and, along with the steady increase in population, contributes to a relatively low average age (38 years). In fact, Umeå's young age profile explains why the municipality is the only one in Norrland, and among 16 of Sweden's 290 municipalities, where the major factor of population change for 2010–2014 was a natural increase in population (SKL 2015). Thus, Umeå's demographic situation is in sharp contrast to adjacent areas of Norrland, which are generally sparsely populated and face ageing and population decline. As a point of reference, the county of Västerbotten (55,400 sq. kilometres) is slightly smaller than Croatia but larger than countries such as Denmark, Switzerland, Slovakia, or Estonia, and has only 268,000 inhabitants. Roughly one out of three Västerbottnians live in the city of Umeå.

The population growth in Umeå is expected to continue. Municipality officials have declared the growth goal of reaching 200,000 inhabitants by 2050. In the structure plan for Umeå, it is stated that urban development should aim for a dense and attractive city settlement, hence enabling sustainable transportation solutions, not least for biking and pedestrians. Developing public spaces and encouraging social inclusion are considered to be of higher importance in a more populous and denser city (Umeå municipality a).

VisitUmeå, the official tourist guide of the Umeå Region, highlights the youthfulness, openness, cultural assets, etc., in promoting visits to Umeå:

> The university city of Umeå, with its 125,000 inhabitants, is the largest city in northern Sweden. Over 30,000 students give the city a youthful, modern touch, but also an international feel and the openness we are so proud of. Here you will find inspirational shopping, high-class restaurants, comfortable hotels, a lot of culture and interesting architecture. Around the corner is beautiful countryside with wide forests, wild rivers and rolling seas for you to discover. Easily accessible trails for hiking, cycling or skiing, rugged dogsled tours, white water rafting that makes the adrenaline pump or looking out for the northern lights that calm the soul.
>
> (visitumea.se VISITORS' GUIDE 2018)

Umeå as part of Sápmi

Situated in northern Sweden, Umeå is also part of Sápmi, the land of the Sami. The Sami are the indigenous people of Finland, Norway, Russia, and Sweden, with a distinct language, culture, and livelihood traditionally based on hunting, fishing, and reindeer husbandry. While Sápmi has no formal border, it is generally perceived as stretching between the central part of Scandinavia and the Kola Peninsula in Russia (see Figure 2.2). It is estimated that the number of Sami is approximately 40,000 to 50,000 in Norway, 20,000 to 35,000 in Sweden, about 6,000 in Finland, and about 2,000 in Russia. These numbers are estimates, as no census of the Sami people has occurred since World War II (samer.se). The popular view of the Sami people is ambiguous; they have been seen either as a group doomed in the modern world or as a kind of noble savages, living in harmony with the nature. In any case, they were seen as different from the majority population in Sweden (Heith 2015). In later times, the Swedish government has attempted to compensate the Sami for historical discrimination. Milestones in this endeavour include the recognition of the Sami as an indigenous people by Swedish Parliament (1977) and the establishment of the Sami Parliament in Sweden (1993). Moreover, in 2000, the Sami language (along with four other historical minority languages in Sweden) was granted official status (Sametinget).

The Sami connections with Umeå are visible in various ways. Some narratives on the Sami presence in Umeå in the early 20th century are provided by Rönér Douhan (2013). To the question of whether the city of Umeå is a good choice for representing the Sami culture, Michael Lindblad, president of the Umeå Sami association *Såhkie*, claims that there is no better alternative if you are looking for a city in Sweden. Several Sami interest groups have Umeå as their base, and Umeå University is a centre for Sami research and offers possibilities to study Sami culture and language (Pettersson 2013). Umeå is one of about 20 municipalities in Sweden that have applied to the Swedish government to be an administrative area for the Sami language: i.e., offering possibilities to use the Sami language in contact with public authorities (Umeå municipality b).

Despite various examples of Sami presence in Umeå, the embracing of Sami themes and Sami cultural expressions has not resonated among all local citizens. This was apparent, for instance, in social media concerning the strong Sami content during the Umeå2014 opening ceremony. Some local citizens expressed doubts as to any Sami connections with Umeå. These alienating segments of the local non-Sami population may also be understood in a historical context of long-running tensions over Sami rights and land-use claims (Fox and Rampton 2015). In the pre-selection report in January 2009, the selection panel expressed some concerns about the 'celebration of Saami Culture, which clearly had to be handled very carefully in dialogue with Saami leaders' (Selection panel a, p. 5).

The ECoC 2014 application and selection

Umeå's application for the ECoC 2014 was made from a strong cultural position. The municipality has striven for many years to enhance its cultural profile. Besides the opening of Umeå University in 1965, the establishment of *Norrlandsoperan* with its symphony orchestra in the 1970s, the erecting of a cultural house through *Folkets Hus* in the 1980s, and the building of a 'musical house' for *Norrlandsoperan* in the early 2000s are among the more visible examples of the cultural ambitions of Umeå municipality. Investments in culture have consciously been used as city development measures. This is evident in the emphasis of turning the 'face of the city' towards the river. As intended in the 'City Between the Bridges' planning initiative from the late 1980s, the quay area, largely occupied by parking spaces, was to be transformed into a public and cultural area (Hugoson 2015; Wåhlin et al. 2016).

The emphasis on culture in Umeå is also evident in the amount of public funding allocated for culture. Umeå is among the municipalities in Sweden with the highest expenditures on culture, more than twice the average for Sweden in recent years. The cost per capita in 2017 was 2,381 SEK (Swedish krona) and 4.5 per cent of the municipality's total operating costs. In 2014, this figure was 2,524 SEK (Myndigheten för kulturanalys 2018).

Cultural life in Umeå is characterized by both cultural activities created by various free associations in the city and by attracting artists to perform at various festivals. Noteworthy is the vital musical scene for local youths, offered through various municipality-funded youth recreational centres. Especially successful was 'Hardcore', a subgenre of punk rock, including its 'Straightedge' profile in Umeå, that evolved in the 1990s (Hugoson 2015). Among the largest cultural festivals are the *Umeå Jazz Festival*, the *Folk Music Festival*, *Littfest*, the *Visfestival* on Holmön, the *MADE* festival and the *Umeå Open*. When it comes to cultural facilities, some of the more important ones are *Norrlandsoperan* and *Folkets Hus*, along with the *Västerbotten museum* and Umedalens sculpture park, as well as the Umeå Arts Campus including the Umeå Institute of Design, the Umeå Academy of Fine Arts, the Umeå School of Architecture, the *Bildmuseet* museum, and HumLab X.

The decision to apply for the Swedish ECoC 2014 was taken by the Umeå municipality in 2005. Four cities in Sweden applied: Gävle, Lund, Uppsala, and Umeå. Lund and Umeå were deemed to best meet the criteria and were invited to submit a full application for the second round of the competition (Selection panel a). Umeå's bid for the ECoC event was named *Curiosity and Passion – the Art of Co-Creation*.

In the bid, Umeå was described as an unusual place: 'large enough to be taken seriously and small enough to make it happen'. The campaign for the ECoC title was 'on behalf of the northernmost region of Europe, which wants to see itself not as on the periphery of Europe, but as part of its heart' (Umeå2014 2008, p. 7). The geographical perspective was stressed, and for the first time, a northern perspective would be exposed through an ECoC year that would 'go well beyond its unique expressions, themes and festivals inspired by the midnight sun, Aurora Borealis, northern nature and Sami culture' (Umeå2014 2008, p. 8).

Later in the bid, it is stated that the goal is to make the entire Northern Room visible. Within Sweden, this region encompasses the country's four northernmost counties: Norrbotten, Västerbotten, Västernorrland, and Jämtland. During Umeå's ECoC year, many things occurred outside Umeå itself. A map on the Umeå2014 website made it easy for visitors to see what was happening in the region (Figure 2.2). The map displayed regional collaborates to Umeå2014: municipalities in Västerbotten, neighbouring counties, and adjacent areas in Finland, Norway, and Russia. Thus, the Northern Room generally corresponds with the Sápmi area. In the final selection report, the panel welcomed the involvement of the wider region but was keen to see the city of Umeå remain at the centre of the ECoC year (Selection panel b).

In 2009 Umeå was selected as Sweden's nominee for ECoC, based on the criteria set out in the European decision. The selection panel also appreciated the strong political engagement, solid governance, high-quality programme, and solid financial support from local authorities. The panel also recommended a number of works to be carried out prior to 2014: for example offering a new European cultural perspective from northern Europe, ensuring full inclusion of the Sami people and Sami culture in the plans, and a confirmation that, while the wider region would be involved, the city of Umeå would be the centre of planning and programme development (Selection panel b).

The ECoC application referred to various examples of investment before the programme year of 2014. In the downtown area of Umeå, the following projects were mentioned: the Art Campus, including *Bildmuseet*/the Art Exhibition Hall; the City Between the Bridges; meeting places for film; an attractive city centre; and an aquatic centre (Umeå2014 2008, Part IV, Q3). As for the cultural programme, open source and co-creation were stressed. The organizers' idea was to set the broad themes for the whole yearlong event and then invite cultural operators to participate and fill the programme themselves (Fox and Rampton 2015).

The Umeå2014 promotional activities

According to the report by Fox and Rampton (2015), a vast number of promotional activities were undertaken to promote Umeå2014. The most important activities started in 2012, when a professional team was established to work on the marketing communication for the event; by 2014, the team consisted of nine people. The budget for marketing activities increased from 7 million SEK in 2013 to 18 million SEK (1.9 million USD) in 2014. Efforts to promote Umeå2014 were aimed at facilitating further culture-driven growth of the city. These endeavours aimed to:

- increase commitment for Umeå2014 and attract co-creation,
- strengthen Umeå's profile as an interesting city of culture, and
- increase the number of visitors to Umeå and to northern Sweden.

The Umeå2014 marketing team placed great emphasis on contacting the city's residents and disseminating information about Umeå2014 in local media. However, in the years 2012–2013, the event was still in its programming phase (which hindered communication) and was the subject of criticism in local media. In 2014, though, more positive comments, and later also assessments, appeared in local media (Fox and Rampton 2015). The local media activities were supplemented by the employment of a group of local Umeå2014 ambassadors, whose goal was to promote Umeå2014 in the city. Many ECoC-related articles were published ahead of the Umeå2014 event in the local newspaper, *Västerbottens Kuriren* (VK). VK is published six days a week and has a coverage of 45 percent of the households in Umeå municipality. From 2005 to 2013, 1,692 articles were published about the ECoC. Some of these articles also contained issues related to growth (286), tourism (127), co-creation (39), Sami (125), and the House of Culture (read *Väven*) (107) (Wåhlin et al. 2016).

Concerning marketing communication on an international scale, this was aimed at attracting tourists and visitors who would not otherwise have heard of the city. Due to time and budget restrictions, it was not possible to influence large groups of potential visitors; instead, other marketing endeavours were undertaken. Prior to the programme year, Umeå2014 organized a promotional tour, Caught by Umeå. The tour encompassed seven European cities and took place in autumn of 2013. It was organized in collaboration with Visit Sweden, Visit Umeå, and Umeå University (Umeå 2014). The tour was financed by the Melina Mercouri Prize, which Umeå2014 had received from the European Commission. Caught by Umeå was the major international communication event, designed to reach out to foreign people and journalists. It is estimated that this tour attracted a total of some 57,000 visitors in various cities. Moreover, it resulted in 14 foreign press visits to Umeå, including one by the Lonely Planet team. In order to promote Umeå2014, a close cooperation was undertaken with Visit Umeå (a local destination company) and Visit Sweden (the national tourism agency). Both agencies cooperated in the organization of the Caught by Umeå tour. The event was also promoted during the Internationale Tourismus-Börse (ITB) travel fair in Berlin in 2013.

Nationally, Umeå2014 was promoted through, among other things, a prelaunch event held in Stockholm in 2014 (Fox and Rampton 2015). However, as stated by Fox and Rampton (2015, p. 25), 'The national media coverage of the ECoC had been disappointing, i.e. less extensive and less positive in tone than international coverage'. A media analysis study commissioned by Umeå2014, which included Russia, China, and eight European countries, confirmed a positive tone in the international coverage. It also included some critical coverage related to the notion of culture-driven growth and a perceived lack of coverage of the Sami. The media coverage peaked in early 2014 and included especially German, Spanish, and Danish press (Fox and Rampton 2015, p. 25).

The Umeå2014 programme year

Like for most ECoC hosts, the cultural programme presented by Umeå2014 during the title year was more extensive and more European in nature than the city's cultural offerings in previous years. The Umeå2014 online calendar contained 1,054 events. To manifest a Sami perspective and legacy, the programme was based on the eight seasons of the Sami calendar, with the intention of giving each season its own character (Table 2.1).

A substantial part of Umeå2014 consisted of recurrent yearly arrangements, like the pop festival *Umeå Open*, the performing arts festival *MADE*, the *Umeå Jazz Festival*, the literature festival *Littfest*, and *Sami week*. Other events were new, like the spectacular opening ceremony **Burning Snow** (Figure 2.1) and the regional project *River Stories*. As indicated in Figure 2.2, some of the Umeå2014 events took place in areas outside Umeå. Among the events with the largest audience were the opening ceremony (also the seasonal inauguration of Dálvvie) **Burning Snow**, with 55,000 spectators; *Leonor Fini/Pourquoi pas?* at Bildmuseet, 47,500; the closing ceremony, *Northern Light*, 11,000; *Littfest*, 10,500; and the opera *Elektra*, 10,000 (Fox & Rampton 2015). The total audience for all Umeå2014 events is estimated at 800,000. About 70 percent of the residents of Umeå attended one or several events (Region Västerbotten 2016). The EU ex-post evaluation (Fox and Rampton 2015) identifies four key cultural results for Umeå2014:

- the focus on the Sami, a highly significant factor in making the programme more unique, innovative and European, and making northern Sweden more visible in Europe;

Table 2.1 The eight seasons of the Sami calendar and the programme year of Umeå2014

Season name	Characteristics	Period
Deep winter	Dálvvie – The Season of Caring	30 January – 27 February
Early spring	Gijrradálvvie – The Season of Awakening	28 February – 29 April
True spring	Gijrra – The Season of Returning	30 April – 19 June
Early summer	Gijrragiessie – The Season of Growing	20 June – 10 July
Summer	Giessie – The Season of Contemplation	11 July – 28 August
Early autumn	Tjakttjagiessie – The Season of Harvesting	29 August – 9 October
True autumn	Tjakttja – The Season of Desire	10 October – 20 November
Early winter	Tjakttjadálvvie – The Season of a Journey	21 November – 29 January

Source: Umeå2014

- enabled Umeå to increase its European and international dimension by strengthening already existing collaborations and creating new links to international partners;
- improved the city's cultural offering during the traditionally weak summer season; and
- the ECoC allowed Umeå to implement larger and more innovative cultural events than previously.

While the effects of Umeå2014 on tourism are not possible to isolate, overall figures give some positive indications. During 2014, the turnover in Umeå's tourism sector exceeded 1 billion SEK, which was an increase of more than 20 percent from the previous year. Changes in accommodation figures are similar, with the number of hotel nights increasing by 21 percent from 2013 to 2014. The number of hits on the Visit Umeå website reached 534,000 (of which 68 percent represented unique visitors) in 2014, an increase of 69 percent (Fox and Rampton 2015; Region Västerbotten 2016).

In the event evaluation commissioned by Umeå municipality from Pricewater-houseCoopers, the focus was on whether or not Umeå2014 had achieved its five empowerment objectives: people, city, culture, Northern Region, and European interaction. According to PwC's report, Umeå2014 managed to empower the city, the culture, and the European interaction. PwC stressed that, while Umeå2104 was not the cause of Umeå's strong development and position, they believed it was a driving force in generating investments and creativity there. Moreover, the municipal contribution of approximately SEK 100 million was augmented about 3.5-fold (empowerment of the city). Thanks to the strong political stance for culture, strong public financing, and support for co-creation, an empowerment of the culture had been achieved. Based on interviews with suppliers and partners, it was assessed that realized value, i.e. generating PR value, exceeded the resources that had been contributed (empowerment of European interaction). Two empowerment objectives were not met, according to PwC. Even though culture consumption had increased, the very ambitiously formulated objective that stated things like 'all citizens have discovered new opportunities' and 'new target groups have been reached' was not realized (empowerment of the people). Activities and events within Umeå2014 were primarily undertaken in Västerbotten and in three cities outside the county. PwC found no clear strategy by which the Northern Regions had identified new forms of interaction with Sweden and Europe (PricewaterhouseCoopers 2015).

People and cultural practitioners were invited to take part in forming the Umeå2014 programme through the open-source approach, based on co-creation and participation. The fulfilment of this approach is also evident in the relatively small proportion of events in Umeå2014 being directly produced or commissioned by the organizing team, compared with previous ECoC events (Fox and Rampton 2015). However, co-creation may disregard unequal terms among those who participate. In a critical review of Umeå2014, Hudson et al. (2017) claimed that most of the co-funded projects were more mainstream cultural activities, like traditional opera performances, that did not challenge existing power relations. Moreover, as stated by Wåhlin et al. (2016), co-creation within the public sector can be seen as a tactic to convince people to share their resources freely, while governments can reduce public spending. Consequently, the overall benefits of co-creation are sensitive to the translation of values between involved partners.

Events of the programme year

A few single events of Umeå2014 are presented in more detail here. Unless otherwise stated, the information was retrieved from the Umeå2014 website. The opening ceremony, *Burning Snow*, on the evening of Saturday, 1 February 2014, was the paramount and signature event of the entire Umeå2014 year. It was accompanied by various other events over the weekend, filling Umeå's city centre. *Burning Snow* attracted the largest number of people at a single time during Umeå2014 (55,000). A number of people held speeches: Marie-Louise Rönnmark, mayor, city of Umeå; Stefan Mikaelsson, president of the Sami Parliament Plenary Assembly; Lena Adelsohn-Liljeroth, minister for culture; Jan Truszczynski, the European Commission's director general for culture; and, finally, the inauguration speech by HRH Crown Princess Victoria.

The accompanying show featured on and above the ice was produced and performed by the interdisciplinary artist network phase7 from Berlin. The show also included performing artists, dancers, a Sami choir, and the well-known Umeå-based Sami artist and songwriter Sofia Jannok. The crowd, larger than expected, made it difficult for many visitors to follow the show as the number of people made it difficult for many to see what was happening on the ice. Complementary screens were too small to compensate for this. Accounts of these difficulties, including doubts regarding the representation of Umeå as a Sami place, were visible in the comment feed on the Umeå2014 website. The feed thus illustrated some counter narratives to the official Umeå2014 discourse:

> *Burning Snow* had everything. Exploitation of a minority culture for commercial purposes, enhancement of stereotyping images of a province. Bad will to local artists and local culture, not allowed to be present. Misleading picture of Umeå culture. Misleading marketing. Poor account of audience. Poor transportation to and from events. Happy organizers. Vielen Dank für *Burning Snow*!
>
> (Umeå 2014, translated by the author)

Sami week, Ubmejen Biejvieh (26 February–12 March 2014), celebrated its 15th anniversary during the Umeå2014 year. In 2014, this event was extended to two weeks. Ubmejen Biejvieh has developed into one of the most important cultural events in Sápmi. It is a meeting place for Sami issues and has a purpose of visualizing and distributing the multifaceted Sami culture through exhibitions, activities for children, lectures, seminars, workshops, concerts, theatre, etc. The programme mainly takes place on the premises of *Västerbottens museum* and attracts Sami from the whole of Sápmi as well as local inhabitants and tourists. Sami week is organized by the local Sami association *Såhkie*.

The *House of Metal Festival* 2014 (28 February–1 March 2014) has been held at *Folkets Hus* in Umeå since 2007, and about 25 bands from Sweden and other countries played at the festival in 2014. Besides heavy metal performances, visitors were offered records, clothing, and other things.

River Stories was the most prestigious regional project during Umeå2014. *Norrlandsoperan* was the main organizer, and the project was one of the most well-funded ones, with contributions from Umeå2014 and the Västerbotten region, as well as state authorities. Among the most visible features of the Västerbottnian landscape are the rivers flowing through the county, from the mountains in the west to the Gulf of Bothnia in the east. River Stories contained a large number of sub-projects, touring through the county and along the rivers to highlight the roles the rivers played as energy sources and communication lines for both timber and people, as well as sources for contemplation. The project was intended to create enhanced regional cultural collaboration and local involvement. Some of the sub-projects partly outgrew the boundaries of the Umeå2014 programme as they were actively supported by Sami associations in other municipalities (Wåhlin et al. 2016).

One example of the sub-projects was the weeklong cultural reindeer raid *Renrajd med Nicolai Dunger och vänner* (25 January–1 February 2014), featuring the artist Nicolai Dunger and friends. The raid departed from Ammarnäs in the mountain areas and went along the river and on old migratory routes for the reindeer herds, with Umeå as its final destination on the inauguration day for Umeå2014. The tour was done on skis, and during it, the small group performed music for and with people who crossed their path. Its final stops were *Sápmi Today* on Umeå's town square (*Rådhustorget*), and later the *Midwinter Jazz* festival at *Folkets Hus*.

Eight Sami Artists at *Bildmuseet* consisted of solo exhibitions by eight Sami artists from Sweden, Finland, and Norway, working with painting, sculpture, photography, film, and performance. The series of exhibitions included:

- Katarina Pirak Sikku, Sweden: Nammaláhpán (2 February–20 April 2014)
- Marja Helander, Finland: Silence (23 February–27 April 2014)
- Per Enoksson, Sweden: The Forest in Me (6 April–1 June 2014)
- Liselott Wajstedt, Sweden: The Lost One (18 May–7 September 2014)
- Carola Grahn, Sweden: A Cry From the Expanses (18 May–7 September 2014)
- Joar Nango and FFB, Norway: Searching for Smooth Space (7 September–2 November 2014)
- Geir Tore Holm, Norway: Fughetta (12 October 2014–18 January 2015)
- Anders Sunna, Sweden: Area Infected (2 November 2014–18 January 2015)

The exhibition at *Bildmuseet*, a museum for contemporary art and visual culture, could be seen as a statement in itself and as an example of a performative turn through counternarratives of Sami culture as it came to be orientated towards the present and the future. Thus, the conventional representation of Sami culture at a museum as primitive and doomed in modernity was challenged and contradicted (Heith 2015).

Baltic Sea – Floating Trunks was both a project and an art installation (20 June–20 September 2014). The project, led by the artistic duo SIMKA, connected young people through art, with the creation of a work of art for the ECoC cities Umeå and Riga as well as Pori in Finland. The work they created was launched on the river as a large floating grove of trees. In the work, the Baltic Sea was seen as a common, floating continent that both unites and divides. When the trees were brought up on land after the summer, they were planted to allow them to take root, giving a long-term aspect to the artwork.

One part of the urban forum project was *Vasaplan, open space design* (3–30 September 2014). Three groups of architects and artists hosted activities on the public square and at the local bus station in central Umeå, *Vasaplan*. The aim was to find new ways to generate dialogue with Umeå's residents about the future shape of *Vasaplan*. The activities ranged from physical installations to film and performances. The organizers were the Umeå municipality, including cooperation with the National Board of Housing, Building and Planning.

The opera *Elektra* (14–23 August 2014) was an interesting blend of classical European cultural heritage, modern performance, and making use of the environmental assets of the outdoor stage on late-summer evenings in Umeå, with their special natural light. The decision to have an outdoor performance allowed for a more spectacular show and extended the reach to larger audiences, presumably challenging the elite culture (Wåhlin et al. 2016).

Norrlandsoperan and the Catalan performing arts group *La Fura Dels Baus* gave a monumental outdoor performance of Richard Strauss's one-act opera. *Elektra* became Norrlandsoperan's largest production ever. The opera took place in the extensive barracks area of Umeå's former infantry regiment I20. The stage was 200 metres long, and the grandstand, with its capacity for 2,000 spectators, also represented the palace where Elektra's family live. The performance included moving steel giants with performers standing inside their chests and containers filled with 'blood'. The Västerbottnian twilight was the perfect background for the burning forest and the river of blood. The opera involved over 250 performers, And the 2,000 seats on the grandstand were sold out for each of the five performances.

The project and travel book *Till häst genom Västerbotten* (On horseback through Västerbotten) (4–5 November 2014). The performing artists were Sven Björklund and Olof Wretling, known from Swedish radio and television and members of the Umeå-based theatre collective *Klungan*. They made a journey through Västerbotten in their hunt for "stories", with the Brothers Grimm as their role models. They left Umeå on horseback for their search, which lasted three seasons. A "Sherpa" provided by the Public Employment Centre assisted them. The journey resulted in a book telling the story of their travel through slurry and depopulated villages, from which new images of the county emerged. The book includes various narratives from different places in the county (Björklund and Wretling 2014). The book was released during a live performance at which Olof

Figure 2.3 Poster with visitor information for the closing ceremony Northern Light in the city of Umeå

Source: Umeå2014

and Sven presented selected stories, illustrated with the fine art photographer Elin Berge's documentation of the seven-month expedition. Tickets to the performance included a book and the opportunity to have it signed after the show.

The show *Northern Light* (13 December 2014, 19:00–20:14) on Lucia Day (Figure 2.3) was the closing ceremony for Umeå2014, with speeches from Fredrik Lindegren, the artistic director for Umeå2014; Marie-Louise Rönnmark, mayor of the city of Umeå; and representatives of the upcoming ECoC cities for 2015, Mons in Belgium and Plzen in the Czech Republic. Northern Light was a colourful show, featuring light projections onto the old town hall and a number of artists from Umeå, Sápmi, and the rest of Sweden.

Cultural infrastructure and city development

The European Commission points out that, besides its cultural imprints, the ECoC event is also an excellent opportunity for regenerating cities. Since the selection of Glasgow as ECoC in 1990, ECoC has been used as a catalyst for urban regeneration strategies. The expected cultural benefits and cultural legacies, such as residents' self-perception and the perception of the place where they live, have justified inward investment (García 2005).

As mentioned, in Umeå's application the ECoC refers to various investments ahead of the programme year of 2014, such as the art campus and an aquatic centre, as well as investments in what would ultimately become the cultural centre *Väven* (Umeå2014 2008, Part IV, Q3). Certainly, all these projects were more or less included in the development plans for the city of Umeå, aside from the realization of the ECoC. However, when Umeå was granted the ECoC title, their timing was coordinated with the Umeå2014 programme (Wåhlin et al. 2016). This is most visible when it comes to the cultural building *Väven*, located in the city centre (Figure 2.4). As a city regeneration project, *Väven* derives partly from the ideas in the programme the City Between the Bridges (also listed in the ECoC application), aiming to upgrade the riverside in Umeå's city centre.

Väven is in itself a co-creation, built as a joint venture between Umeå municipality and the real estate company Balticgruppen AB and co-owned through the company Väven i Umeå AB (Så byggdes väven). The building was designed by the Swedish White Arkitekter and the Norwegian Snøhetta, with the aim of creating an architectural landmark. The building's façade resembles the trunk of a birch, a tree that is common in Umeå. As with other projects designed by Snøhetta, *Väven* also invites people to enter the building through a terrace circumscribing the part of it that faces the river. Thus, the building also becomes a social monument, with the intention of breaking down the barriers between internal activities and public

Figure 2.4 The culture centre *Väven* in Umeå

Source: Håkan Appelblad

space (Snøhetta). *Väven* is said to be a platform for culture and experiences in Umeå, where people and ideas are woven together: hence, the name *Väven* (Eng. 'weave'). Within its premises are Umeå City Library, the Museum of Women's History, the cinema *Folkets Bio*, and other facilities for workshops, venues, etc. As indicated by the building's name, there are no sharp borders between the different sections, inviting cross-border and co-creation activities. *Väven* was inaugurated on 21 November, the same day as the inauguration of the last season of the programme year, Tjakttjadálvvie. Its external premises had been used earlier as part of the stage during the official Umeå2014 opening ceremony on 1 February, with the Sami children's choir performing on its terrace.

Concluding remarks

Various indications suggest that the Umeå2014 event allowed Umeå to reap some of the expected benefits that cities hosting an ECoC event experience. The rich cultural programme, co-creation with international partners, joint projects with local and regional cultural operators, investments in cultural facilities, etc. have strengthened its cultural sector, contributed to growing numbers of visitors, and presumably enhanced and extended its image as a place in northern Europe. In retrospect, the Umeå2014 event year could possibly be understood as an event that very much enhanced the strong cultural profile Umeå already possessed, bringing it to an even higher level. Meanwhile, local opinions may still include sentiments concerning a lack of inclusion and the promotion of mainstream culture to the exclusion of alternative forms of locally based culture.

It can be argued that the Umeå2014 event promoted Umeå with respect to all of Thrift's (2009) four conceptions of space:

First: Investments in cultural facilities, like the cultural complex *Väven* including the new waterfront, have contributed extensively to city development in Umeå. Even if *Väven* was not purely the result of Umeå2014, the ECoC year became a catalyst and set the time frame for this 'empirical construction' that became *Väven*.

Second: Umeå2014 came into being in cooperation with cultural organizers, partners, and tourists. These links contributed to connections between Umeå and areas beyond, as an 'unblocking space'.

Third: The promotion of Umeå as a place and the Umeå2014 event drew on different images of Umeå but also on images of other areas in the Swedish – and consequently the European – north and Sápmi: enriching Umeå's 'image space'. This strengthened image was obviously stronger on the European level, outside domestic areas. The international communication event, as intended with the Caught by Umeå tour, likely contributed to this.

Fourth: Umeå2014 may have contributed to changing Umeå's image in the eyes of its own inhabitants, as well as of others who have now gotten to know Umeå. Whether Umeå is permanently different in people's minds in this post-Umeå2014 era, however, is a legacy that will be difficult to reveal.

Still, promotional activities and the Umeå2014 programme enhanced qualities of the north, many of which draw on themes related more to waste areas
and realms not encapsulated within the city of Umeå alone. The River Stories project is a tangible example of how Umeå2014 came to embrace areas
stretching beyond the city, representing both the north and Sápmi.

With reference to main dimensions of events, the *content, temporalities*, and
spatialities; Umeå2014 provides examples partly challenging the notion of what
an event is all about:

Content: A cultural yearlong programme, including more than 1,000 sub-
events, indeed forms a complex overall event. The ECoC year in Umeå
contained many sub-events more or less connected to the overarching programme of Umeå2014.

Temporalities: An event is limited in time. Visitors attending an event have to
be there to experience it. A yearlong event sets aside the temporal motives
dictating when to arrange an event, as there are no seasons to overbridge.
Further, visitors cannot be expected to remain for a full year. Even culturally devoted local citizens may have difficulty enduring keeping themselves
updated on a yearlong programme.

Spatialities: The main concern in this study is the spatial references connected
to Umeå2014. Umeå2014 took place mostly within the city. However, the
Northern Room, Sápmi, and other northern notions refer to larger spaces.
Further, many of the events included in the Umeå2014 programme were
physically located in places well outside the city of Umeå. In this sense,
Umeå2014 serves as an example of how place and space are, so to say,
interwoven overarching geographies.

For Umeå, a small city in the north with cultural ambitions, the ECoC event
was in some sense the perfect opportunity. The co-creation approach, despite its
risks and problems, was a strategy appropriate for this small city. Building upon
existing cultural sources, and forming alliances with other cultural sources outside Umeå, was strategic and necessary. This inevitably included a re-negotiation
of place and space. The city of Umeå won the ECoC title while stressing the
geographical perspective and embracing European dimensions including northern
realms and Sápmi. Umeå as a place was promoted to also being a space.

References

Åkerlund, U., & Müller, D. K. (2012). Implementing tourism events: The discourses of
Umeå's bid for European capital of culture 2014. *Scandinavian Journal of Hospitality
and Tourism*, 12(2), 164–180, doi:10.1080/15022250.2011.647418
Andersson, I. (2014). Placing place branding: An analysis of an emerging research field
in human geography. *Geografisk Tidsskrift-Danish Journal of Geography*, 114(2),
143–155.

Anholt, S. (2010). Places: Identity, Image and Reputation. London and New York: Palgrave Macmillan.

Björklund, S., & Wretling, O. (2014). *Till häst genom Västerbotten*. Stockholm: Bonnier.

Eriksson, M. (2010). *(Re)producing a Periphery, Popular Representations of the Swedish North. GERUM 2010:2*; Department of Social and Economic Geography, Umeå University.

EUR Lex 11997E151. Treaty Establishing the European Community (Amsterdam Consolidated Version); Part Three: Community Policies; Title XII: Culture; Article 151; Article 128 – EC Treaty (Maastricht consolidated version); Article 128 – EEC Treaty. Retrieved from https://eur-lex.europa.eu/legal-content/EN/TXT/?uri=CELEX:11997E151

European Commission. (2018a). European Capitals of Culture. Retrieved from https://ec.europa.eu/programmes/creative-europe/actions/capitals-culture_en. Accessed 2018.

European Commission. (2018b). European Capitals of Culture 2020 to 2033: A Guide for Cities Preparing to Bid. Retrieved from https://ec.europa.eu/programmes/creative-europe/sites/creative-europe/files/capitals-culture-candidates-guide_en.pdf. Accessed 2018.

European Communities. (2009). European Capitals of Culture: The Road to success, from 1985 to 2010. Retrieved from https://ec.europa.eu/programmes/creative-europe/sites/creative-europe/files/library/capitals-culture-25-years_en.pdf

European Parliament. (2013). European Capitals of Culture: Success Strategies and Long-Term Effects. Directorate-General for Internal Policies, Policy Department, Structural and Cohesions Policies. Retrieved from www.europarl.europa.eu/RegData/etudes/etudes/join/2013/513985/IPOL-CULT_ET(2013)513985_EN.pdf

Fox, T., & Rampton, J. (2015). Ex-post Evaluation of the European Capitals of Culture, Final Report. European Commission. Retrieved from https://ec.europa.eu/programmes/creative-europe/sites/creative-europe/files/files/ecoc-2014-report_en.pdf

García, B. (2005). Deconstructing the city of culture: The long-term cultural legacies of Glasgow 1990. *Urban Studies*, 42(5/6), 841–868.

Garcia, B. (2017). 'If everyone says so. . . ' Press narratives and image change in major event host cities. *Urban Studies*, 54(14), 3178–3198.

Gdaniec, C. (2000). Cultural industries, information technology and the regeneration of post-industrial urban landscapes: Poblenou in Barcelona – A virtual city? *GeoJournal*, 50(4), 379–387.

Getz, D. (2008). Event tourism: Definition, evolution, and research. *Tourism Management*, 29, 403–428.

Heith, A. (2015). Indigeneity, Cultural Transformations and Rethinking the Nation: Performative Aspects of Sámi Elements in Umeå 2014. Culture and Growth: Magical Companions or Mutually Exclusive Counterparts?/[edr] Britta Lundgren & Ovidiu Matiu, Lucian Blaga University of Sibiu Press, 7, 110–126.

Hudson, C., Sandberg, L., & Schmauch, U. (2017). The co-creation (of) culture? The case of Umeå, European capital of culture 2014. *European Planning Studies*, 25(9), 1538–1555, doi:10.1080/09654313.2017.1327032.

Hugoson, R. (2015). *Umeå stads historia 1950–2010*. Umeå: Umeå kommunfullmäktige.

Liu, Y. D. (2015). Event-led strategy for cultural tourism development, disP – *The Planning Review*, 51(2), 28–40, doi:10.1080/02513625.2015.1064645.

Müller, D. K., & Jansson, B. (2007). The difficult business of making pleasure peripheries prosperous: perspective on space, place and environment. In D. K. Müller and B. Jansson (eds). *Tourism in Peripheries, Perspectives from the Far North and South*. Oxfordshire: CABI.

Myndigheten för kulturanalys. (2018). Samhällets utgifter för kultur 2017. Kulturfakta 2018:5. Retrieved from https://kulturanalys.se/wp-content/uploads/2018/11/samhallets-utgifter-for-kultur-2017_webb.pdf

OECD. (2017). OECD Territorial Reviews: Northern Sparsely Populated Areas.

Pettersson, S. (2013). Umeå: Co-creation and the City, A Study on Culture-led Growth and Participatory Approaches to Urban Development in the Planning of the European Capital of Culture 2014. Master thesis in Human Geography, 30 credits. Department of Geography and Economic History. Umeå University.

PricewaterhouseCoopers. (2015). Evaluation of Umeå2014, Summary in English. Retrieved from http://umea2014.se/wp-content/uploads/2015/09/Report-Umeå2014-english-version-FINAL.pdf

Region Västerbotten. (2016). Region Västerbotten och det europeiska kulturhuvudstadsåret I Umeå 2014. Retrieved from http://umea2014.se

Rönér Douhan, G. (2013). Renrajd över Tegsbron och renkappkörning på Haga. In L. Olsson, S. Haugen, L. Edlund & L. Tedebrand (eds). *Umeå 1314–2014, 100 berättelser om 700 år. Johan Nordlander-sällskapet* (Vol. 30). Skellefteå: Artos & Norma.

Rough Guides Top 10 Cities. (2014). Retrieved from www.roughguides.com/best-places/2014/top-10-cities/

Så byggdes väven. The Construction of Väven. Retrieved from http://sabyggdes.vaven.se/c1/

Sametinget. The Sami Parliament in Sweden. Retrieved from www.sametinget.se

Schulze, G. (2005). *The Experience Society*. London: Sage.

Selection panel a. Designation of a European Capital of Culture for 2014 Pre-selection report. January 2009. Retrieved from https://ec.europa.eu/programmes/creative-europe/sites/creative-europe/files/files/ecoc-2014-preselection-report-sweden_en.pdf

Selection panel b. Selection of a European Capital of Culture 2014 in Sweden, Final selection report, September 2009. Retrieved from https://ec.europa.eu/programmes/creative-europe/sites/creative-europe/files/files/ecoc-2014-panel-sweden_en.pdf

SKL. (2015). Urbanisering, Utmaningar för kommuner med växande och minskande befolkning. Sveriges kommuner och landsting.

Snøhetta. The project Väven. Retrieved from www.snohetta.com/projects/30-vaumlven

Statistics Sweden. www.scb.se/en/

Sykes, O. (2011). Introduction: European cities and capitals of culture – A comparative approach. *Town Planning Review*, 82(1), *European Cities and Capitals of Culture*, 1–12, doi:10.3828/tpr.2011.8

Thrift, N. (2009). Space: The fundamental stuff of geography. In N. Clifford, S. Holloway, S. Rice and G. Valentine (eds). *Key Concepts in Geography* (2nd edition, pp. 85–96). London: Sage.

Umeå municipality a. Översiktsplan Umeå kommun, 2011, Fördjupning för Umeå, Umeås framtida tillväxtområde. Available through, http://umea.se/umeatillvaxt

Umeå municipality b. www.umea.se/umeakommun/kommunochpolitik/manskligarattigheter/nationellaminoriteterochminoritetssprak/samisktforvaltningsomrade.4.2ec28df4125d2ef852080004901.html

Umeå2014. (2008). Curiosity and Passion: the Art of Co-Creation. A Bid from Umeå to Become the EU's Northernmost European Capital of Culture Ever. Retrieved from http://umea2014.se/wp-content/uploads/2013/01/ansokan_1_eng.pdf

Umeå2014. Website of Umeå2014, European Capital of Culture. Retrieved from http://umea2014.se/en/

Wåhlin, N., Kapsali, M., Näsholm M. H., & Blomquist, T. (2016). *Urban Strategies for Culture-Driven Growth, Co-Creating a European Capital of Culture*. Cheltenham, UK: Edward Elgar Publishing.

3 Branding authenticity

Perceptions of La Patum de Berga, a complex place marketing event in Catalonia, Spain

Alba Colombo and Natàlia Cantó-Milà

Introduction

This chapter deals with the festivity of La Patum in Berga, Catalonia, Spain, focusing especially on the authenticity which many locals and visitors alike see in this traditional cultural event related to the Corpus Christi celebrations. La Patum was declared a UNESCO Intangible Cultural Heritage of Humanity in 2005, and its existence has been documented since the 16th century.[1]

Local and regional marketing through events is not a new idea, as it is now one of the most popular instruments to promote cities, regions or towns. Thus, events may be used as strategic tools in many different areas (Gibson and Stevenson 2004; Hannigan 2003; Evans 2001) such as for economic development, as a tourist attraction or for city branding, among others (Getz 1991, 2012; Smith 2012; Colombo 2009; Richards and Wilson 2004). Therefore, local branding through events is a common strategy not only for cities but also for towns and villages, where one can observe how events transform the locality in economic terms as well as in cultural and social aspects (Getz 2008; Cudny 2016).

This chapter aims to observe the relation between the promotion and branding of Berga through La Patum and its authenticity. The celebration consists of diverse performances by symbolic and mythical figures dancing to traditional music accompanied by pyrotechnics. It takes place in a relatively small square, Saint Peter's (Sant Pere) Square, but, as some interviewees have emphatically pointed out, it would not be thinkable to move it elsewhere to a larger location. The Patum's inexorable link with this particular square restricts the number of people who can take part in it. Moreover, the possibility to physically perform in it (and thus transition from being an observer to becoming a performer) is even more restricted. Some interviewees have depicted accessibility as being practically impenetrable, as local networks secure participation in these groups of mythical figures for some, thereby excluding others. This issue of inclusion/ exclusion has gained importance and sparked some debate, especially since the festivity has become so well known beyond the borders of its region of origin.

Thus, although La Patum Festival's frame has spread internationally and it has become a clear branding and place-marketing event for Berga, it hides strongly structured and restrictive regulations regarding who is entitled to do what during the event.

The analysis presented in this chapter is based on structured interviews conducted during the festival in 2016 and three focus groups held in Berga (2016–2018) during and after the event, including participants, artists, local experts and audience. The data gathered have helped the authors analyse the discourse that emerged concerning the value of this event, particularly focusing on aspects of authenticity.

The chapter concludes with some reflections on the effects of branding and promoting a city or region through an event such as La Patum over the years, the underlying perceptions and the mutual dependence between the event and its social context. Local branding seems to produce value in different areas even though the authenticity of the events appears to be perceived differently by participants, attendees and experts.

The current Patum in contemporary Berga

Berga is a municipality in the province of Barcelona 100 kilometres north of the Catalan capital. It is a small town by Catalan standards; in 2016 it had 16,175 inhabitants. Since the recovery of democracy in Spain (after 40 years of Franco's dictatorship), Berga has elected the conservative Catalan nationalist party Convergènvia i Unió (CIU, now defunct) to its local council for eight of its ten legislatures. The Socialist Party of Catalonia (PSC) has won the local election only once (2003–2007). After the last municipal election, the Candidatura d'Unitat Popular (CUP) won the majority of the votes, leading to some significant changes in the established order and power structures. Thus, while the city council's recent history (illustrating the recent political history of Berga) paints a picture of a conservative and Catalan-nationalist society, the politically turbulent times Catalonia has been experiencing in the last few years have deeply affected Berga. For example, the current mayor is a young female politician from CUP undergoing an ongoing judicial process due to her political stance about Catalonia's independence from Spain. However, none of this changes the fact that Berga is a Catalan town in which culture, traditions, language and identity are important and worth communicating, enjoying and preserving.

Among these traditions, this culture and these identity markers, Berga is the host and the birthplace of one of the most representative centuries-old cultural festivities in Catalonia: La Patum. A celebration of fire and culture, this religious and ancestral representation has survived until today with a fidelity to its origins which its participants (and interviewees researched for the purposes of this chapter) acknowledge, respect and praise. This celebration has evolved over the years and centuries, and despite the fact that the popular imaginary views, experiences and narrates it as unique and authentic, La Patum has not always been the same. In fact, in 2016, when the authors started the research into this festivity, its authenticity and its meanings, the Patum had just introduced a musical piece by Bruce Springsteen ("If I Fall Behind") as a new song danced to by the event's iconic giants.[2]

The first written documentation of La Patum (from 1264) closely linked it to the Corpus Christi processions, a Catholic celebration of the mystery of the body of Jesus Christ. However, it did not become popular until the beginning of the 15th century, as the first reference to the celebration of a public Corpus Christi event in Berga dates from 1454 (Carrera 2014). La Patum is a traditional cultural event and one of the most emblematic among Catalan Corpus Christi festivities; therefore, the dates of celebration are variable, depending on the Corpus Christi calendar – generally between the end of May and the end of June. It is composed of several representations of fights between Moors and Christians and between devils and archangels, and it also includes dances of diverse *entremesos*[3] or interludes (Colombo et al. forthcoming). The number of *comparses* (performers) and groups and the intricate choreography of the whole event make this festivity complex and difficult to understand from outside. As Soler i Amigó (2001) claims, La Patum is highly complex and unique due to its symbolic density, its frenetic rhythms, the multitudes and the outbreak of a contained emotion. Nowadays, it is organized by the independent body Patronat Municipal de La Patum, constituted in 2001 with political representatives, heads of groups (taking part in the event), *patumaires* (anyone who takes part in the festivity) and experts such as historians or folklorists. This body has the goal of administrating, preserving and coordinating the organization of the festivity, ensuring respectful celebrations as well as everything related to the corporate image, advertising or publicity. During the festivity, the town population may increase six times (generally, its population is around 16,000); most of these are people from Catalonia although, during recent years, the number of other national and international visitors also increased.

As Joan Amades (1983), an eminent Catalan folklorist describes, "the ensemble of La Patum represents a very remarkable, and probably unique, popular play. We do not know of anywhere else that still maintains so actively old episodes and elements of ancient *entremesos* with such harmonic and spectacular staging. The whole of La Patum is a remarkable document of archaeological value, forming one of the performances that took part in the height of the Eucharistic festivities". Thus, La Patum is one of those cultural folklore festivities that link the present with the past, encompassing mysticism, emotion, memory, traditions and contemplation.

Accordingly, La Patum is a complex event composed of several processions, dances and performances. During the three days of La Patum festivities, there are several Patums taking place at various times on different days, sometimes addressed to different audiences, incorporating different content, dances or both, such as "*the children's Patum*", "*the ceremonial Patum*" (being a sort of showcasting) and "*the complete Patum*". The latter is held during the nights of Thursday and Sunday of Corpus Christi and is the most representative. Diverse groups of *comparses* perform for several days emulating a procession, which is organized hierarchically. Some of the most representative figures in these parades portray flora and fauna divinities, with zoomorphic and anthropomorphic features. Other elements are also important, such as fire and pyrotechnics. The fire is generally carried by devils and some other figures such as beasts called "*guites*" (mule-dragons). There are also "*fuets*", representative long and thin pyrotechnic elements made especially for this event and named after a very typical Catalan sausage. These fireworks are flares that sparkle for a while before exploding in a final thunder.

La Patum has evolved over time, improving the quality of the figures and the performer's representations, restoring some figures and recovering others. Nevertheless, there are certain representations that are considered essential, original and authentic, such as those involving fire and pyrotechnics (wielded by the *diables* or devils), and changing them would lead to heated debates and discussions, to say the least. The *diables* appear at two moments during the festivity: in the performances of the "*maces*" and the "*plens*". The *maces* perform during the ceremonial and the complete Patum and take their name from the instruments they carry: long staffs with a circular box filled with stones at one end, which makes a noise like a drum. It is at the end of these staffs that the *fuets* are located. The *plens* are another type of *diables* (devils). They dress in red and green, wear diabolic masks and carry large bunches of herbs and leaves. The dance of the *plens* is a diabolical representation linked to the ancient rites of agricultural and livestock renovation. They carry six *fuets* on their heads, and three more hang from the tails of their costumes. Since the performers of the *plens* cannot see much due to the masks they are wearing, they always have a companion by their side who guides them and helps them during the dances. They represent the zenith of the festivity, its culmination. They perform at the complete Patum (Thursday and Sunday night) in Sant Pere's square, and they mix with the crowd. There are more than a thousand *fuets* burning at the same time in the square during the dance of the *plens*, and the whole crowd is "forced" to move anticlockwise in a synchronized manner. A step in the wrong direction can be dangerous, as our interviewees assured. The crowd, the fire, the music, the smoke and the movement create an impressive spectacle that generates a collective catharsis (Carrera 2014; Noyes 2003). It is a liminal moment, far beyond the quotidian everyday life that inhabits this square during the rest of the year (Turner 1979). This moment is recognized as the peak of the festivity, the moment of real participation, the instant of complete communion among people and festive groups and probably also the time to set repressed energies free. Nowadays, this moment also serves the purpose of commemorating the survival of this festivity and perhaps even of Catalan culture in general, year after year. Thus, La Patum is the binding element of a society, and no political powers have been able to harness the true significance of the feast, which is the deepest love for the land, Berga and its surroundings (Rumbo and Soler 2001).

· **Methodology**

The data for this research were gathered between May 2016 and October 2018. In fact, this study was part of a much wider research project dealing with "Imaginaries of the future in times of austerity", financed by the Spanish Ministry of Economy and Competitiveness.[4] This project has a strong foundation in the fields of sociology of culture, emotions, social imaginaries and economic sociology. Its goal is to analyse the imaginaries of the future of people living in the areas of influence of Barcelona (Catalonia, Spain) and Leipzig (Saxony, Germany) by focusing on the narrations of their own life trajectories and what they have considered/consider important and relevant in their lives.

Between 2016 and 2018, 23 structured interviews were conducted; three focus groups were held with experts, participants and cultural activists and the researchers engaged in field observation. The interviews were undertaken during La Patum itself, so there was limited time to ask questions, as interviewees were preparing for a dance or passing by heading towards the next dance or to lunch, home or work. The interviewees were chosen randomly from the street, resulting in more than 20 interviews. However, the focus groups did not take place during the festivity or in the immediate vicinity but in more relaxed situations in which the time pressure on informants was much lower. Several participant profiles were invited to join these groups, from organizers, attendees, participants, insiders (people from Berga) and also outsiders (people not from Berga). The focus groups included between three to five informants.

In the interviews the authors asked what the respondents thought of the festivity, how often they had visited it and why, what their relation was to the event and how they came to know about it. The authors also asked about participation, experience, traditions, what the festivity meant to them, how they thought it would carry on in the future, how they felt about it and how they valued the different options they gave as possible futures for the festivity. In contrast, during the focus groups, the authors asked very general questions regarding matters such as the participant's relationship with the festivity; their role or roles in it (as participant, organizer, audience); what they knew, thought and valued about La Patum and how they thought it would evolve in the future. The authors did not need to prompt the participants any further because the conversations were so lively that each of these very general questions yielded remarkably long answers. First, there was a brief round of individual replies, followed by dialogue and debate among the participants during which we only needed to intervene occasionally to clarify a point. Otherwise, the authors were able to just observe, listen and take notes while the conversation evolved naturally among the participants towards issues regarding social structure, nationalism, classism in the local society, commitment, change and what the festivity meant to each of those sharing their time and insights with us. One of the focus groups was the spontaneous result of one structured interview that developed into a fascinating conversation with a group of young (male) migrants from Morocco, who also spoke about how as outsiders (this was their self-given label) they experienced and regarded the festivity. Two of our interviews, also conducted with migrants, offered further and complementary insights into the issues raised during this focus group. Interestingly, the authors did not need to introduce the object of this study as the authenticity dimension arose in both cases, during the interviews and the focus groups.

The triangulation of qualitative methods has allowed us to reach a deeper understanding of this event and its manifold meanings, structures and dynamics and the social and power relations among its participants and audiences as well as to grasp the singular relation between the city, the event and wider society that has made its long history possible and significant. Furthermore, we have sought to understand the special place that La Patum has in the imaginaries of the past, present and future, both of Berga and of Catalan culture in general.

Results

As already mentioned, this study is part of a wider research project, the general results of which encouraged the authors to focus on La Patum as an interesting and unique case study. One of the most striking results obtained from this research was the importance that our interviewees conferred upon the issue of "authenticity". It was an underlined issue in responses regarding their consumption patterns and preferences; their evaluation and valuation of people, objects, cultural products and circumstances and their experience and participation in events (festivals, festivities etc.). Indeed, events have remarkable importance within people's narrations regarding their lives and what they hold dear. Events have framed, made possible and become cherished or dreaded moments in their lives and include not only marriages, births, funerals and rites of passage but also the modern equivalents of liminal moments. Events are moments in which people may touch the (now secularized) sacred: special concerts, theatre plays, a night at the cinema or local festivities (Turner 1979). This was also spontaneously referred to in interviews conducted for the purposes of this chapter. La Patum is one of these very special moments, an event that takes place once a year, every year, following the lunar calendar as the celebration of Corpus Christi does. La Patum was a key event for one of the interviewees in the wider sample, who mentioned that it was the first time he had gone out alone with his friends at night and qualified it as a "magic moment", when he was dancing and jumping in the square surrounded by the peers he loved. At this moment, he claimed that he had felt ". . . alive, for the first time really alive, young, strong, healthy . . . like holding the world and the future in the palms of my raised hands" (Jordi, 39).[5]

These insights led us to focus in greater detail on the special events that may become important, even crucial, in our life stories, and thus make them unique in many ways. Events such as La Patum can be lived and experienced as authentic in two ways: authentic in the sense of "original", of having remained faithful to its origins and thus (relatively) unaltered over time, or as having been the setting or even "the cause" for unique experiences in one's life that have conferred an aura of authenticity on these places in a way no other place can have. Hence, they are authentic in a way because we were (or felt like) our truest selves in them.[6] As one interviewee framed it when speaking of the "special places" she had shared with her partner: "Before splitting up, we actually went back to that place . . . We had gone there every time we visited Weimar, and it felt so special, so *ours*, if you know what I mean. This time . . . it just felt like a normal restaurant, even ugly, ordinary . . . all that was special about it was gone . . . what we had thought so unique, so authentic . . . it was only in our minds. It was never there to begin with" (Anna, 32).

Strong personal bond with the festivity

Among the most relevant elements observed are the feelings and emotions our informants expressed when talking about La Patum. For example, when considering La Patum in her life, one of the interviewees stated: "I come here, and I do it because it's a feeling, it's something that attracts me, it's like a drug, you need it. My years are organized from Patum to Patum . . . being able to celebrate another Patum is like thinking, look, it's been a year. For me La Patum is happiness, and I remember it all year round" (Marta, 28). In Marta's case La Patum is not an event that happens once a year; it is the beginning and the end of her experiential year, a moment of celebration but also of remembrance of years gone by and all the past Patums in her life. Joaquim (81) also underlined the importance of La Patum arguing, "For me it means festivity, party, participating, it is something that comes from inside me, it's like loving someone; you don't know why you love that girl precisely, but you do know that you love her. With La Patum it is like this. I love La Patum because I was born with it, and it's my life". These examples illustrate how La Patum is part of people's lives, especially for those born in Berga and who have therefore been experiencing it since their early childhood. It is something irreplaceable, a "special place" in the sense mentioned earlier, and they could not imagine their lives without it. But this does not only happen to people who were born in Berga. Xavi (40) told us, "I've been coming here with my family since I was a kid. . . . I come from Barcelona, but we had a house here, and we spent our summers here. You have friends, you spend holidays . . . and you come to La Patum . . . and I simply love it. I have been coming here almost every year, every time I can, with my parents first, then with my friends and now [points at his wife and baby], and I hope she'll do the same one day [pointing at the baby in the cradle]".

Other elements that emerge from our data are experiences and memories of being part of La Patum, of being there and witnessing the moment and/or actively participating (dancing or otherwise) in it. As we gathered in our interviews and focus groups, those who attend La Patum speak mainly about two different kinds of experience.[7] On the one hand, they refer to the event itself: the dances, the times, the figures, the fire . . . and they do so in a language full of sensorial clues: they speak about what they have sensorially experienced. They talk about the smells, the touch, the sounds and what they see, and one even spoke about tasting gunpowder on his girlfriend's skin.[8] On the other hand, the informants also speak about social interactions (and wider relational networks) that surround and are involved in the celebration of this festivity.

Both kinds of experience are viewed and interpreted by our interviewees through the lens of "authenticity": the sensorial experiences as well as the social interactions that take place during La Patum are lived as necessary experiences without which the festivity would not be the same anymore. Its meaning and its very "materiality" would be lost to those who attend it year after year and keep faithful to the local traditions in the most late-modern way. To put it in their words: "La Patum wouldn't be La Patum without that gunpowder smell" (Anita, 64), or "The celebration is so special because of the people you are with; if we [the locals] are not there anymore and it becomes a mere show for the tourists, everything will be lost" (Pau, 41).

The sensorial Patum

Of all the senses, the sense of smell is the one that normally receives the least attention.[9] However, when speaking of and remembering La Patum, our interviewees made the sense of smell an anchoring point for their depictions. Thus, for instance, one interviewee highlighted: "the smell of fire. My children experience it differently since they have grown up with the smell of fire, but for me, it is very difficult; sometimes I suffer" (Lourdes, 60), and also "What I like most about the La Patum is the smell of gunpowder. At home when the crowds jumped, the smoke used to come into the house through one window and go out through another. It was like a kind of chimney. This is probably the thing that I like most and which awakens the most memories" (Joaquim, 81). Another respondent stated that "It is indescribable . . . it is that feeling of being in the midst of the jumping crowd, seeing all those lights and smelling the gunpowder as if it were a drug. You cannot get enough of it" (Arnau, 35).

These examples underline the idea of fire, gunpowder and its smell as a great experience but also as a danger, and therefore it is treated with respect. "Of course you protect yourself, and you try to be careful. At the end of the day, you're playing with fire, I mean, literally!" (Arnau, 35). Besides smell, the senses of hearing and sight also played an important role in the interviewees' recollections of the festivity, highlighting above all the music, the light of a thousand fires and the -perspective when seeing the square from above (from balconies or the top of the church step): "You see all those people jumping together, and this combined with the lights, the music, the smell . . . it is really quite hypnotic" (Pau, 41).

The Patum of social relations

Regarding social interactions, and relations in general, the interviewees and focus groups highlighted the great importance as well as the particularities and specificities of social relations during this festivity. We would like to emphasize two different levels of relationality, which are crucial in the depiction of being with and being among others in La Patum. The interviewees addressed the importance of being part of a crowd, of being among others or relating to many other people – some known, some unknown – in the same here and now of Saint Peter's square, all dancing, jumping and moving together like waves in a great sea. However, the interviewees also addressed the issue of being with others, interacting with others, at La Patum. Thus, they spoke about those particular people with whom they go to La Patum, those specific people they had met and regularly meet there, turning La Patum into a very "special moment and place" in their lives. In fact, one of the most remarkable things the authors learned from the interviewees and from focus groups was that locals do not necessarily go to La Patum with their regular friends and families, but some have their "Patum friends" (Aitor, 29). These are people they have been going to La Patum with for many years and who are not necessarily the people they currently share most of their time with. Furthermore, during La Patum, the normal rules of life do not apply in the same way. "If I went at night without my wife and came back home the next day drunk and [a] mess, she'd be so angry with me! During La Patum, that is no problem. She'll have been out with her Patum friends too" (Aitor, 29). Or: "At La Patum everything is an excess, the fire, the noise, the music, the sweat, the sleepless nights, the alcohol, the drugs, and sex . . . It's a bit like in *Sons of Anarchy*: what happens in La Patum stays in La Patum. There are many infidelities that are tolerated during La Patum just because it's La Patum, and things happen" (Jordi, 33). This illustrate the idea that the festivity provides the opportunity for transgression, changing the social normative behaviour, providing unusual activities, feelings and emotions, such as different authors considered as transgressive festivals or events (Cudny 2016; Davies 2015; Picard and Robinson 2006).

Despite the crowds, the festive atmosphere and the suspension of the usual social norms that the last quotes illustrate, La Patum does not function without any social rules or forms of distinction and differentiation. In fact, the differentiation between insiders and outsiders is remarkable as the authors have learned from the gathered data. Thus, while in the midst of the crowds, all types of people may seem undifferentiated, among this crowd the lines of difference between insiders and outsiders – people from Berga and elsewhere/people from the area and elsewhere/active participants (dancers, organizers, performers, "jumpers" and audiences) – are palpable and never erased. As we discovered from the focus groups with locals, the differentiation between insiders and outsiders is relevant in the festivity, to an extent that we could not have detected in the observations. Furthermore, these differences were made clear in the interviews with both locals and outsiders. However, through the focus groups, we were able to comprehend dynamics even within the dancing and the jumping and in the square at the zenith of the festivity of which we had been previously unaware. First, the case of a young woman who attended the event for the first time and saw a great relation between experienced and inexperienced attendees: "You think that you already know what you are doing, but sometimes, as you are an outsider, you have some respect [when you get into the square], and I noticed that people help you even though you are an outsider; they help you a lot. I have seen people fall, and they were caught rapidly, and sometimes when I was unsure about what to do next, the person beside me helped me out. I really liked it because it is kind of madness and anarchy, but with some control" (Maite, 21). This participant expressed how grateful she was to see how the community of participants and attendees help each other in complex and extreme moments, such as when entering the square, probably during the *salt dels plens*, when it is filled with jumping performers and fire. She also stressed that this aspect is a great characteristic of La Patum, as this same sense of protection and community cannot be found in other towns with similar festivities such as Vilafranca del Penedès. Nevertheless, what is also remarkable is how the interviewee differentiated between being an insider and an outsider, local and foreigner, and also how the local people treated her as an outsider. We could speculate that a crucial element in these events is the social perception of differences: of being an insider, who knows the event, the groups, the trajectories and probably also the threats and the complexities of this festivity, or being an outsider who does not know.

In fact, one of our interviewees explicitly addressed this difference, saying, "Sometimes people who come from elsewhere and do not know the jumps [the dance] just drive in, and of course . . . you watch them fall over. They hurt themselves and harm others because if somebody is lying on the ground, you may not see them and fall over them yourself, and then another falls, and another . . . and then what? So you help them when you can, not only because they need help, but for the sake of the group; it cannot go wrong. They are not being responsible . . . but if someone from Berga did this, we would be really angry with them . . . They would have to be extremely drunk to do something like that. We would kick them out without a second thought" (Pau, 41).

Past and future of event structures

As explained earlier, La Patum is a traditional and popular Catalan cultural event with a long history. Originally secular in nature and with civil goals, La Patum was rapidly adopted by ecclesiastical authorities and linked to the Corpus Christi celebrations. The tradition has been passed down from generation to generation, with efforts made to maintain both the outstanding festive elements and the essence of the event. Nevertheless, there has been some evolution and changes over the years. As a traditional event, the audience's and participants' imaginary regarding the festivity is rather conservative when considering the evolution of the representations and performances. For example, adaptation to contemporary society and any subsequent modification may be something complex and not accepted or well perceived. As Dídac (34) stressed: "I do not think it will evolve; the Patum will continue to be the same traditional Catalan celebration". However, some other informants hesitantly identified a certain evolution: "It will not evolve; I do not believe it; it must be the same. When other cities have made changes, such as the location, it is no longer the same; here it is here. La Patum is the heart of the whole traditional festivities in Catalonia . . . It has to evolve, but it cannot change completely since it must maintain its warmth because it would stop being what it is" (Ramon, 58). Although Joan (62) considered that evolution is needed and logical with a traditional and also historical event such as La Patum, he stated,

> Tradition is like a seed planted in the new generations through parents and families; therefore, this seed will never stop growing. The Partit Popular [conservative Spanish Christian-democratic political party] would have to win the election to really spoil this event, but still it would be very difficult to ruin and damage La Patum. The kids will maintain it.

Accordingly, it could be considered that even if the participants and audience perceived some modifications, the imaginary is conservative and reluctant to accept change, underlining the importance of maintaining the tradition to ensure the essence and perhaps also the authenticity of this event.

In this way, and as we have argued before, the experience of La Patum in the narrations of our interviewees wonderfully combines the two dimensions of authenticity we are pointing at: on the one hand, the faithfulness to a(n imagined) origin and original festivity, and on the other, the experience of the festivity in a way that so deeply connected with one's own "authentic core" that it sort of melts with it and thus becomes part of oneself. These two dimensions (the sensorial and the relational Patum) are therefore untouchable regarding the felt authenticity of the festivity. One interviewee combined in his narration both dimensions in a way that we think stands for what the other interviewees also expressed in a more scattered way: "La Patum is so beautiful, unique and attractive . . . My biggest fear is that somebody comes and sees a business opportunity and tries to turn all this into a theme park, moves it to a larger place with safety marks all over, uses fake powder for insurance policy reasons, instructs the dancers at a previous workshop with safety instructions . . . and they reproduce the rest one to one: without the people, without the square, without the powder. You'd have almost the same thing, yet nothing would be the same" (Ignasi, 37).

There are other dimensions of La Patum, which are certainly more negotiable and open to change, and even aspects of the festivity which are thought of as worth changing, as some of our interviewees briefly pointed at and as it became very clear during the discussions held in the focus groups.

For instance, regarding the structures behind the scenes, the organization and coordination of the groups (*comparses*), it seems that nowadays, there is more openness than many years ago, and therefore, it could be considered that the groups have become more accessible: a development which has been depicted as "positive" within the interviews and focus group discussions. "Each *comparsa* is organized individually, but there is now a board to coordinate all of them. Each *comparsa* is a group with a leader and collaborators, which ranges from three to forty people. Depending on each *comparsa*, entry can be gained one way or another, since they have different internal guidelines. In mine, for example, it is very important to attend regularly, and over the years, you end up officially joining the group" (Pere, 41). However, there are still situations in which people must have certain contacts and a social network in order to become a member of a specific group: "I plan to do it [be part of the group and a performer] when they allow me to jump; they will do so as I have connections" (Clara, 20). This could help us understand that the complexity surrounding the access to the groups is also an aspect that may be considered unique to this event as the structures within all these different *comparses*, each with its own guidelines, is nothing more than a mirror of the social power structures of the city.

Perceptions of consequences of city branding through the event

As is well known, during recent decades, events have been seen by government, social organizations and the private sector as tools not only for achieving social and economic goals and developing urban portfolios, but also for promoting cities and municipalities (Colombo 2017; Cudny 2016; Smith 2012; Richards and

Wilson 2004). Therefore, promoting a municipality through events is not new and clearly perceived: "La Patum brings visibility to Berga, and especially since it was recognized by the UNESCO; when people think of La Patum, they think of Berga" (Lourdes, 60). But the case of Berga and La Patum is complex as the festivity does not directly and specifically aim to market the city. However, this event has been promoting the city indirectly, and, as a consequence, citizens and participants do perceive promotional effects in different dimensions. The promotion strategy has been developed directly and indirectly, since such a traditional event has had a long history in the municipality's own trajectory: therefore, indirectly by mundane people, participants or attendees willing to be there again and promote it through a huge word-of-mouth strategy process. Direct promotion is made by communication bodies such as magazines, radio, TV stations and social media but also administrations as well as public and civil bodies. For example, the event has its own website with different languages and social media,[10] it is mentioned in the different administrations' websites, such as the city council and regional government[11] and the tourism offices from Berga and also from Spain[12] and it is also listed at the UNESCO intangible heritage website.[13]

Nevertheless, there is a popular reaction against incising interest to La Patum as generating massification, and this is perceived negatively: "Each time, there will be more people; maybe we should take some measures and control who can jump in the square. Nowadays, there are some *comparses* that are unable to move about and go out correctly" (Marta, 28). Also Ramon (58) stressed that: "Now with too many people, we are no longer able to participate. We do not go inside the square; it is not the same now". However, there are participants who consider the massification in the square as an important characteristic of the experience: "For the amount [sic] of people, the square has become too small, but if it were bigger, it would not be the same" (Pepi, 59). Some interviewees also consider the atmosphere generated by this massification in the square somewhat authentic: "What I really don't like is the quantity of people, but it is inevitable, since there is that atmosphere of warmth and good mood" (Dídac, 34).

La Patum does not differ greatly from many other events that have become economic boosts for the municipality and the region. Consequently, it is perceived as an important pillar of Berga's economic development. "It is an important source of income for those who have their own businesses as well as for us workers" (Rosario, 34), and "I think that La Patum contributes to Berga; many bars survive thanks to the Patum and not just thanks to tourism. This is the case both for the region and for the city" (Marta, 28). Moreover, as this event was declared UNESCO Intangible Cultural Heritage of Humanity, it is also perceived as an event that entails the preservation of cultural wealth and the diversity of its ritual components. "La Patum is of a great cultural importance; it is the heritage of humanity and a cultural asset that reaches beyond Catalonia. Everyone identifies us; locally everyone knows that La Patum is in Berga, and the city is linked to cultural traditions" (Antoni, 35). Some participants also stated: "It provides the city with tradition, friendship and *Catalanity*" (Joaquim, 81).

Accordingly, there is a strong feeling of linking the city with the event locally, nationally and internationally, understanding La Patum as a strong identifying feature of Berga. In other words, "Berga without La Patum is not Berga, and La Patum without Berga is not Patum. It is like a mother and a child; it is the same. Berga and La Patum are one and the same. La Patum means everything to Berga" (Pere, 41).

Conclusions

This chapter focuses on the analysis of place marketing through a traditional and popular cultural event. We observed the perceptions of participants and audiences, which led to identifying authenticity as a branding element for the locality. As underlined, this event has the characteristic of keeping ancestral figures and rituals from ancient times alive. Therefore, the popular imagery of this event is strongly related to traditional aspects of Catalan culture and, consequently, also to authenticity. We understand this authenticity through two different dimensions: firstly by its "originality", preserving original elements of representation, and secondly by perceptions of the participant experience.

Although this study is not a classical observation of place branding through events, due to the analysis perspective of participant perceptions, the authors believe that it is of great interest to the academic debate: firstly as it underlines the importance of social experience and personal interpretation of the event when considering it as an attraction, and secondly the authors consider authenticity as a structural pillar for attracting visitors to destinations. In this sense, this perspective helps us understand popular interpretations of events, an aspect we consider crucial when analysing place branding through events.

As place marketing through events has become a contemporary instrument for promoting cities (Bodet and Lacassagne 2012), transforming them economically as well as socially (Getz 2008; Cudny 2016), city marketing is not only a matter that concerns the municipal authorities, it also involves all the actors that make up a city: for example, companies, inhabitants and visitors, who can be regarded as consumers and producers of urban products (Van Mierlo 2014). Nevertheless, although events may help open up spaces for other uses (Neal et al. 2015), they may also introduce some physical, symbolic and financial barriers that exclude some people from participating (Smith 2016). Therefore, the authors interpret that perception and popular interpretation are fundamental when defining an event or a place as a brand. If we consider a brand as a part of a product (in our case, an event) with relevant, unique and symbolic values closely aligned to consumer needs (Chernatony and McDonald 1992), that brand can powerfully offer promise and quality.

The data gathered regarding La Patum shows us that authenticity, as explained earlier, may be perceived in two dimensions. The first is the recovery and continuation of centuries-old representations through the presentation of heritage and cultural wealth, although some changes in and the evolution of said representations are accepted. Among these changes, there are general evolution and changes such as increased accessibility to the groups of performers. The second is in the experience of personal imagery as an authentic aspect linking the event, as a special place, with feelings, emotions and memories. These two dimensions are also illustrative of how those emotions and experiences are nodes that firmly link audiences and participants to the event. Both those born and living in Berga and outsiders who have an intense emotional link to this festivity perceive the event as theirs and integrate La Patum into their lives.

This study also revealed results which could be interpreted beyond the goals of this research: for example, the case of Berga's social power pattern mirrored in the event structures, as Bullen and Egido (2004) stressed in their research about the Alardes in Hondarribia and Irun (Basque Country, Spain). Our study has not focused on the depth of the relationship between authenticity and city branding; nevertheless, the participants' and audiences' perceptions reveal that authenticity is an important aspect that firmly links this event, and consequently the city, with inhabitants and visitors. This link could also generate some contra-reaction, as some informants mentioned that there are now too many people as a result of the popularity of the event, and some of them even feel that the city should limit access rather than promote it further. Nevertheless, the strong emotions expressed by those who like this festivity and participate every year (inhabitants or not) reveal aspirations and the possibility of excitement, promises, respect and fear. Consequently, in the case studied here, this promise is strongly related to the popular imaginary of La Patum as an authentic experience.

Notes

1 The Patum is first mentioned in ecclesiastical documents, such as those written by the Council of Terraconense in 1564, which prohibited popular representations not linked to ecclesiastical authorities. Since the Bulla (what we now call La Patum) was a purely civil and secular celebration designed to honour civil authorities, this festivity was included in those ecclesiastical prohibited texts (Amades 1983).

2 For more information and details about this, consult the following: www.vilaweb. cat/noticies/bruce-springsteen-cedeix-una-canco-a-la-patum-de-berga/; www.ara.cat/ cultura/Patum-ballaran-Bruce-Springsteen-Corpus_0_1564043796.html.

3 An entertaining interval between the first and second acts of a play. It is thought to have been performed on the Spanish stage in the 16th century and derives from the influential Italian *comedia dell'arte*.

4 The project was titled "Everyday Life Futures: Reshaping Urban Lives in Times of Austerity and Change" (CSO2013–48232-D) and focused on imaginaries of the future in crisis times.

5 The names of our informants have been anonymized through pseudonyms.

6 These "authentic" experiences, narrated in these terms, may echo Schulze's concept of "experience society" (Schulze 1992, 1999) and Pine and Gilmore's (1999) theories regarding the experience economies; however, we would like to highlight that while Pine and Gilmore's analyses and, to a certain extent, Schulze's are directed towards the creation and marketisation of events regarding the exchange value of experiences (and thus arguing the creation of a new type of added value in the process), La Patum is not a festivity that has been created or kept for its market value. Despite the undeniable fact that Berga profits from hosting La Patum, it is also true that the city could profit much more from it if its format were adapted to the demands of the "experience society and

economy", but this adaptation takes place very partially, and it is still possibly to dance at La Patum without having to enter into any economic transaction.

7 Of course, the experience is one, a whole, but we can distill and highlight aspects of it for analytical purposes.

8 In a similar manner as Duffy et al. (2011) explore regarding the interrelation of rhythms and qualities of sounds with bodies in music festivals in Australia.

9 See Georg Simmel's "Sociology of the Senses" (Simmel 1997, pp. 109–120).

10 For more information, please visit www.lapatum.cat, www.facebook.com/La-Patum-252859778161630/, https://twitter.com/lapatum?lang=es.

11 For more information, please visit the city council website www.ajberga.cat/ajberga/apartats/index.php?apartat=132 or the regional Catalan government website http://patrimoni.gencat.cat/es/coleccion/la-patum.

12 For example, www.femturisme.cat/es/rutas/la-patum-de-berga, www.turismoen catalunya.es/fiesta-Patum-de-Berga.html, www.turismeberga.cat/index.php/la-ciutat/la-patum, www.spain.info/es/que-quieres/agenda/fiestas/barcelona/fiesta_de_la_patum_de_berga.html.

13 For more information, please visit https://ich.unesco.org/en/RL/patum-of-berga-00156?RL=00156.

References

Amades, J. (1983). *Costumari Català. El curs de l'any*. Barcelona: Ed. Salvat i 62, ISBN: 84-345-3673-0.

Bodet, G. S. P., & Lacassagne, M. F. (2012). International place branding through sporting events: A British perspective of the 2008 Beijing olympics. *European Sport Management Quarterly*, 12(4), 357–374.

Bullen, M., & Egido, J. A. (2004). *Tristes espectáculos: las mujeres y los alardes de Irún y Hondarribia*. Bilbao: universidad del País Vasco.

Carrera, M. (2014). Calendari de les festes amb pirotècnia. Barcelona: Botaga Producciones.

Chernatony, L., & McDonald, M. H. B. (1992). *Creating Powerful Brands: The Strategic Route to Success in Consumer, Industrial and service Markets*. Oxford, UK: Butterworth-Heinemann.

Colombo, A. (2009). Expansive waves of festivals: Approaches in economic impact studies of arts festivals. *La revista d'economia della cultura*, 3, 351–359.

Colombo, A. (2017). Music festivals and eventfulness: Examining eventful cities by event genres and policy agendas. *Event Management*, 21, 563–573.

Colombo, A., Oliver, E., Massager, M. (forthcoming). *Shifting Narratives in Catalan Popular Culture: The "Samba Invasion" in Devils Groups of Barcelona*. Identities. Global Studies in Culture and Power Taylor & Francis.

Cudny, W. (2016). *Festivalisation of Urban Spaces: Factors, Processes and Effects*. Cham: Springer.

Davies WKD. (2015). Festive cities: Multi-dimensional perspectives. In W. K. D. Davies (ed). *Theme Cities: Solutions for Urban Problems* (pp. 533–561). Cham: Springer.

Duffy, M., Waitt, G., Gorman-Murray, A., & Gibson, Ch. (2011). Bodily rhythms: Corporal capacities to engage with festival spaces. *Emotion, Space and Society*, 4(1), 17–24.

Evans, G. (2001). *Cultural Planning: An Urban Renaissance?* London: Routledge.

Getz, D. (1991). *Festivals, Special Events and Tourism*. New York: Van Nostrand Reinhold.

Getz, D. (2008). Event tourism: Definition, evolution, and research. *Tourism Management*, 29(3), 403–428.

Getz, D. (2012). *Event Studies. Theory, Research and Policy for Planned Events*. Oxford: Elsevier.

Gibson, L., & Stevenson, D. (2004). Urban space and the uses of culture. *International Journal of Cultural Policy*, 10(1), 1–4.

Hannigan, J. (2003). Symposium on branding, the entertainment economy and Urban place building: Introduction. *International Journal of Urban and Regional Research*, 27(2), 352–360.

Neal, S., Bennett, K., Jones, H., Cochrane, A., & Mohan, G. (2015). Multiculture and public parks: Researching super-diversity and attachment in public green space. *Population, Space and Place*, 21(5), 463–475.

Noyes, D. (2003). *Fire in the Plaça. Catalan Festival After Franco*. Philadelphia: University of Pennsylvania Press.

Picard, D., & Robinson, M. (eds). (2006). *Festivals, Tourism and Social Change: Remarking Words*. New York: Chanel View Publications.

Pine, J., & Gilmore, J. (1999). *The Experience Economy: Work Is Theater & Every Business a Stage*. Harvard: Harvard Business School Press.

Richards, G., & Wilson, J. (2004). The impact of cultural events on city image: Rotterdam. cultural capital of Europe 2001. *Urban Studies*, 41, 1931–1951.

Rumbo i Soler, A. (2001). *Patum!* Berga: Edicions Amalgama.

Schulze, G. (1992). *Die Erlebnisgesellschaft: Kultursoziologie der Gegenwart*. Frankfurt, AM: Campus.

Schulze, G. (1999). *Kulissen des Glücks. Streifzüge durch die Eventkultur*. Frankfurt, AM: Campus.

Simmel, G. (1997). Sociology of the Senses. In: *Simmel on Culture* (pp. 109–120). London: Sage.

Smith, A. (2012). *Events and Urban Regeneration. The strategic Use of Events to Realise Cities*. New York: Routledge.

Smith, A. (2016). *Events in the City: Using Public Spaces as Event Venues*. Abingdon: Routledge.

Soler i Amigó, J. (2001). *Cultura Populat Tradicional*. Barcelona: Editorial Pòrtic.

Turner, V. (1979). Frame, flow and reflection: Ritual and drama as public liminality Japanese. *Journal of Religious Studies*, 6(4), 465–499.

Van Mierlo, J. (2014). *Events and City Marketing: The Role of Events in Cities* (pp. 127–157). on Gerritsen, D., & Van Olderen, R. *Events as a Strategic Marketing Tool*. Cabi Tourism Texts. Oxfordshire: CABI.

4 Participatory cultural events and place attachment

A new path towards place branding?

Zafeirenia Brokalaki and Roberta Comunian

Introduction

In the last 30 years, academics, policy makers, and city planners have explored extensively the role of art in urban development, urban revitalization, and city planning (Bassett 1993; Müller 2018). Placing the emphasis on culture, urban studies researchers have elaborated on the positive effects of art on urban place-making (Redaelli 2018; Richards and Duif 2018). Scholars working in the field of events and festival studies have also discussed the relationship between cultural events and place identity, festivals and place branding; artistic public celebrations; and place image-making (Cudny 2016). Additionally, marketing scholarship has offered valuable insights in relation to the impact of aesthetic, artistic, and cultural experiences on place marketing and branding strategies (Bain and Landau 2017). In other words, interdisciplinary academic work and real-life cases suggest that art has a significant role to play in our spatial experiences, perceptions, and behaviours. As a result, the employment of art has been crucial for the development, promotion, inhabitation, consumption, and sustainability of contemporary urban space.

However, the literature on arts and place is often focused on institutionally led, publicly funded, or market-based creative strategies applied for the planning, development, and promotion of nations, regions, or metropolitan centres for external audiences, such as investors, tourists, and visitors (Comunian and Mould 2014). As a result, existing research has not fully examined the relationship between non-institutional, audience-led, and crowd-sourced cultural events and place marketing. Furthermore, the role of participation in the production, dissemination, and consumption of grassroots arts events has not been fully explored yet. This is especially true in relation to how internal audiences, such as local communities, may perceive, feel about, and experience their cities. Third, existing studies concentrate on the implications, effects, and outcomes of hallmark cultural programmes, major festivals, and large-scale art events. However, they overlook smaller artistic happenings, everyday creative practices, and informal cultural activities.

In response to this research gap, the purpose of this chapter is to explore the affordances of everyday creativity in relation to the development of human-place bonds between internal audiences and urban public spaces, investigating the role that pocket-size participatory cultural events may play in place branding endeavours. For this research, we define participatory art events as those space-bound, informal, and grassroots cultural happenings that are initiated, produced, implemented, and consumed by audiences, local communities, and everyday creative people. Participatory cultural events, in our context, are non-institutional, audience-led, and spontaneous cultural expressions of non-expert creatives and emerging and professional artists.

Our work brings together theoretical contributions and literature from diverse disciplines with the aim of addressing the following overarching research question: How do participatory art events affect the perceptions, sentiments, and attitudes towards a place? The findings of our multi-sited ethnographic research help us conceptualize what happens when creative citizens use their imagination, storytelling capability, and artistic self-expressive faculties to co-create, share, and co-consume the cultural content of their urban public space. This enables us to critically examine whether place marketing theory could also engage with non-institutional, grassroots, audience-led cultural initiatives. Do existing institutional marketing approaches contribute to the promotion of the original character of a place? Or should we turn our attention to alternative organic initiatives of citizen participation in the arts that can help us extend our place branding theorizations and practices?

Place attachment and creativity in place branding

Our work bridges two diverse sets of academic arguments, which might in many ways seem disconnected but will be key in the development of our conceptual framework. On one side, we aim to review the academic knowledge in relation to place attachment. On the other end, we aim to consider how culture and creativity become instrumental tools for place marketing and branding strategies. Finally, we question the current lack of research on bottom-up participatory arts events. Hence, we highlight the need for further research that investigates how participatory art events connect with place attachment and place branding.

Understanding place attachment

The study of affective relationships that people develop towards their environments is a subject that has received considerable scholarly attention across various disciplines. Our work concentrates on the theory of *place attachment*, which is used as the conceptual foundation that enables us to explore the emotion-laden human-place bonds stimulated, developed, and sustained through participatory art events. Using place attachment as a broad theoretical framework, we discuss how individuals – locals and visitors – experience, form, interpret, negotiate, and assign meanings to their urban environments through participatory art experiences.

To explore the role that participatory art events may play in place attachment, we draw on the work of the British psychologist John Bowlby, who was the first to conceive the basic tenets of *attachment theory* (Bowlby 1951, 1969). Bowlby studied the bonds that are developed between a baby and a mother, introducing *attachment* as the emotional parent-infant relationship. Later, Bowlby (1982) looks at potential negative effects that may arise in case of disruption of this relationship due to events of deprivation, separation, or bereavement. Today, attachment theory has moved beyond the parent-infant relationship to include studies which explore attachment to communities (Manzo and Perkins 2006), social environments (Milligan 1998), neighbourhoods (Manzo 2005), brands (Thomson et al. 2005), and places (Kyle et al. 2004). In other words, attachment theory currently covers a wide domain in terms of research and application, embracing bonds to persons, objects, and places. The key characteristic of the concept of attachment, which is common across all different research areas, disciplines, and practical manifestations, is the desire of the attached individual to maintain closeness to the object of attachment (Bowlby 1969).

To delve deeper into the human-place relationships that can be developed through participatory cultural events, we focus on the notion of *place attachment* (Manzo and Devine-Wright 2013). Place attachment refers to the long-lasting affective, cognitive, social, cultural, symbolic, and physical ties that are developed between a person and a particular setting through processes of human-place bonding (Low and Altman 1992). The theory of place attachment builds on research initially conducted by Fried (1963), who demonstrates that people suffer from grief when they have to be removed from a place they feel attached to. As Relph (1976) reveals, in our everyday life situations, we are not aware of the strong bonds and commitments that exist between our lives, our places, and ourselves. The significance of our places "become[s] apparent only in time of loss and hardship" (Relph 1976, p. 40).

Spaces become places through experience, symbolisms, and sentiment (Tuan 1974). In this sense, people experience, form, and transform urban space through their daily routines, their everyday practices, their senses (Duffy et al. 2011), and their mundane meaning-making processes. Steele (1981) also supports that places do not exist independent from us. Humans create their own places, which are defined by the physical attributes of the space and the meanings we bring to them. This human-place bond, conceptualised as place attachment, "is based on an accumulation of physical, social, historical, and cultural meanings that become associated with the place through time and experience" (Debenedetti et al. 2013, p. 905).

Flourishing in the fields of different scientific disciplines, the theory of place attachment holds the same premise as attachment theory: the desire and tendency of the individual to maintain closeness to a particular place (Shumaker and Taylor 1983). It is because peoples' identity and values are shaped within and by places they consider significant that strong human-place bonds are developed. In a similar vein, place identity is not only a component of self-identity, but also an aspect of social identity (Stedman 2002). Physical sites become arenas for social interaction, which forms individuals, communities, society, politics, and cultural life. Social sites define and are defined by collectively constructed processes, local group meanings, and the largest cultural and socio-political contexts (Milligan 1998). In other words, our physical environments can be viewed as an essential part of ourselves and a defining part of our shared identity regardless of, or in addition to, the physical qualities of the space.

Although place attachment has been explored in many contexts, there is limited work that theorises how human-place bonds are developed in the contemporary market-driven urban space and what circumstances might facilitate this. For example, there are a few studies which look at the processes in which mundane or commercial places can arouse strong emotions for their visitors (Debenedetti et al. 2013). There is also literature suggesting that art events, public celebrations, and festivals, through collectively shared symbolic processes, can ascribe meaning to publicly accessed spaces (Kozinets 2002; Visconti et al. 2010; Patsiaouras et al. 2018). However, these papers do not examine the role of smaller-scale symbolic, cultural, and aesthetic experiences in the development of human-place bonds within everyday urban contexts.

We propose that an analysis of the practices, experiences, and manifested outcomes linked to city attachment through participatory art events will help us better articulate the relationship between everyday creativity, human-place bonding, and place branding. According to Johnston and Conroy (2008, p. 381), "The reasons why people become attached to different locations extend well beyond the location's physical characteristics, the types of products it sells and/or the level of service it provides". Hence, our research explores how informal participatory arts events may trigger, develop, and sustain human-place bonds, discussing the implications of place attachment for place branding.

The role of arts, culture, and creativity in urban regeneration, placemaking, and place branding

In this brief review, we first explore how art has recently found a new role in local, city, and regional development interventions. Secondly, we focus more closely on the role that festivals have played in this broader landscape as artistic event-based intervention. Finally, we review the limited attention given in the literature to participatory art events.

In the last three decades, art, culture, and creativity have been key in the regeneration processing of many cities around the world (Evans 2005). They have been used – alongside physical regeneration and urban renewal – for a range of instrumental objectives. These objectives can be summarised under three main headings: (1) economic, (2) image/rebranding, (3) social interaction. They have been used as an opportunity to re-think local economic development and specifically focus on new sectors of the economy – such as the creative industries (Mould and Comunian 2015). However, while investments in cultural events, arts, and creativity can have potentially positive impact in developing local creative production, many authors highlight that this is not necessarily an easy strategy for many cities competing for talent (Jayne 2005; Comunian 2009; Comunian and Jewell 2018). Second, García (2004) underlines how cultural activities can maximize the impact of city branding, supporting the view of Tibbot (2002), who argues that "cultural projects give emotional 'fuel' for successful destination brands. And cultural brands can be adopted by commercial regeneration projects" (Tibbot 2002 quoted in García 2004, p. 316). Part of this is due to the increasing competition among cities to attract capital and investments. In a sort of competitive place marketing, the cultural assets and attributes of a city have been acquiring a central position (Griffiths et al. 2003). Miles (2005), however, questions this because it promotes a standardized understanding of culture. This is the culture associated with big flagship projects and event-led advertising campaigns developed by public authorities. Rebranding old urban spaces to attract new residents, tourists, and investors is often at the expense of local communities. Furthermore, as Pratt (2000) suggests, "the question of whose representation of the city is used to promote and advertise it is about which set of values, which aspects of the city are invested with legitimacy, which parts are visible and which are not" (Pratt 2000, p. 45). Nonetheless, a third objective often put forward for using arts and culture in regeneration is their role in engaging communities and fostering new interactions amongst old and new residents (Miles 2005).

Festivals play an important role in the arguments illustrated here as a sub-field within event studies. They are an important component of cities' cultural strategies for regeneration and attraction of investment and people. Refocusing our previous arguments for the value of cultural intervention in relation to (1) economic impact, (2) image/branding, and (3) social interaction, we can reflect on how festivals can become instrumental on all three levels. In respect to social engagement and interaction, festivals celebrate community values, ideologies, identity, and continuity (De Bres and Davis 2001). For example, Derrett (2003) argues that community-based festivals in New South Wales, Australia, contribute to a sense of community. In this sense, festivals shape experiences, meanings, spatial patterns, and processes. They inspire creativity and generate emotional responses. However, they can also attract large (external) attention and crowds. The latter are of specific interest for the economic and image/place branding value of culture. In relation to image and branding, festivals are being employed as tools in destination image-making, branding, and re-positioning strategies. Harcup (2000) examined how a festival was developed to deliberately help change the image of Leeds. Jago et al. (2003) in Australia studied how to build events into destination branding. Boo and Busser (2006) examined how a festival could improve a destination's image. With this branding and image potential, festivals are strategically used to create economic impact and jobs, which constitute our third theme (Crompton and McKay 1994). This is also celebrated by local policy makers as a great tool for job creation. However, as previous research suggests, most career opportunities created tend to be in the service sector and often lead to low-paid jobs (O'Sullivan and Jackson 2002). Ultimately, while festivals have been considered useful instruments for destination branding and economic development, their multiplication has also had a negative impact on the level of quality and authenticity that a city can present and promote.

Despite the richness of the existing studies on the relationship between art festivals and place marketing, as previously mentioned, the role of grassroots, audience-led, bottom-up cultural events in spatial consumption has not been fully examined yet (Sasaki 2010). Limited previous work in marketing and consumer research has suggested that participatory aesthetic practices can contribute to the collective consumption of urban public space (Visconti et al. 2010), a sense of community (Kozinets 2002), and social cohesion (Patsiaouras et al. 2018) for dwellers, local communities, and citizens. However, there is not adequate research conducted that investigates the role of smaller, informal, and more spontaneous participatory cultural happenings in the city.

Case study, methodology, and research framework

Athens Fringe Festival

Athens Fringe Festival (AFF) is a multifaceted arts festival organised annually since 2008 in the city of Athens in Greece. AFF is one of the first contemporary participatory art initiatives in the city. Its participatory character is manifested by its intention to invite every form of art; a range of creative practices, methods, and mediums; and diverse publics to learn, prepare, develop, present, and promote artistic work during the festive period. The key characteristic of the festival is its unique capacity to invite any member of the society to showcase their creative talents; everyday creative people; craftsmen; makers; amateur, emerging, and professional artists; local community members; designers; activists; students; academics; marginalised groups; immigrants; media professionals; local authority representatives; tourists; and city visitors are welcome to participate with their own creative ideas and self-expressive works.

The festival usually takes place for a month every June/July, hosting some hundreds of people presenting their art and attending others' events ranging from visual and fine arts; music, theatre and dance; poetry; installations and screenings; crafts; fashion; and cooking to learning, community and children's programmes, workshops, seminars, and public discussions. The artistic activity of the festival is formed by the proposals received from the audience through a series of open calls. All proposals are accepted for realization by the organizing team since the objective of the festival is to support every form of everyday creative self-expression. In this sense, it could be argued that no clear preference of an art form, medium, practice, or cultural producer is privileged. The "curation" of the programme is more a practice of scheduling.

The organising team consists of local community members and volunteers, who collaborate to put together the festival schedule, to establish partnerships with local businesses and venues, and to spread the word about the events. AFF is an independent platform that operates as a network for the creative individuals of the city and operates as a registered charity. Any income generated from the events is reinvested in the organisation of next year's festival.

The aim of the festival is to operate as an open platform for everyday creative people who wish to engage with artistic self-expressive practices and aspire to produce, organise, and showcase their cultural work. Usually, the participants of the festival set up arts events to try new self-expressive activities; take part in collaborative projects; meet with the public; and cooperate with other creative individuals, artistic collectives, and activist communities. They get involved in processes of reciprocal learning and public discussion and contribute to the organising of social activism through the arts. In other words, AFF's ultimate objective is to trigger an active interaction between the city, its citizens, and its visitors through the arts.

The events of the festival take place in numerous public spaces, such as streets, gardens, squares, public transport vehicles, parks, beaches, and neighbourhoods. Some events also take place in a variety of indoor spaces more or less commercial in nature, such as cafes, restaurants, bars, cinemas, and theatres. These urban settings operate as exhibition spaces, performance venues, screening areas, meeting places, arts schools, and platforms for dialogue. During the festival period, many different events take place in multiple sites around the city simultaneously. The participants can attend all the events for free, and the spectators who do not actively participate in the art-making process can enjoy others' creative output using a daily pass that gives them access to all festival spaces (public and commercial) at a cost of five to ten euros per day.

The space-bound, informal, and audience-led character of AFF makes it an appropriate context to explore arts-stimulated interactional processes; participatory practices; and human-place dynamics, relations, and bonds in urban settings. We limit our research only to spaces that are publicly owned and accessed, such as streets, parks, plazas, public transport vehicles, and beaches in the city.

Methodology and research questions

To research the relationship between participatory art events, place attachment, and place branding, we conducted a multi-sited ethnography in Athens, Greece (Marcus 1995; Falzon 2016). The stories found in this chapter are generated through active participation in a variety of art events initiated, developed, and produced by everyday creative people, who occupy, use, and experience a number of public spaces across the city with the aim to create, develop, and present their artistic work. Our data collection and analysis methods are not applied across all festival sites and events as this would not be feasible. AFF takes place in multiple public and privately-owned locations simultaneously for many days every year. This means that an intensive and sustained immersion in all different events of each site would not be a realistically achievable plan. One of the researchers participated in some of the events in more than ten public sites (streets, parks, means of public transportation, beaches) during a five-year period between 2011 and 2016, collecting empirical data comprising field notes, observations, photographs, videos, and interviews with festival participants.

During the first two years, the researcher witnessed and experienced the artistic events taking place across the city as an active participant, jotting field notes, taking photographs, and getting immersed in the creative events. In the next three years, the researcher tried to engage in participatory art activities, such as observing the physical context of the participatory art events; keeping notes about the physical activity of festival participants; and interacting with them about their embodied, emotional, and mental engagement with the space through informal discussions. Throughout this period, the researcher conducted ten interviews with festival participants, who ranged from first-time festival attenders to returning festival goers and from creative people who take part in the festival showcasing their work to organisers and volunteers. The focus of the research was placed specifically on participants' spatial experiences during the festival period. Based on this, we examine the relationship between grassroots participatory art events and place attachment towards urban public spaces. We then discuss what happens when participatory forms of art are brought into our everyday urban sites.

More specifically, the research has been focused on responding to the following four questions:

- How do grassroots participatory arts events emerge?
- How does audience involvement in the creation, preparation, and implementation of cultural events affect human-place bonds?
- How does audience participation in cultural events influence spatial experiences, perceptions, and sentiments?
- In what ways can art-stimulated participatory events contribute to placemaking, marketing, and branding endeavours for our cities?

Responding to these questions enables us to develop our theoretical understanding of the relationship between participatory art events and place branding. For our data analysis, we have decided not to describe, evaluate, or delve into every aesthetic experience, artistic project, and creative event recorded, lived, and interpreted through our fieldwork, as this would be neither feasible nor productive. We, therefore, do not follow a chronological or event-focused narration, but we develop emic-to-ethic themes that respond to our initial research questions. Reflecting on the theoretical perspectives and the literature discussed previously, we focus our attention on those stories that can shed some more light on the role that participatory art events may play in place attachment, marketing, and branding efforts.

Findings

The origin and meaning of the AFF: how participatory arts events emerge in our cities

AFF started in a serendipitous way as a non-planned demand by many citizens of Athens to create an open artistic platform. Such a platform allowed them to creatively, discursively, and aesthetically interact, share, and exchange their dreams and fears, passions and loves, emotions and hopes through art. As one of the festival organisers has publicly stated:

> We keep falling into each other. Our paths cross at the tube entrance. We drive next to each other on Kifissias Avenue; we look at each other from the trolley windows. We are seeking reasons to talk to each other, and we are happy when we find one, even if this reason is to yell at each other. We live in the same city. We are the first generation that feels that we own it. We love it. Athens belongs to us, and it's the extension of our living rooms. Reality is nice; it can even be magical. Fringe is the Festival of Athens.

The philosophy behind the festival is revealed through its slogan: *Athens Belongs to Us*. The founding team of the festival consists of a group of everyday creative people, who were struggling for years to find a cultural institution, organisation, or venue to accept their creative work in Athens. So, interestingly, while significant investment in urban arts tends to concentrate on building new cultural infrastructure and iconic cultural landmarks, these same institutions often promote an institutional perspective on culture, which does not facilitate everyday creativity (Comunian and Mould 2014). Before the launch of AFF, creative Athenians who were not professional artists were not feeling welcome to present their work in arts-dedicated venues, art festivals, or cultural institutions for decades. They were not recognised as legitimate cultural producers, and they were not encouraged to artistically express themselves in urban public contexts. This is the main reason AFF was established. Everyday citizens who felt the need to interact with others in creative ways tried to find non-arts, public, or privately-owned spaces that would allow them to share their stories through art and would enable them to aesthetically communicate with others. Inspired by the Edinburgh Fringe Festival, they came up with the idea of AFF and launched this festival as an act of resistance to the mainstream art offerings in the city. As one of the core organising team members of the festival recalls:

> We were begging the well-established art festivals . . . to become more open, to accept the work of more people. There was an intense need to express ourselves, but there was no platform willing to host us. We have sent countless letters to artistic directors and cultural programmers asking them to allow more people to participate in the Greek artistic scene. Everything was rejected. We were not "professional" enough. They were looking for "quality". They have been claiming that the Greek artistic scene "should progress", so they have been trying to focus on developing partnerships with international artistic companies. In 2008 AFF was born out of this need for participation in the cultural production of the city. AFF, in this sense, is a political action. An action of participation in the cultural commons.

In response to our first research question, we can see that, far beyond being launched as an urban top-down strategy, participatory events often seem to appear as a response to the stifling of art and creativity in institutional frameworks. This highlights a general discontent of people in being treated just as consumers in the broader creative economy and the importance of social interaction and everyday creativity (Wilson 2010). Further, recent academic work highlights the importance of the "creative citizen" (Hargreaves and Hartley 2016) and the need to take seriously the role they play, not simply as audiences but as cultural producers. As our interviewees argue, the value of non-professional creative self-expression is not always recognised within institutions and professional settings (Comunian 2011). This structural inadequacy creates the need for organic participatory and collaborative art events and inspires their emergence in cities (Comunian 2017).

Participatory cultural practices and place attachment

The second area of inquiry relates to how participatory cultural events inspire place attachment. Our informants' stories reveal that participatory creative activities are undertaken through *practices of physical familiarization, spatial experimentation, interaction, and control*. The arts-based multisensory, experimental, relational, and authoring practices make citizens come closer to the physical context of the city. They offer a protected environment in which people can creatively experiment; express themselves; and share ideas, emotions, and experiences with others. Participants' stories articulate how human-place bonds develop through such participatory creative practices.

Physical familiarisation

Our data indicate that audience participation in the making, experience, and consumption of cultural events contributes to spatial familiarisation, risk-taking, and sensory exploration. Many respondents highlighted how their involvement with events in the AFF provided an opportunity to familiarise themselves with the city. This was the case for individuals who lived there for decades as well as newcomers.

> I participate almost every year in AFF. Although I have been living in this city for more than four decades, I had never felt that I know my city much. Through the festival, I have come to know little corners, underground areas, and hidden places of the city that I had never noticed before. The discovery of these places happens in a unique way. Passing by a new building or walking on the same street every day is not enough; it takes many creative ways to discover your city with all of your senses.

Participatory art events request the active involvement of the audience in creative productive processes; it is not simply about attending an event but about being physically, mentally, and psychologically immersed in the creative happening. As a result, the type of familiarisation that takes place through participatory art events

Figure 4.1 AFF, 2011. Dancing on Syntagma Square
Source: Authors

involves multi-sensorial experiences and a deep level of engagement that brings an embodied understanding of the city (Duffy et al. 2011).

> During the festival, we spend so much time listening to the sounds of the city and producing our own sounds or acting and dancing in central spots. Yesterday, I had to lie down on the most central commercial street of Athens because of an improvisational act we were presenting. I had never smelled, touched, or felt the temperature of Ermou Street before. I don't know why, but I feel closer to it now. It's not just a street any more. You know . . . it's a street that I know . . . a street that I can recognise with all my senses. I don't know why, but I think that I love it more. It means more to me now. I shared a part of my life and myself on that street with all my honesty and emotion . . . in front of friends, strangers, and family members . . . How could it be the same again?

Experimentation

Participatory art events also encourage artistic self-expression, experimentation, and risk-taking practices. Creative participatory practices give audiences the opportunity to try new things, to be brave and open themselves to the public, and to explore new forms of public interaction. This is what two returning festival participants stated when commenting about their city experiences during AFF.

> [During the AFF], the city is transformed into this friendly place, where you can just experiment. If I start singing alone in the middle of the street in any given moment, people would probably think that I am crazy, but during the festival, such acts of self-expression are acceptable and welcome.
>
> You identify the most unsuspected space, you try to familiarize yourself with it for a minute or two, and then off you go. Anything that comes to your mind becomes possible.

These place-embedded practices of self-experimentation support the inclusivity of diverse, often conflicting, creative voices in the city, the broadening of representation in the Athenian urban landscape, and the pluralism of public expression (Wilson et al. 2017; Mason and Scollen 2018).

Interaction

Another significant practice that contributes to the development of human-place bonding is the interaction and dialogue needed in order to create grassroots participatory cultural events. Space-bound participatory cultural events facilitate meaningful verbal and non-verbal exchanges with others. This is an important dimension of participatory art because it builds on our knowledge of how culture can bring people together (Amin 2008). It also highlights the role of festivals in creating spaces for artistic self-expression (Kozinets 2002), dialogue (Wilks 2011), and collaboration (Comunian 2017).

> In a time where all forms of participation in the public dialogue – except the national and municipal elections – have been taken away from us, that citizens cannot decide on the matters of their everyday lives . . . we have found a way to take part in the public debate and to intervene. We do this through art, the most genuine form of human self-expression. We turn our city into an arena of interaction. We use sounds and rhythms, our bodies and our moves, our stories and our poems, to share our experiences, our dreams, our troubles. Athens becomes a domain of creative self-expression, exchange, and dialogue.

This statement comes from an older local amateur participant referring to the problematic social effects of the economic crisis in Greece. The respondent is arguing that art and creativity offer an alternative avenue towards public debate.

Control

The last significant characteristic of participatory art events identified through our research concerns the practices of control that are encouraged. Participatory cultural opportunities empower the consumer's role in the attached space but also enable participants to gain control over the space. Participatory artistic practices relate to the ability of individuals to creatively contribute to the context in which they express themselves but also to feel empowered to act on, shape, and control their physical environments. The following statement comes from a younger emerging artist who has taken part in the festival repeatedly.

> For 360 days every year, Athens is a place where things happen, and I have to adjust. I have to drive faster, I have to walk faster . . . I have to be quiet, I have to divert because of the demonstrations, I have to wait, I have to move again, I have to ask permission to enter into particular buildings. But there are a couple of days during the year . . . when I can just experience my city in the way that I want to. There is not a better feeling than knowing that for some days, you can take back control. You can live on your own terms. You produce your own work on the spot and in the moment, and it feels like the city is just there for you, waiting to be crafted according to your wishes, inspirations, and ideas. The city becomes yours again, even if it's just for a few fleeting moments.

Here, it becomes clear how participatory art events can relate to issues of cultural democracy (Wilson et al. 2017). Participatory art events can be powerful ways to redefine collective identities (Miles 2005) as well as group experiences, perceptions, and sentiment towards the city. In other words, participatory art events enable ordinary people to creatively shape, form, and define their urban context and content (Strydom et al. 2018).

From place attachment to place image

The aforementioned narratives suggest that participatory art events encourage consumer practices that contribute to the development of human-place bonds. But how are these experiences of spatial familiarisation, experimentation, interaction, and control manifested? How are human-place bonds translated in terms of audiences' spatial associations and evaluations? First, festival participants in the study stated that participatory art events contribute to a sense of authenticity for Athens. Second, participants expressed a sense of safety, security, and protection experienced in the context of their city. Third, place attachment was manifested through post-event nostalgia. Last, festival participants expressed perceptions and sentiments of closeness, ownership, and collective possession.

Authenticity

Many authors highlight how using art as a tool to improve the city image for tourism has become a common urban strategy. While this kind of investment might lead to local economic development, this tends to be very short term (García 2005), often leaving empty buildings and displacing the local community in the long-term analysis (Gaffney 2010). On the other end of the spectrum, recent research has engaged with the concept of authenticity in cultural and tourism experiences (Jive´ n and Larkham 2003; Knudsen and Waade 2010). This is very close to our findings in Athens, where participants reported the importance of spontaneity, informality, and authenticity in how the AFF events took place and involved real people. The following opinion comes from a local audience member who was visiting the festival for the first time:

> Events like this are genuine. Here, we find real stories, from real people for real people. Everything is real. It's real art. There is nothing curated, nothing refined; nothing is created with the aim to be sold. There is no formal stage, no props, no designed settings. All the events happen in real time, in real settings, in impulsive and spontaneous ways. It's a sincere act of communication.

Usually, art events are delivered by professional organisers with the risk of losing the authentic local, community, and participatory character of the festive activities (Edensor and Sumartojo 2018; Rota and Salone 2014). Professionally staged events run the risk of offering standardised, impeccable, and often uninspiring experiences to audiences. Grassroots participatory art events offer a rare opportunity to audiences to show the city's own idiosyncratic merit, anarchic creativity, and beauty without constructing stages, auditoriums, and luxury holiday packages for tourists. This creates a unique, valuable, and distinctive character for Athens, which might have greater potential for communicating a more authentic, original, and organic place identity.

Safety

As highlighted in the literature, place attachment depends on and connects with our primal need for safety and security (Fried 2000). It also contrasts with many of the contemporary fears which are developed and experienced in our cities (Low 1997). Furthermore, from a city marketing and tourism perspective, it connects with one of the key issues that cities aim to address to attract visitors (Dolnicar 2005). The following statement comes from a younger participant who is taking part in the festival for the first time:

> The city feels safer and more open. There is this homey feeling everywhere . . . you feel like you are in your shower, you know. Singing for yourself . . . but people are actually there . . . present . . . and they care. They stop, they listen . . . they try to understand . . . they sometimes ask questions. For a few days, Athens becomes cosier and less threatening.

Human-place ties developed through participatory creative practices have the potential to make our urban spaces feel safer, less threatening, and friendlier. They create a sense of homeyness, coziness, and intimacy (Debenedetti et al. 2013).

Post-event nostalgia

Art-stimulated place attachment also creates a strong post-event nostalgia. This reflects the arguments of Bowlby (1982), Fried (1963), and Relph (1976) about grief in cases of place loss and separation. A young participant who travelled to Athens from abroad to present her work in the festival discusses the positive associations, dear memories, and treasured recollections developed during the festival period.

> It doesn't feel the same . . . you know. It's the same place, the same city . . . and at the same time, it isn't. Because it becomes impersonal, in a sense, again. But the memories are still so warm and vivid. We keep talking about our memories when we performed and had our rehearsals here. And every single time that I pass by, I remember these intense feelings . . . There was fairy dust . . . there was heartbeat . . . you know . . . there was anxiety and excitement. It was just magical! Now, we just have to wait for next year's events.

As this participant argues, the memories of the events create an idealised image of the city; Athens is felt and remembered as a magical, charming, innovative, and alive place. Participatory creative practices stimulate strong associations for individuals with the experience of excitement for the moment. Participants' experiences, sentiments, and shared moments give meaning to the city, their lives, and their spatial-based interactions (Tuan 1974; Steele 1981).

Collective possession

Participatory art practices also stimulate a sense of ownership and collective spatial possession. The stories from the field allow us to imagine how a city, through extra-governmental participatory aesthetic practices, can be experienced as collectively possessed by the citizens.

> When other big events take place in particular parts of Athens, we know that we can't have access to those parts of the city if we don't aim to attend the event. You know . . . big concerts, parades, marathons. They just close the streets down. So, if it's not your type of thing to attend as a spectator, you can't be there; you are excluded. When AFF takes place, we come together to create, collaborate, and change our city. Access is free . . . We all get the opportunity to express ourselves in our common shared space. Everyone can use the city to tell their own stories. In this sense, the city becomes yours. But at the same time, you know that it belongs to others, and you are there to hear their stories as well. And, in this way, you feel that you belong in something bigger, in something collective.

In this sense, it could be argued that AFF acts as a political arena of non-institutionalised participatory aesthetic experiences that has the potential to shift

Figure 4.2 AFF, 2011. Athens Fringe Bus, Interventions in the City
Source: Authors

the shape, the outlook, and the experience of the city, encouraging a more collective sense of spatial possession (Visconti et al. 2010).

From place image to place branding

As discussed earlier, participatory cultural events, such as AFF, have the potential
to arouse individually experienced attachment towards urban space. This happens
through participatory art practices undertaken by diverse creative citizens. However, such human-place bonds may also lead to further macro-level implications;
participatory art events foster a new playful, creative, polysensory identity for the
attached place for both citizens and external visitors to the festival. As one of our
local informants explains, these events make inhabitants feel closer to their city and
also enhance their desire to remain close to it – something that reflects the existing
literature on place attachment (Bowlby 1969, 1982; Shumaker and Taylor 1983).

> I would never change this city for anything in this world – where else can you
> find this burst of creativity? This artistic excitement in every corner? I have
> travelled all around the world, and there is no other place right now that offers
> this feeling of creativity. Although Athens is not an easy city, actually,
> it's one of the hardest cities to live in, it offers you something that no other
> place can. It's this feeling of creative resistance . . . you know . . . this sense
> of whatever may happen to us, we still have power, and this is our creative
> spirit. We still have ways to respond to the problems of modernity, and this

is our creative urge. This is what keeps me in this city . . . and it will keep me forever. Athens is a place irreplaceable. I wouldn't change it for any other city in the world.

Participatory art events here clearly contribute to a sense of connection to and pride in the city, its vivid character, and creative flair. This results in commitment, loyalty, and fidelity from the side of the citizens. Our participants demonstrated advocacy and loyalty towards the city of Athens because of this participatory artistic activity. This is another manifestation of place attachment, which is related to place branding (Faullant et al. 2008). While loyalty seems to connect with external visitors and their affiliation and return patterns to places, in this case, we find that loyalty – and, in some respect, pride of a place (Bailey et al. 2004) – is experienced by local citizens who are not willing to leave, replace their cherished place, or associate their lives with another city (Fried 1963; Relph 1976). This is richly expressed by a young professional, who lives in Athens and has participated in the festival several times.

> The atmosphere is so lively and vivid. When the events take place, Athens is a colorful city! Full of art, paintings, music, balloons, songs, plays, dances, poems. There are stories everywhere . . . You never get bored; there are unique happenings everywhere in the city. There are people who create in every corner. They create because they hope in something better, because they want to express their disappointment and disagreement, because they want to change their society, and they want to be changed. They long to communicate. And when the words we have are not enough, we resort to whatever form of communication is left – and this is art. I love this sense of surprise and unpredictability in a city. I love this artistic flair.

This is an image of the city which is not created and shaped by policy makers or place managers but emerges among the networks of participants, citizens, and visitors who engage in the grassroots creative activity in the city. Participatory art events can create a long-term enhancement of the appreciation for the city's offerings, its creative profile, and its surprising gifts. Through stories that are reproduced by international media (Sooke 2017) and by the festival's own channels and social media, the mosaic of the city image is enriched. However, this enhanced perception of Athens because of its grassroots creative events is not only evident in internal audiences' stories. Our discussions with local business owners and tourists revealed that:

> This creative vibe brings so many people downtown. Athens has many disadvantages, but this artistic activity going on brings in people, commerce, positive reputation, and more artists from around the world. It brings excitement to Athenians and visitors.
>
> This is why I wanted to travel to Athens! I had heard so many stories, and I kept reading that it's a city where crowd-sourced art is evidenced in any

unimaginable and unexpected place. And I wanted to experience that. It's true. Athens is like an adult playground. There is a sense of freedom, creativity, and playfulness everywhere. It's a place full of sounds, images, smells, and tastes.

Because of these grassroots lived aesthetics experienced across the city, Athens now embodies the meaning of underground creativity and uncompromised artistic self-expression. It is broadly recognized because of this unexpected, anarchic, and surprising artistic disposition that its citizens present. Athens, as a place brand, through its crowd-sourced art events, manages to organically connect ideals of resistance, self-expression, and genuine creativity, changing how people think, feel, and act (Jones 2017). We believe that this last impression from a tourist we met during the festival brilliantly summarises our findings:

> We all have the same perceptions about Greece . . . a place of debt, lazy people, and poverty. So, as a foreigner, you are a bit sceptical about travelling there. We hear many negative stories. And, obviously, these are not completely fake. But if you find a glimpse of spontaneous and genuine craziness in the sea of commercialisation that we all have to swim in, you forget all the rest and you dive in.

Discussion and concluding remarks

Our stories from the field suggest that participatory art events in urban public spaces contribute to the development of human-place ties that extend, enrich, and deepen usual spatial experiences in the city. Through participatory art practices, people get the opportunity to familiarise themselves with the city, experiment and interact with others in its context, and ephemerally control the space around them. Our findings indicate that participatory art practices stimulate place attachment, which has an impact on participants' spatial experiences, perceptions, and sentiments towards the city, manifested through a sense of authenticity, security, possession, and post-event nostalgia. This results in an overall enhancement of the city image for internal and external audiences, an appreciation of its offerings, and loyalty towards the place.

Reflecting on the stories from the field, we developed a framework (Figure 4.3) to conceptualise how the participation of citizens and visitors in informal arts events in the city can (1) foster human-place bonds; (2) affect spatial experiences, perceptions, and sentiments; and (3) impact macro-level implications in the overall place brand. In our analysis, we identified four key stages that connect the possibility for participatory cultural events to stimulate place attachment and, consequently, enhance the place brand.

Our concluding remarks highlight some conceptual propositions, some remaining open questions, and some venues for further research, which, hopefully, colleagues will be interested in exploring with us. Our findings suggest that, against a copycat strategy of culture-led regeneration (Evans 2003) and the boosting of

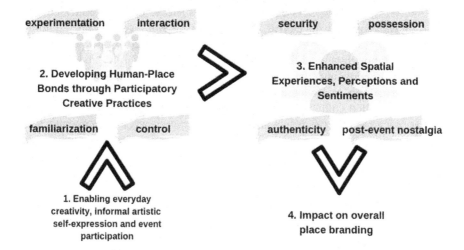

Figure 4.3 Relationship between participatory cultural events, place attachment, and place branding

Source: Authors

marketing-led festivals (Quinn 2005), grassroots participatory cultural events will become more important in supporting and sustaining an authentic identity for places (Kagan et al. 2018). In a similar vein to Mould's (2015) readings of subversive creativity, we propose that participatory festivals have the potential to question existing urban politics, unleash radical urban creativity, and offer opportunities for self-experimentation, social interaction, and spatial reconfiguration. In the case of AFF, we have demonstrated how the participatory, spontaneous, and audience-led nature of the artistic events has created a new dialogical platform for the city and an alternative place brand, which has affected the spatial experiences, perceptions, and sentiments of locals and visitors towards the city (Richards 2017). However, to understand whether this change in place image can affect and transform broader socio-cultural spatial dynamics, perceptions, and sentiments in the long-term, we would require further research.

Another crucial issue is whether participatory cultural events can be encouraged, supported, and/or developed through institutional channels. We would argue that participatory art events stimulate place attachment and contribute to the development of human-place bonds exactly because of their spontaneous, organic, fluid, bottom-up, and independent character. It is the emergence and experience of this resisting counterculture that creates this sense of authentic, non-compromised, and autonomous identity that makes places distinctive, original, and creative. While the encouragement of institutions would go a long way in ensuring the festival keeps on growing and embracing more places and people in the city, policy interventions – through funding or other means – might stifle the event's freshness, genuineness, and impulsiveness, changing the nature of the festival itself

(Comunian 2011). Therefore, the question remains open for place policy makers, managers, and marketers on how to connect and sustain the authenticity of independently initiated, developed, and delivered grassroots participatory cultural events to city branding endeavours (de Brito and Richards 2017).

Finally, although beyond the scope of this book, we hope this study can also contribute to a better understanding of the role of participatory cultural events and everyday creativity in academic discussions, policy endeavours, and managerial aspirations around cultural democracy (Richards 2007; Wilson et al. 2017), as well as in a more creative development, positive experience, and democratic living of our cities.

References

Amin, A. (2008). Collective culture and urban public space. *City*, 12(1), 5–24.

Bailey, C., Miles, S., & Stark, P. (2004). Culture-led urban regeneration and the revitalisation of identities in Newcastle, Gateshead and the North East of England. *International Journal of Cultural Policy*, 10(1), 47–65.

Bain, A. L., & Landau, F. (2017). Artists, temporality, and the governance of collaborative place-making. *Urban Affairs Review*, doi:1078087417711044

Bassett, K. (1993). Urban cultural strategies and urban regeneration: A case study and critique. *Environment and Planning A*, 25(12), 1773–1788.

Boo, S., & Busser, J. A. (2006). The hierarchical influence of visitor characteristics on tourism destination images. *Journal of Travel & Tourism Marketing*, 19(4), 55–67.

Bowlby, J. (1951). *Maternal Care and Mental Health*. Geneva: World Health Organization.

Bowlby, J. (1969). *Attachment and Loss v. 3* (Vol. 1). New York: Random House.

Bowlby, J. (1982). Attachment and loss: Retrospect and prospect. *American Journal of Orthopsychiatry*, 52(4), 664.

Comunian, R. (2009). Questioning creative work as driver of economic development: The case of Newcastle-Gateshead. *Creative Industries Journal*, 2(1), 57–71.

Comunian, R. (2011). Rethinking the creative city: The role of complexity, networks and interactions in the urban creative economy. *Urban Studies*, 48(6), 1157–1179.

Comunian, R. (2017). Creative collaborations: The role of networks, power and policy. In M. Shiach and T. Virani (eds). *Cultural Policy, Innovation and the Creative Economy*. London: Palgrave Macmillan.

Comunian, R., & Jewell, S. (2018). '*Young, Talented and Highly Mobile*': Exploring Creative Human Capital and Graduates Mobility in the UK New Frontiers in Interregional Migration Research (pp. 205–230). Cham: Springer.

Comunian, R., & Mould, O. (2014). The weakest link: Creative industries, flagship cultural projects and regeneration. [Article]. *City, Culture and Society*, 5(2), 65–74. doi:10.1016/j.ccs.2014.05.004

Crompton, J. L., & McKay, S. L. (1994). Measuring the economic impact of festivals and events: Some myths, misapplications and ethical dilemmas. *Festival Management and Event Tourism*, 2(1), 33–43.

Cudny, W. (2016). *Festivalisation of Urban Spaces: Factors, Processes and Effects*. Cham: Springer.

De Bres, K., & Davis, J. (2001). Celebrating group and place identity: A case study of a new regional festival. *Tourism Geographies*, 3(3), 326–337.

de Brito, M., & Richards, G. (2017). Events and placemaking. *International Journal of Event and Festival Management*, 8(1), 8–23.

Debenedetti, A., Oppewal, H., & Arsel, Z. (2013). Place attachment in commercial settings: A gift economy perspective. *Journal of Consumer Research*, 40(5), 904–923.

Derrett, R. (2003). Making sense of how festivals demonstrate a community's sense of place. *Event Management*, 8(1), 49–58.

Dolnicar, S. (2005). Understanding barriers to leisure travel: Tourist fears as a marketing basis. *Journal of Vacation Marketing*, 11(3), 197–208.

Duffy, M., Waitt, G., Gorman-Murray, A., & Gibson, C. (2011). Bodily rhythms: Corporeal capacities to engage with festival spaces. *Emotion, Space and Society*, 4(1), 17–24.

Edensor, T., & Sumartojo, S. (2018). Reconfiguring familiar worlds with light projection: The gertrude street projection festival, 2017. *GeoHumanities*, 4(1), 112–131.

Evans, G. (2003). Hard-branding the cultural city – From Prado to Prada. *International Journal of Urban and Regional Research*, 27(2), 417–440.

Evans, G. (2005). Measure for measure: Evaluating the evidence of culture's contribution to regeneration. *Urban Studies*, 42(5–6), 959–983.

Falzon, M. A. (2016). Introduction: Multi-sited ethnography: Theory, praxis and locality in contemporary research *Multi-sited ethnography* (pp. 15–38). New York and Abingdon: Routledge.

Faullant, R., Matzler, K., & Füller, J. (2008). The impact of satisfaction and image on loyalty: The case of Alpine ski resorts. *Managing Service Quality: An International Journal*, 18(2), 163–178.

Fried, M. (1963). *Grieving for a Lost Home, the Urban Condition: People and Policy in the Metropolis* (ed). New York: Leonard J. Duhl.

Fried, M. (2000). Continuities and discontinuities of place. *Journal of Environmental Psychology*, 20(3), 193–205.

Furman, W., & Buhrmester, D. (2009). Methods and measures: The network of relationships inventory: Behavioral systems version. *International Journal of Behavioral Development*, 33, 470–478.

Gaffney, C. (2010). Mega-events and socio-spatial dynamics in Rio de Janeiro, 1919–2016. *Journal of Latin American Geography*, 7–29.

Garcia, B. (2004). Cultural policy and urban regeneration in Western European cities: Lessons from experience, prospects for the future. *Local Economy*, 19(4), 312–326.

García, B. (2005). Deconstructing the city of culture: The long-term cultural legacies of Glasgow 1990. *Urban Studies*, 42(5–6), 841–868.

Griffiths, R., Bassett, K., & Smith, I. (2003). Capitalising on culture: Cities and the changing landscape of cultural policy. *Policy & Politics*, 31(2), 153–169.

Harcup, T. (2000). Re-imaging a post-industrial city: The Leeds St Valentine's Fair as a civic spectacle. *City*, 4(2), 215–231.

Hargreaves, I., & Hartley, J. (2016). *The Creative Citizen Unbound: How Social Media and DIY Culture Contribute to Democracy, Communities and the Creative Economy*. Bristol: Policy Press.

Jago, L., Chalip, L., Brown, G., Mules, T., & Ali, S. (2003). Building events into destination branding: Insights from experts. *Event Management*, 8(1), 3–14.

Jayne, M. (2005). Creative industries: The regional dimension? *Environment and Planning C: Government and Policy*, 23(4), 537–556.

Jive′n, G., & Larkham, P. J. (2003). Sense of place, authenticity and character: A commentary. *Journal of Urban Design*, 8(1), 67–81.

Johnstone, M. L., & Conroy, D. M. (2008). Place attachment: The social dimensions of the retail environment and the need for further exploration. In A. Y. Lee and D. Soman (eds). *NA – Advances in Consumer Research Volume 35* (pp. 381–386). Duluth, MN: Association for Consumer Research. http://www.acrwebsite.org/volumes/13327/volumes/v35/NA-35

Jones, I. (2017). 'He's still the winner in my mind': Maintaining the collective identity in sport through social creativity and group affirmation. *Journal of Consumer Culture*, 17(2), 303–320.

Kagan, S., Hauerwaas, A., Holz, V., & Wedler, P. (2018). Culture in sustainable urban development: Practices and policies for spaces of possibility and institutional innovations. *City, Culture and Society*, 13, 32–45.

Knudsen, B. T., & Waade, A. M. (2010). *Re-investing Authenticity: Tourism, Place and Emotions*. Bristol: Channel View Publications.

Kozinets, R. V. (2002). Can consumers escape the market? Emancipatory illuminations from burning man. *Journal of Consumer Research*, 29(1), 20–38.

Kyle, G. T., Mowen, A. J., & Tarrant, M. (2004). Linking place preferences with place meaning: An examination of the relationship between place motivation and place attachment. *Journal of Environmental Psychology*, 24(4), 439–454.

Low, S. M. (1997). Urban fear: Building the fortress city. *City & Society*, 9(1), 53–71.

Low, S. M., & Altman, I. (1992). *Place attachment* (pp. 1–12). Cham: Springer.

Manzo, L. C. (2005). For better or worse: Exploring multiple dimensions of place meaning. *Journal of Environmental Psychology*, 25(1), 67–86.

Manzo, L. C., & Devine-Wright, P. (2013). *Place Attachment: Advances in Theory, Methods and Applications*. New York and Abingdon: Routledge.

Manzo, L. C., & Perkins, D. D. (2006). Finding common ground: The importance of place attachment to community participation and planning. *Journal of Planning Literature*, 20(4), 335–350.

Marcus, G. E. (1995). Ethnography in/of the world system: The emergence of multi-sited ethnography. *Annual Review of Anthropology*, 24(1), 95–117.

Mason, A., & Scollen, R. (2018). Grassroots festival keeps city alive during severe drought. *Journal of Place Management and Development*, 11(3), 266–276.

Miles, M. (2005). Interruptions: Testing the rhetoric of culturally led urban development. *Urban Studies*, 42(5–6), 889–911.

Milligan, M. J. (1998). Interactional past and potential: The social construction of place attachment. *Symbolic Interaction*, 21(1), 1–33.

Mould, O. (2015). *Urban Subversion and the Creative City*. London: Routledge.

Mould, O., & Comunian, R. (2015). Hung, drawn and cultural quartered: Rethinking cultural quarter development policy in the UK. *European Planning Studies*, 23(12), 2356–2369.

Müller, A. L. (2018). Voices in the city. On the role of arts, artists and urban space for a just city. *Cities*, 91, 49–57.

O'Sullivan, D., & Jackson, M. J. (2002). Festival tourism: A contributor to sustainable local economic development? *Journal of Sustainable Tourism*, 10(4), 325–342.

Patsiaouras, G., Veneti, A., & Green, W. (2018). Marketing, art and voices of dissent: Promotional methods of protest art by the 2014 Hong Kong's Umbrella Movement. *Marketing Theory*, 18(1), 75–100.

Pratt, A. C. (2000). Cultural tourism as an urban cultural industry. A critical appraisal. *Cultural tourism*, 33–45.

Quinn, B. (2005). Arts festivals and the city. *Urban Studies*, 42(5–6), 927–943.

Redaelli, E. (2018). Creative placemaking and theories of art: Analyzing a place-based NEA policy in Portland, OR. *Cities*, 72, 403–410.

Relph, E. (1976). *Place and Placeness*. London: Pion.

Richards, G. (2017). Tourists in their own city – Considering the growth of a phenomenon. *Tourism Today*, 16, 8–16.

Richards, G., & Duif, L. (2018). *Small Cities with Big Dreams: Creative Placemaking and Branding Strategies*. New York: Routledge.

Richards, R. E. (2007). *Everyday Creativity and New Views of Human Nature: Psychological, Social, and Spiritual Perspectives*. Washington, DC: American Psychological Association.

Rota, F. S., & Salone, C. (2014). Place-making processes in unconventional cultural practices. The case of Turin's contemporary art festival Paratissima. *Cities*, 40, 90–98.

Sasaki, M. (2010). Urban regeneration through cultural creativity and social inclusion: Rethinking creative city theory through a Japanese case study. *Cities*, 27, S3-S9.

Shumaker, S. A., & Taylor, R. B. (1983). Toward a clarification of people-place relationships: A model of attachment to place. *Environmental Psychology: Directions and Perspectives*, 2, 19–25.

Sooke, A. (2017). Can Athens become Europe's new arts capital? Retrieved Date Accessed, 7 January 2019 from www.bbc.com/culture/story/20170509-can-athens-become-europes-new-arts-capital.

Stedman, R. C. (2002). Toward a social psychology of place: Predicting behavior from place-based cognitions, attitude, and identity. *Environment and Behavior*, 34(5), 561–581.

Steele, F. (1981). *The Sense of Place*. Boston: Cbi Pub Co.

Strydom, W., Puren, K., & Drewes, E. (2018). Exploring theoretical trends in placemaking: Towards new perspectives in spatial planning. *Journal of Place Management and Development*, 11(2), 165–180.

Thomson, M., MacInnis, D. J., & Whan Park, C. (2005). The ties that bind: Measuring the strength of consumers' emotional attachments to brands. *Journal of Consumer Psychology*, 15(1), 77–91.

Tibbot, R. (2002). Culture club: Can culture lead urban regeneration. *Locum Destination Review*, 9, 71–73.

Tuan, Y. F. (1974). *Topophilia: A Study of Environmental Perception, Attitude, and Values*. Englewood Cliffs: Prentice Hall.

Visconti, L. M., Sherry Jr, J. F., Borghini, S., & Anderson, L. (2010). Street art, sweet art? Reclaiming the "public" in public place. *Journal of Consumer Research*, 37(3), 511–529.

Wilks, L. (2011). Bridging and bonding: Social capital at music festivals. *Journal of Policy Research in Tourism, Leisure and Events*, 3(3), 281–297.

Wilson, N. (2010). Social creativity: Re-qualifying the creative economy. *International Journal of Cultural Policy*, 16(3), 367–381.

Wilson, N., Gross, J., & Bull, A. (2017). *Towards Cultural Democracy: Promoting Cultural Capabilities for Everyone*. London: King's College London.

5 The impact of outdoor cultural festivals on the city image

Lublin case study

Aleksandra Kołtun

Lublin, which is one of the biggest cities in Eastern Poland, has long been considered underdeveloped and unattractive for tourists, investors, and even its own inhabitants. This shabby image has not improved until recently, largely due to a major mobilisation accompanying the city's candidature for the title of the European Capital of Culture 2016. Although the title was awarded to another city, the events created then still contribute to some profound changes in the way Lublin is perceived today.

The purpose of this chapter is to provide information on the ways outdoor cultural festivals improve the image and brand of their host city, in terms of attracting tourists and stimulating urban development. The analysis is based on an extensive study of four major annual events held in Lublin: the Night of Culture, the East of Culture – Different Sounds Art'n'Music Festival, the Carnaval Sztukmistrzów (which can be translated as "Conjurors' Carnival") and the Jagiellonian Fair. Although none of these events were preceded with any marketing activity or ascribed any specific promotional aims, their impact on Lublin's image, both inside and outside the city, is extremely powerful.

The chapter starts with a brief description of the festivals' host city. Basic geographical and demographic details are provided, together with some crucial information on Lublin's recent change from a typical, so-called "Poland B" town into an ambitious, dynamically growing urban area. This is followed by some essential data on the methodology and course of the study. The third and fourth sections of the chapter contain an overview of the four studied festivals. The authors describe the main artistic and organisational assumptions, as well as the scope of the marketing activities that accompany each event. The authors also provide some information on the role performed by the festivals according to official urban development strategies. The subsequent parts of the chapter focus on the key research findings. They regard the effects of festival tourism as well as some more extensive and longer-lasting transformations of the city image. Moreover, the research findings show some important changes to the ways inhabitants treat the place where they live, thus influencing the city's internal image. In this case, we can identify effects pertaining to socialisation and reinforcement of social integration. They encompass fostering a sense of local pride and confidence as well as the influence on the perception and evaluation of the urban space. The final section of the chapter is a recapitulation of the key findings, in relation to the goals set in Lublin's branding and development strategies.

Introducing changes through culture: the festival host city

Lublin is a city in Eastern Poland, the capital of a voivodeship and an important cultural, educational and economic centre. In 2017, it was inhabited by about 340,000 people and the ninth largest city in Poland (Central Statistical Office Poland). Traditionally, Lubelskie Voivodeship was associated with agriculture and weak industry. Despite fairly small distances to Warsaw, the capital of Poland, and to the Ukrainian border, Lublin for decades remained disconnected from the main national and international transportation systems. It was situated in an underdeveloped region, called "Poland B". The city was treated as unattractive in terms of career opportunities and tourism assets. Although the popular distinction between the well-developed region of "Poland A" and the underdeveloped "Poland B" is an oversimplification, it has a strong influence on the way people perceive different parts of Poland.

In recent years, many attempts have been made in Lublin to improve the local job market, the living standard, and the city image, following the assumptions of the Lublin Development Strategy for 2013–2020. The global strategy is supported with several sector strategies (e.g., pertaining to culture or tourism development). Like many other economically declining cities, Lublin has turned to culture and the creative sector as a major urban development factor (see Cudny 2016; Landry 2008; Florida 2002). A turning point in Lublin's recent transformation was the decision to enter the competition for the European Capital of Culture 2016 (further on referred to as ECoC 2016). The process of preparing a formal application not only invigorated local artistic and cultural circles, but also encouraged Lublin inhabitants to cooperate for the sake of the city's development. Although Lublin finally lost in the competition, the very fact of being short-listed in its second stage proved that the city was capable of introducing changes and had an interesting cultural offer. The competition for ECoC 2016 made it evident that culture could act as an effective, locally attainable and fairly appealing impetus for a major urban change (see Kondrasiuk 2012; Kubicki 2012).

Today, Lublin has made up for many infrastructural inadequacies, both in terms of transportation and public facilities. The number of tourists has been constantly on the rise (according to the Central Statistical Office, in 2015, it had grown by 33 percent, compared to 2006). The cultural sector has been steadily growing in importance, offering not only large events, but also a dense network of organisations and informal initiatives. At the same time, local authorities have become more participative, encouraging the inhabitants to actively engage in the local governance. Lublin is still facing several problems, typical of an average large Polish city, such as the out-migration of young, educated people; gentrification; and privatisation of public spaces. However, over the last few years, the city has managed to change its image of a far-flung, retarded and completely uninteresting periphery. It has created an increasingly attractive job market, diversified its cultural offering and has been gradually improving people's standard of living. As presented next, festivals are an important contributor to this reputational success.

Research methodology

The results presented in this chapter are based on a comprehensive empirical study conducted in 2017. The study, entitled "The impact of Lublin's outdoor cultural festivals on the city's social and economic growth", was co-authored by the authors of this chapter.[1] Its purpose was to carry out a systematic, wide-ranging and in-depth analysis of the network of socio-economic relations, developed and reinforced by organising the largest regular outdoor cultural festivals in Lublin.

The research problems included several issues. First, the role and functions of festivals from the perspective of major urban growth strategies. Second, the structure of festival audiences (basic demographic structure, visitors' motivations and expenditures), the audiences' evaluations as well as the very experience and practices of festival participation. The third element was the effect of doing volunteer work during festivals on the volunteers' educational and professional careers. Another issue was the evaluation of festivals by the local entrepreneurs. All research participants were also asked about their perception of the impact of festivals on various aspects of urban growth, including its internal and external image.

The study was based on several primary and secondary sources of data. Desk research involved available reports and expert opinions on the evolution of festivals over time, as well as their impact on the city's growth. Selected quantitative indicators concerning local economy, culture and tourism were analysed in order to get a picture of Lublin's transformations between 2006 and 2016. Also, some qualitative content analyses were performed on a body of formal documents created by various city hall agendas (e.g. development strategies; their implementation assessments; information packs available for inhabitants, tourists and potential investors).

The audience of each festival was investigated by means of a uniform survey questionnaire. Researchers handed paper questionnaires to the respondents and collected them after they had been filled in. The respondents were selected randomly. Each researcher had their own starting point at which they were supposed to choose every tenth person walking by (with an additional criterion for groups: the person who'd celebrated their birthday most recently). A total of 1,562 questionnaires were included in the analysis, allowing statistical generalisation of research conclusions for each festival separately. Also, in order to obtain richer and more substantial data, the study included qualitative semi-structured interviews with a purposefully selected sample of festival participants, as well as qualitative visual analyses of social media content (Instagram and Facebook, visual materials uploaded by festival participants).

Moreover, the research included a paper questionnaire for entrepreneurs operating in the hospitality, gastronomy and commerce sectors within the geographical premises of Lublin Old Town and city centre. A list of 130 entrepreneurs who met the criteria was prepared and included in the study. Eventually, 81 question-naires were taken into account.

All the quantitative analytical procedures were performed using the SPSS soft-ware. The qualitative analyses were based on the constructivist grounded theory methodology (Charmaz 2006). They consisted of dense data coding (open coding and axial coding), as well as in writing memos.

The whole research process (e.g. constructing research tools, elaborating on the results at every stage of the research, writing reports, holding workshops etc.) was discussed and clarified with festival organisers. Moreover, in order to ensure a holistic approach to research, the team of researchers was interdisciplinary (including specialists on urban sociology, economy, philosophy and organisa-tional studies) and intra-generational (consisting of both seasoned academics and novice researchers and students).

If not stated otherwise, all the data and information concerning participation in and evaluation of the festivals come from the research described in this section.

Themes and organisation of the festivals

The events analysed in this chapter are festivals. A festival was defined by Cudny (2016, p. 18) as "an organised socio-spatial phenomenon, taking place at a spe-cially designated time, outside the everyday routine, shaping the social capital and celebrating selected elements of human tangible and intangible culture" (Cudny 2016, p. 18). All events included in the research are regular summer festivals that have been organised in the last ten years. They vary in length from one-night events (i.e. the Night of Culture) to three- or four-day-long festivals (i.e. East of Culture – Different Sounds Art'n'Music Festival, Carnaval Sztukmistrzów, and the Jagiellonian Fair). The majority of festivals are not ticketed and free for event goers. Most of them are open-air events or are held in venues owned by various public institutions, located in Lublin's Old Town and in its vicinity.

The festivals' programmes include a variety of artistic and cultural activities (from live performances, exhibitions, screenings and temporary street art to more participative workshops and events aimed at specific groups). The events are sup-plemented by additional services, such as evening entertainment, food and drink (offered by clubs and restaurants) and guided tours.

Although the four investigated festivals share some common organisational and artistic principles, it should be stressed that each of them has its own indi-vidual character, crucial for its experience and evaluation.

The Night of Culture focuses on transforming and rediscovering urban spaces. Every year, it offers hundreds of indoor and outdoor events, together with count-less art objects and installations located at various places (e.g. on buildings' facades or above the streets). The Night of Culture participants described it as an extremely intense, time-bound condensation of something extraordinary, magical and surprising, even if it took place in everyday urban spaces.

The core of the East of Culture – Different Sounds Art'n'Music Festival is live musical performances, with a particular focus on the cultural context of East

European countries. The festival participants appreciated its high artistic quality (uncompromised by the free admission policy) and a unique location in the immediate vicinity of the Old Town. This festival definitely differs from other music festivals due to its unprecedented accessibility – both in economic and geographical terms.

Carnaval Sztukmistrzów presents a combination of the so-called new circus, theatre and alternative art. Buskers, jugglers, slackliners and performers of all kinds take over the city centre, giving an impression of a carnivalesque suspension of everyday norms and social order. The majority of spectacles take place in the streets, which means that their constitution and course rely upon the interaction between the artist and the audience. The research shows that such mutual engagement and joint creation were crucial to participants' experience of Carnaval Sztukmistrzów.

The ambition of the Jagiellonian Fair organizers is to present the richness of authentic folk art, tradition and local handicraft. This is the only festival with a strong market function. However, that does not overshadow its main aim, which is exhibiting craftwork, demonstrating traditional trades and passing on skills that are dying out with the last generations of artisans. The fair participants highlighted the importance of the atmosphere of mutual interest and cordiality. They stressed how astonished they felt not only by the beauty of the presented objects, but, above all, by the openness and friendliness shown by the craftsmen presenting their goods during the event.

In terms of formal management, all four festivals are organised by a municipal institution – the Workshops of Culture, responsible to the mayor of Lublin. Most of the festival budget comes from the city and is supplemented with grants from other public institutions (e.g. the Ministry of Culture and National Heritage) and private sponsors.

The role of the Workshops of Culture as the main organiser varies, depending on the event. On the one hand, the institution deals with all management problems and the artistic programme. On the other hand, it delegates the realisation of activities to the artists, animators and volunteers who are directly organising the events. Two of the investigated festivals are organised jointly by the Workshops of Culture and other cultural institutions. The East of Culture – Different Sounds festival is organised by the National Centre for Culture together with the Ministry of Culture and National Heritage. Carnaval Sztukmistrzów is organised in cooperation with the marketing department of the City of Lublin. Every year, all four festivals are partnered by numerous public institutions, including NGOs, informal groups, individuals and other institutions which carry out various tasks connected with the technical and artistic aspects of the events' programme.

Festival audiences and communication strategies

In 2017, the four festivals attracted approximately 500,000 visitors, about half of whom attended Carnaval Sztukmistrzów. The Jagiellonian Fair was visited by another 150,000, the Night of Culture by 100,000, and the East of

Culture – Different Sounds festival by 50,000 people.[2] The festival participants were mostly young people (the average age of a festival participant was 35; the median age was 33), well-educated (75 percent declared continuing education after graduating from high school) and fairly affluent (70 percent described their own financial situation as "good" or "very good").

The differences in audience sizes and their structure depended on the aims of an individual festival and its target groups. These, in turn, influenced the scope and range of communication strategies. It must be stressed that none of the studied festivals was started as a promotional event, and the marketing-oriented goals did not determine their organisation. Originally, they were created by local artistic and cultural circles and based on Lublin's cultural assets: rich history, strong theatre and performance traditions, ambitious animators and educators. Over the last decade, the scope of events, artistic orientation and promotional range have certainly spread beyond their hometown. However, the festivals are still organised by local people, based on a variety of local assets and directed primarily towards the local inhabitants.

As was said earlier, the scope of festival communication strategies varies, while the basic marketing tools are fairly recurrent. All festivals have their own websites, Facebook pages and Instagram accounts (apart from those maintained by their organisers and partners). They are run all year round, more intensively before the date of a given event. Moreover, the events take advantage of the media patronage (local and national radio, TV, press), ensuring a wide range of informative and promotional coverage (articles, press releases, advertisements etc.). Other marketing tools used in all festivals include various outdoor media in Lublin and the Lublin region. They include billboards and posters displayed at bus stops, at the headquarters of various institutions and organisations and on public advertising columns. Finally, all festivals have a large distribution network for their printed programmes and additional promotional materials (e.g. postcards for the Jagiellonian Fair, funny gadgets for Carnaval Sztukmistrzów and the Different Sounds Festival).

Regarding the target groups and the communication range, the Night of Culture remains predominantly regional. It is focused on Lublin's public space and was created mainly by local institutions, organisations and artists. The majority of the festival goers are city inhabitants and people living in the neighbouring municipalities. They often combine attending the festival with visiting their friends and families (out of the four festivals in question, the Night of Culture had the highest proportion of participants who chose this option as one of the motivations for their presence at the festival). The festival communication strategy focuses on Lublin and its region, occasionally reaching out to audiences in the whole country, mainly through social and traditional media.

The case of the East of Culture – Different Sounds Art'n'Music Festival is quite different. It aims at people interested in high-quality, niche music styles (the motivation of "seeing a particular artist/particular event" was chosen most frequently by the audience of this festival, compared to other events). The festival also welcomes all "passers-by" willing to try out something new but not necessarily familiar with the programme. A significant part of its audience comes from Lublin and its region, as well as from other large Polish cities (e.g. Warsaw, Cracow, Wroclaw, Katowice, Poznan). On the one hand, the festival communication strategy is targeted at the opinion leaders (e.g. via Facebook, media patronage etc.) and the media specialising in music and culture (websites, blogs, magazines). On the other hand, it focuses on the inhabitants of Lublin and the largest Polish cities, as well as cities in the neighbouring countries which have flight connections with Lublin.

Among the four festivals in question, Carnaval Sztukmistrzów certainly stands out in terms of the scope of communication activities, due to the fact that it was chosen as the flagship cultural event promoting the city's brand. (More information on its position is provided later in the chapter.) Its media patrons are usually the most popular nationwide TV and radio stations. Also, Carnaval holds the most extensive and far-reaching outdoor campaigns in Warsaw and almost all other large cities in Poland. Accordingly, among its target groups are tourists and families with kids, both of whom make up a significant proportion of the Carnaval's audience.

The Jagiellonian Fair is targeted at groups varying in terms of age, origin or areas of interest, but at the same time, it is intended for those who are specifically interested in folk arts and crafts. Its communication strategy is therefore twofold. On the one hand, it aims at various specialists, professionals as well as amateurs and DIY (do it yourself) fans. On the other hand, it is open to large audiences from Lublin, the region and selected large cities in Poland.

The survey results show that the communication strategies applied by the festival organisers were fairly successful. Two out of three most frequently indicated motivations to visit the festival were "the information [on the festival] seemed inviting to me" and "I've heard it's an appealing event" (quoted by 44.2 percent and 31.5 percent of all festivals' audiences, respectively). Finally, regarding the sources of information about the festival, the answer "I have been participating [in the festival] for many years" was one of three chosen most often for each of the studied events. This shows that festivals have become commonly recognised, especially among the local visitors, who often treat them as the "must-go" of the day. One of the respondents said it point-blank: "So, this evening is the Night of Culture. If you're not here, then where are you?" (a 30-year-old male Lublin resident).

The role of the festivals in the city development and promotion strategies

At the time of the research, plans for Lublin's development were included in the city brand development programme ("The Brand of Lublin"), under the slogan "*Lublin. City of Inspiration*". The city brand was to develop according to the socio-economic development strategy, supported by a number of sector strategies focused on tourism and culture (*Lublin Development Strategy 2013–2020, Lublin Strategy of Tourism Development until year 2025, Lublin Strategy of Culture Development 2013–2020*).

According to the information provided by the city of Lublin, the "The Brand of Lublin" project aims to "prepare a coherent, solid image of Lublin and tools for its short- and long-term promotion".[3] The project was launched in 2007 after a multi-stage preparation process, including product analysis, public investigation, public consultations and strategic workshops. It was decided to position Lublin as a multicultural urban centre, combining the culture of the Western civilisation with Eastern spirituality, resulting in a rich and unique heritage. The slogan coined then was "*Lublin. City of Inspiration*", envisioning the city as capable of freeing people's desire to change and act creatively. Consequently, cultural events which provide unique, locally embedded, engaging experiences have become vital elements of the brand. Carnaval Sztukmistrzów has been chosen as a flagship promotional product, which is particularly well-suited for branding purposes. Since 2010, it has been organised in cooperation with the marketing department of the city of Lublin, providing significantly more promotional and PR support and a larger marketing budget than other festivals included in the study.

Formal documents including plans for Lublin's development contain elements establishing and building its brand. However, they also treat culture and the festivals presented in the study as factors developing other socio-economic areas, not considered in the city's marketing. *Lublin Strategy of Development 2013–2020* treats culture as an important factor of social growth, especially in terms of fostering openness and tolerance. According to the strategy, festivals support the development of leisure activities, build regional and metropolitan bonds and develop the urban creative sector (City of Lublin 2013a). The four festivals included in the study are also mentioned in two reports evaluating the strategy implementation for 2013 and 2014 (City of Lublin 2016, 2017). They are listed in the part regarding the development of leisure activities, among "the most important regular cultural events", along with 28 other events in 2013 and 50 in 2014 (City of Lublin 2016, pp. 94–98; City of Lublin 2017, pp. 106–111).

Similarly, the festivals appear in *Lublin Strategy of Tourism Development until year 2025* (City of Lublin and Landbrand 2013a, 2013b). They are listed alongside 20 other events with the greatest potential to attract tourists (City of Lublin and Landbrand 2013a, pp. 50–57). Three of them – the Night of Culture, the East of Culture – Different Sounds Art'n'Music Festival and the Jagiellonian Fair were classified as nationwide events; Carnaval Sztukmistrzów was given the status of an international event.

Finally, *Lublin Strategy of Culture Development 2013–2020* mentions all the festivals included in the study (City of Lublin 2013b). It states that Carnaval Sztukmistrzów "should be created to become an event from Lublin which is best recognised across Poland and Europe" (City of Lublin 2013b, p. 90). Other projects described as crucially important are the Night of Culture (due to its socialising character) and the Different Sounds Festival (for bringing the Eastern and Balkan music to Lublin). It is noteworthy that this is the only major official document that stresses the need to balance the promotional and tourist aspects of all cultural events with their role in reinforcing local communities and the *genius loci* of Lublin.

Consequently, the festivals are strongly promoted in various information packs available to inhabitants, tourists and potential investors. The body of materials that were used by the research team dated back to 2009 and encompassed a total of 40 ephemeral prints (brochures, flyers, presentations, business offers, folders). Sixteen (40 percent) of them included a variety of economic data and were aimed at entrepreneurs, 15 prints (37.5 percent) concerned different aspects of culture and leisure, 7 (17.5 percent) were published by the tourism office, 1 (2.5 percent) presented very general information about Lublin and 1 (2.5 percent) was devoted to Lublin's brand, "City of Inspiration". Together, they provide a fairly comprehensive view of how the strategic aims related to the festivals translate into more specific official documents that are widely distributed on a daily basis.

In the materials mentioned earlier, the festivals are usually presented as an attractive way of spending free time and an important element of cultural life, as well as one of the biggest advantages of Lublin. The materials include different information about the events, ranging from festival names to the full data concerning their dates, venues and organisers. The festivals also appear in pictures, visually reinforcing what is stated in the text – Lublin as a vibrant, engrossing, very attractive place of unique experiences. Thus, they convey the qualities that are described here as the core of Lublin's brand. What is important is that the pictures showing festivals generally convey what their participants described in the course of research as vital to their experience. Accordingly, they show groups of people filling embellished, transformed public spaces; ecstatic crowds dancing to live music; slackliners walking between the roofs of buildings and craftsmen proudly presenting their works.

Not surprisingly, the four festivals appear most commonly in brochures/catalogues concerning culture. All the publications that the researchers had access to included information about each of them. Other types of printed materials present the events depending on the level of specificity – the more detailed a brochure/catalogue is, the less frequently the festivals appear in it. However, it should be stressed that even materials regarding the economic situation of Lublin mention the festivals alongside other information on culture and entertainment.

To sum up, the festivals included in the study are clearly an important part of the developmental plan for Lublin and its marketing communication strategy. In general, they are all treated primarily as promotional products targeted at both the tourists and the inhabitants. This means that festivals are viewed either as versatile products (e.g. Carnaval Sztukmistrzów) or as elements of other promotional undertakings directed towards different groups. Apart from the strategy for the cultural sector, almost no attention is paid to the artistic or educational dimension of festivals.

At the same time, neither the branding strategy nor any of the formal documents described here provide specific information on the role or functions of the festivals. Almost all the materials acknowledged their value, yet none laid out their goals or assigned them specific tasks. Therefore, the next sections of this chapter are based upon what are assumed to be indicators of festivals' success. This, however, does not mean that the selection of research topics was entirely arbitrary. The propositions put forward by the research team were complemented and approved by the key festival stakeholders, i.e. their organisers and the representatives of several city hall departments. Hence, the following sections present information on the scale of festival tourism and its impact on the local economy, the importance of cultural events for improving the city image and the process of reinforcing the local identity and the sense of attachment to the city, as well as the effect of urban space regeneration. The information provided next is based on three elements of the research project presented in the article: the desk research, the survey and interviews conducted among festival audiences and the survey of the local entrepreneurs.

Festivals tourism and the impact of cultural events on the image of Lublin

The results of the survey conducted among the festival audiences showed that 190,000 participants were not inhabitants of Lublin, which made up around 38 percent of the whole audience. Nearly half of them came from the region, i.e. the municipalities surrounding Lublin (17 percent of all participants). Of all festival participants, 12.3 percent lived in one of the 15 largest Polish cities (other than Lublin).

Carnaval Sztukmistrzów, as the key promotional product for Lublin's branding system, attracted the greatest number of tourists – around 86,200 people, which made up 43.1 percent of its audience. Out of all the festivals under study, it was the Night of Culture that had the smallest proportion of tourists (approximately 24.5 percent of the whole audience; 24,000 people). This figure confirms its regional focus, mentioned earlier.

Of the respondents from outside Lublin, 63 percent declared that the events were among the main reasons for their trip to the city of Lublin. They most frequently indicated the Jagiellonian Fair and Carnaval Sztukmistrzów. This finding is supported by two previously published empirical studies, conducted among tourists in Lublin. According to Tucki (2013, 2014), participation in cultural events was among the three top-ranking reasons for visiting Lublin in each year of his research.[4]

Table 5.1 The audience structure with regard to the participants' place of residence

	The size of audience – total value	*The size of audience residing in Lublin*	*The proportion of audience residing outside Lublin (%)*
The Night of Culture	100,000	24,500	24.5%
The East of Culture – Different Sounds Festival	50,000	22,100	44.3%
Carnaval Sztukmistrzów	200,000	86,200	43.1%
The Jagiellonian Fair	150,000	60,000	40.0%

Source: Author's elaboration

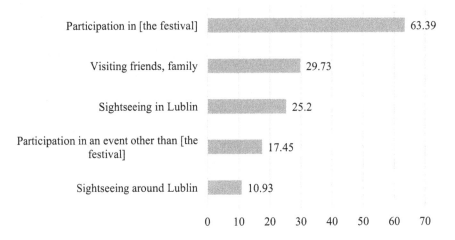

Figure 5.1 Reasons for visiting Lublin indicated by the respondents residing outside the city

Source: Author's elaboration

Table 5.2 Average spending on festival participation, considering the participants' place of residence

	Average spending by a festival participant residing in Lublin	*Average spending by a festival participant residing outside Lublin*
The Night of Culture	14.6 EUR	39.5 EUR
The East of Culture – Different Sounds Festival	15 EUR	53.6 EUR
Carnaval Sztukmistrzów	23.9 EUR	45.3 EUR
The Jagiellonian Fair	34.4 EUR	51.3 EUR

Source: Author's elaboration

The second most frequently indicated reason for coming to the event was visiting family and friends – it was indicated by around 30 percent of tourists. Finally, approximately one in four festival participants was interested in sightseeing in Lublin.

Festival tourism brought significant economic benefits to the city. Taking part in the events was predominantly free of charge, so any financial costs concerned the consumption of additional goods and services. The survey included two questions about the audiences' spending. One question referred to the cost of participating in the festivals, and the other was about the expenditures resulting from the whole stay in Lublin. Thus, the data provided in response to these two questions should be read as separate information.

The sum of money spent by tourists in connection with participating in the festivals amounted to around 9,150,000 EUR (54.7 percent of the total amount of expenditures of the festivals' audience). The survey results showed that the tourists' spending exceeded the city inhabitants' expenses at each of the festivals in question. On average, the expenditures of people from outside Lublin made up 240 percent of the residents' costs.

The other type of spending, covering the cost of the whole stay in Lublin, mainly concerned food and drinks consumption. Of the festival tourists, 67.1 percent used restaurant services; 57.2 percent intended to visit pubs. Moreover, almost half the respondents admitted buying food in grocery stores (49.9 percent, the average values unbalanced by the number of festival participants). One in three people declared using public transport. There was a significantly smaller demand for accommodation services. Only 22.5 percent of festival tourists claimed that they had booked a place to stay (a hotel room, an apartment, a place in a hostel). This relatively small expenditure on hospitality services resulted from the fact that the majority of people had come to Lublin for one day only, and they often combined attending the event with visiting friends and family.

These results were confirmed by the local businesses. The survey conducted among the entrepreneurs who ran their businesses in Lublin's Old Town and its vicinity shows that the highest rise in revenue occurred in the catering industry (an increase of 76 percent, compared to an average non-festival day), next in commerce (by approximately 50 percent) and the hospitality sector (about 25 percent).

The audience of Carnaval Sztukmistrzów brought in the largest sum of money as regards their whole stay in Lublin – a total of 7,150,000 EUR. This resulted mainly from the fact that the Carnaval had the highest number of tourists among its participants. The overall sum of expenditures declared by tourists attending all four festivals amounts to 17,410,000 EUR.

Festival tourism not only generated significant income for the city, but also contributed to its image improvement. Nearly all festival tourists (95 percent) declared their willingness to come back to Lublin in the future. This favourable stance towards the city corresponded to the respondents' general opinion about their stay. They could evaluate their stay choosing an answer on a scale of 1 to 7, ranking from "fantastic" to "disastrous", with the neutral grade of "neither good nor bad". Over half marked "very good" (52.5 percent), another one third chose "fantastic" (31.8 percent) and a further 14.8 percent described their visit in Lublin as "good". This means that 99.1 percent of the festivals' participants living outside Lublin were satisfied with their stay.

According to the respondents, the festivals "show that there are a lot of interesting things going on in Lublin" and "allow the people of Lublin to be proud of their city". Most of the festival audiences from outside Lublin strongly agreed and agreed with both statements.

Several other empirical studies also indicate that people who visit Lublin describe it as a city with an interesting and attractive cultural offer. More than half the people surveyed by Tucki (2013, 2014) regarded Lublin as a city of numerous cultural events (in 2013, 65 percent of them agreed and strongly agreed with this

statement, this proportion rising to 71.7 percent in 2014). A significant proportion of them supported the opinion that cultural events organised in Lublin had a
unique formula (48.9 percent in 2014; 60.6 percent in 2013). The proportion of
answers stating disagreement and strong disagreement with both statements never
exceeded 15 percent.

In yet another study, conducted in 2016 by a large consulting agency, Kantar
Public, on a representative sample of Poles (computer-assisted telephone interviews), those who had ever visited Lublin were asked to evaluate several elements
of its tourist offer. Of the respondents, 65 percent indicated the city's history as the
most attractive; 27 percent pointed to the city's atmosphere; 19 percent mentioned
cultural and sports events. The research conducted by Tucki and Kantar Public
did not specifically refer to the festivals that were analysed and presented in this
chapter. However, they demonstrate a strong tendency among tourists to associate
the city with a rich cultural offer.

Finally, these positive evaluations from tourists are part of a wider and longer-
standing process of improving Lublin's image. The research contracted by the
city of Lublin in 2007 (ARC Rynek i Opinia 2007; Studio Fokus 2007),[5] the year
when the brand identity programme for the city was launched, showed that Lublin
evoked no specific associations among one third of Poles. The attributes that were
brought up most frequently were universities and academic life. The researchers
concluded that Lublin was a city lacking personality, offering barely any stimulus
to the potential visitors.

Quite differently, a study carried out in 2015 demonstrated a significant improvement in terms of Lublin recognition and the associations it evokes (ARC Rynek
i Opinia 2015a, 2015b).[6] The respondents were asked what made Lublin more
attractive for tourists than other cities in Poland. The three most frequent answers
were "a lot of interesting monuments" (chosen by 51 percent of the respondents),
"a city with atmosphere" (40 percent) and "many interesting cultural/entertain-
ment attractions" (28 percent). According to the research report, Lublin can be
described as, first of all, "a cultural melting pot": that is, a city in which diverse
traditions, energies and artistic styles meet and intersect. Secondly, Lublin can be
treated as "a creator", which highlights its specific vibe as well as its interesting
history and monuments.

Summing up, the arguments presented in this section clearly show that the festivals included in the study contribute to the development of Lublin's economy
and its image. It should be stressed, however, that the success measured by audience numbers and the amount of additional income is actually becoming one of
the threats to the festivals' future. The quantitative focus ignores less tangible
effects of festival organisation, such as the integration of local urban community
or rediscovering neglected spaces, both of which are described in detail in the
next part of this chapter. To make matters worse, the core of the festivals studied herein – namely, their artistic and cultural quality – is currently granted less
attention than the economic benefits they provide. This means that the festivals
can easily become increasingly oriented towards meeting "the market demands"

rather than providing unique content. As a result, the event experience can deteriorate, eventually leading to smaller audiences and weaker reputational effects.

The impact of festivals on the internal image of Lublin and urban regeneration

The four festivals presented in the article also improved the image of Lublin in the eyes of its inhabitants. First and foremost, they played an important role in reinforcing the local urban community. In a very simple sense, festivals were, by nature, occasions for spontaneous bonding and socialising. The interviewees in the study appreciated the fact that festivals were capable of "dragging people out of their homes, away from their TV sets" (a female, 50 years old, Lublin resident). Another advantage mentioned by the research participants was that, during the events, one could accidentally run into some old friends and relatives, refresh relationships and often meet new people. Finally, the events presented in the chapter were treated as perfect occasions to invite guests living outside Lublin. This, in turn, gave the inhabitants an opportunity to boast of their exceptional town.

However, more importantly, participating in festivals let people feel that they still shared some interests, values and ways of behaviour (see also Arcodia and Whitford 2006, pp. 12–14; Richards and Palmer 2010, pp. 21–24). The feeling of being pleasantly surprised that so many other people, seemingly very different from one another, were doing the same thing and maybe even enjoyed it (like me!) was an important factor in sustaining the elusive bond with other city residents. After all, apart from sports and cultural events, there were few opportunities to share some experience together, on site and at the same time. In this sense, the festivals lend themselves exceptionally well to fulfilling the mission of integrating the city residents.

Furthermore, festival participation triggered a sense of pride and identity with the place. The visual analyses of the social media content showed clearly that participating in an event was an opportunity not only to show off, but also to present oneself as being a part of something bigger – a citizen of Lublin. Exclamations such as "I love this town!" or simply #lublin and #lublinmiastoinspiracji (in English: #lublincityofinspiration) were not unusual. Photos and videos uploaded on Facebook and Instagram were often accompanied by words of fascination and delight with the poster's own place of residence. As one of the users expressed it, "Such things happen only in Lublin".

The results of the survey conducted among the audiences included the following findings: Lublin residents declared that festivals made them proud of their city and that they had a positive impact on the city's image. The respondents were asked to define their level of agreement with some statements concerning the city image and the role of festivals. The question was provided with a selection of answers on a scale from 1 to 5, in which 5 stood for "strongly agree", 3 for "neither agree, nor disagree", and 1 for "strongly disagree". Figure 5.2. shows the distribution of answers provided by Lublin residents only.

To what extent do you agree or disagree with the following statements?

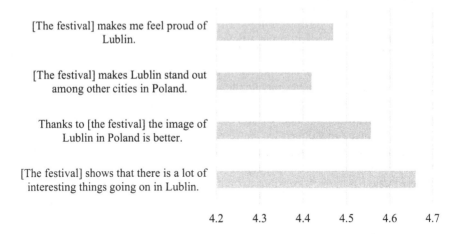

<table>
<tr><td>[The festival] makes me feel proud of Lublin.</td></tr>
<tr><td>[The festival] makes Lublin stand out among other cities in Poland.</td></tr>
<tr><td>Thanks to [the festival] the image of Lublin in Poland is better.</td></tr>
<tr><td>[The festival] shows that there is a lot of interesting things going on in Lublin.</td></tr>
</table>

4.2   4.3   4.4   4.5   4.6   4.7

Figure 5.2 Resident participants' evaluations of the festivals' impact on Lublin's image
Source: Author's elaboration

Another aspect of the impact of festivals on Lublin is the transformation of urban space. The events included in the study contributed to wide-ranging urban regeneration, from increasing the attractiveness of certain places to enriching the residents' "mental maps" of the city.

Arguably, the festivals are partly responsible for the metamorphosis that Lublin's Old Town has undergone in recent years. In 2005, two years before the first two events presented herein were created, *A Local Revitalisation Programme for City of Lublin* had described the Old Town as a "museum of antique buildings" or "scenography" (City of Lublin 2005, p. 9). The Old Town had been treated with due respect but lacked activity, liveliness. The same document had also highlighted the role of entrepreneurship as well as cultural and artistic activity. Twelve years later, it was obvious that the Old Town had become one of the most popular and inviting areas for both inhabitants and tourists. The results of external research (ARC Rynek i Opinia 2015a; Kantar Public 2016) and the study conducted during the festivals fully endorsed the popularity of the Old Town – it was usually chosen by residents and non-residents as their favourite area in the city. Although the Old Town bustled with social life even on a regular day, during the festivals, it was literally flooded with crowds. Even local entrepreneurs admitted that the numbers of people were so huge that it was impossible to cater for all of them.

At the same time, the festivals used the Old Town space as "material" that could be, to some extent, moulded and refashioned (see the city as a stage for festivalisation, Richards and Palmer 2010, pp. 25–28). Building upon monuments and historical objects, the festivals added to their popularity and, again, worked for the desired image of Lublin as a city of rich and interesting heritage. Yet there was a much more meaningful effect of refashioning the Old Town. It was the experience of certain places literally turned from completely innocuous detours or spaces that were neglected or even tattered into the most attractive spots for "selfies", taken with constant sighs of amazement. Festival participants were mostly shocked that relatively little effort and practically no renovation could make a real difference. Eventually, not only did the Old Town cease to function as a "scenography" or "museum" (City of Lublin 2005, p. 9), but the citizens themselves also realised that public spaces were much more "flexible" and open to positive changes than was usually thought.

Finally, festivals often symbolically opened certain spaces to the public (see Cudny 2016, p. 82). Lublin still had a lot of centrally located streets and whole neighbourhoods that, for various reasons, remained socially and culturally isolated. On a daily basis, the passers-by who did not live there simply did not enter them, not out of fear, but simply because they chose standard, most popular paths. As one of the research interviewees explained: "You visit places which you would normally not enter or even walk through. They [the festivals] kind of force us to explore wider and deeper and to look for distinct places in the city, ones that you slip past every day" (a female, 30 years old, residing outside Lublin).

The festivals included in the study often penetrated such neglected spaces, choosing them as locations for various attractions. To give an example, Cyrulicza and Furmańska Streets were made significant elements of the Night of Culture in 2017. Although the two streets were located within the Old Town, in the direct vicinity of some of the most popular tourist attractions and one of the high streets, almost every festival participant that heard of them asked how to get there. Finally, the artistic installations attracted dozens of people and were portrayed by the local media on numerous occasions. The area was not just popularised but literally put on the mental maps of Lublin inhabitants.

Conclusions

The data and arguments put forward in this chapter illustrate the importance of cultural events for shaping the image of the city of Lublin. For decades, Lublin was a "blank spot" on the map of Poland – a poor and secluded place that brought no particular associations. Today, Lublin is widely considered to be a city with an interesting, varied cultural offer and a characteristic, appealing vibe.

The direction that Lublin took by following its development and branding strategies is not uncommon in many urban areas around the world. Striving to become "an eventful city" (Richards and Palmer 2010) and departing from the notions of cultural economy and the economy of experiences (see Cudny 2016), Lublin adopted cultural events as one of the key stimulators of urban growth.

Consequently, the festivals presented in this chapter became instruments for attracting tourists and supporting the "*Lublin. City of Inspiration*" brand. In this respect, they seem to have satisfied the expectations, attracting about 190,000 people from outside Lublin in 2017. They spent significantly larger sums of money than the inhabitants, greatly contributing to the local economy, which was also widely recognised by entrepreneurs. At the same time, almost all visitors declared a high level of satisfaction with their stay and the willingness to come back to Lublin in the future.

The results of the qualitative analysis showed that the experiences resulting from participating in each event varied, but they all brought unique benefits as regards developing the *"Lublin. City of Inspiration"* brand. Carnaval Sztukmistrzów symbolically turned the world upside down and pulled its audience into a game against routines and social norms. The Night of Culture was exceptional in its capability of encouraging people to discover urban spaces anew, while the East of Culture – Different Sounds Art'n'Music Festival and the Jagiellonian Fair explored and recreated various motifs originally coming from Eastern cultures.

Moreover, festivals organised in an eventful city perform important functions in the local community and urban regeneration. The events included in the study became a reason to be proud of one's own place of residence, thus strengthening local identities and self-confidence. Furthermore, by inviting the participants to sites that were neglected and often avoided, they acted as catalysts for changing the way that public spaces were perceived and evaluated.

The article may then appear to be presenting a perfect story of success. This, obviously, is not the case. There are potential problems that became apparent in the course of research, which result directly from what is today commonly regarded as an achievement – the huge audiences every year.

First of all, it is essential to discriminate between a crowd that gives a special vibe to the event and one that is tiresome. In 2017, the participants of the study expressed predominantly positive opinions concerning other people attending the festivals. However, some signs of a growing feeling of excess and overpopulation could be seen as well. On one occasion, the crowds made it impossible to move around or see anything and turned the event experience into a burden. All in all, the attempts to achieve the goal of constantly increasing the audience numbers will inevitably lead to a situation when Lublin's Old Town becomes too small to fit everybody in comfort and safety.

Second of all, what originally made the festivals so successful was their authenticity. The research clearly showed that it was the uniqueness of the experience it provided that made each event special. Their participants did not look for anything that they had already known or practised elsewhere. They came to the festival because it offered something that they could not have otherwise. Having said that, the fact that the official developmental strategies for Lublin virtually ignore the artistic and social dimensions of the festivals seems a serious misunderstanding. This is one of the key issues that Rose Fenton addressed years ago in her expert opinion on the process of applying for the title of the European Capital of Culture (Fenton 2011). Putting the festivals under the common label of promotional or tourism products can easily undermine their individual, intrinsic character, paradoxically having an adverse effect on . . . tourism and Lublin's image.

Recapitulating, as Richards and Palmer (2010) argue, eventfulness can be greatly beneficial to urban spaces in economic, social, and symbolic terms. However, "eventfulness should not be an aim in itself, but a means of improving the city and making it more attractive and liveable" (Richards and Palmer 2010, p. 4). Lublin seems to have achieved most of its promotional and tourist goals. Scarcely anyone would now hesitate to give culture and cultural events their due for enhancing the city's development. With these conclusions in mind, it seems sensible to focus again on some of the less evident culture-related benefits, mainly related to the influence of events on the social cohesion and general quality of living.

Notes

1 The research was financed by the Workshops of Culture in Lublin from a grant funded by The Ministry of Culture and National Heritage of Poland in 2017 (grant programme "Creative sectors development"). The final report (Kołtun et al. 2017) and 11 working reports that summarise results from each stage of the study are available online.
2 Numbers of individual participants were estimated by the Workshops of Culture and Lublin City Office.
3 All information concerning Lublin's branding is available online at https://lublin.eu/lublin/marketing-miasta/marka-lublin/ (Accessed 1 October 2018).
4 The methodology of Tucki's research (2013, 2014) included standardised interviews conducted on a representative sample of tourists drawn in areas located near tourist attractions and main transportation hubs, as well as in hotels and other accommodation facilities.
5 The research encompassed a survey conducted on a representative sample of Poles (computer-assisted telephone interviews) and six qualitative focus interviews realised on a purposeful sample of residents of five voivodeship capitals.
6 The research consisted of two surveys conducted on a representative sample of Poles (computer-assisted telephone interviews and computer-assisted web interviews).

References

ARC Rynek i Opinia. (2007). *Wizerunek Miasta Lublin. Prezentacja przygotowana dla Biura Promocji Miasta Lublin.* Warsaw: ARC Rynek i Opinia.
ARC Rynek i Opinia. (2015a). *Raport z badania wizerunku Lublina. Część CATI.* Warsaw: ARC Rynek i Opinia.
ARC Rynek i Opinia. (2015b). *Raport z badania wizerunku Lublina. Część CAWI.* Warsaw: ARC Rynek i Opinia.
Arcodia, Ch., & Whitford, M. (2006). Festival attendance and the development of social capital. *Journal of Convention & Event Tourism*, 8(2), 1–18.
Charmaz, K. (2006). *Constructing Grounded Theory: A Practical Guide Through Qualitative Analysis.* London and Thousand Oaks (CA): Sage.
City of Lublin. (2005). *Local Revitalisation Programme for City of Lublin.* Lublin: City of Lublin.
City of Lublin. (2013a). *Lublin Development Strategy 2013–2020.* Lublin: City of Lublin. [Online]. Available from: https://lublin.eu/gfx/lublin/userfiles/_public/pliki_do_pobrania/strategia_rozwoju_lublina_na_lat/lublin_development_strategy_2013-2020.pdf (Accessed 1 October 2018).

City of Lublin. (2013b). *Lublin Strategy of Culture Development 2013–2020*. Lublin: City of Lublin. [Online]. Available from: https://lublin.eu/gfx/lublin/userfiles/_public/pliki_do_pobrania/projekty_zalaczniki/strategia_kultury_2013-2020/strategia_rozwoju_kultury_lublin.pdf (Accessed 1 October 2018].

City of Lublin. (2016). *Jak rozwija się Lublin? Raport monitoringowy z realizacji* Strategii rozwoju Lublina na lata 2013–2020 *w 2013 r*. Lublin: City of Lublin. [Online]. Available from: https://bip.lublin.eu/gfx/bip/userfiles/_public/import/strategia-i-planowanie/strategia-rozwoju-plan-dzial/strategia-rozwoju-lublina-na-l/145239_strategia_rozwoju_lublina_na_lata_2013_2020._raport_moni.pdf (Accessed 1 October 2018).

City of Lublin. (2017). *Jak rozwija się Lublin? Raport monitoringowy z realizacji* Strategii rozwoju Lublina na lata 2013–2020 *w 2014 r*. Lublin: City of Lublin. [Online]. Available from: https://bip.lublin.eu/gfx/bip/userfiles/_public/import/strategia-i-planowanie/strategia-rozwoju-plan-dzial/strategia-rozwoju-lublina-na-l/145240_strategia_rozwoju_lublina_na_lata_2013_2020._raport_moni.pdf (Accessed 1 October 2018).

City of Lublin & Landbrand. (2013a). *Lublin Strategy of Tourism Development Until Year 2025. Part One: Analytical*. Lublin: City of Lublin. [Online]. Available from: https://lublin.eu/turystyka/strategia-rozwoju-turystyki/ (Accessed 1 October 2018).

City of Lublin & Landbrand. (2013b). *Lublin Strategy of Tourism Development Until Year 2025. Part Two: Strategical*. Lublin: City of Lublin. [Online]. Available from: https://lublin.eu/turystyka/strategia-rozwoju-turystyki/ (Accessed 1 October 2018).

Cudny, W. (2016). *Festivalisation of Urban Spaces. Factors, Processes and Effects*. Cham: Springer.

Fenton, R. (2011). *Festiwale i organizacje kulturalne Lublina. Raport dla zespołu Europejskiej Stolicy Kultury 2016 Urzędu Miasta Lublin*. Lublin: City of Lublin.

Florida, R. (2002). *The Rise of the Creative Class*. New York: Basic Books.

Fokus Studio. (2007). *Postrzeganie i ocena miasta Lublin pod względem turystycznym – raport z badań jakościowych. Prezentacja przygotowana dla Prezydenta Miasta Lublin*. Unknown place: Fokus Studio.

Kantar Public. (2016). *Badania turystyczne miasta Lublin*. Warsaw: Kantar Public.

Kołtun, A. (ed). (2017). *Wpływ lubelskich festiwali plenerowych na rozwój gospodarczy i społeczny miasta: Noc Kultury, Wschód Kultury – Inne Brzmienia Art'n'Music Festival, Carnaval Sztukmistrzów, Jarmark Jagielloński. Raport końcowy z badania*. Lublin: Warsztaty Kultury. [Online]. Available from: www.warsztatykultury.pl/raport/ (Accessed 1 October 2018).

Kondrasiuk, G. (2012). ESK, wiedza kultury, instrumentalizacja, in: Hudzik, J. and Celiński, P. (eds). *Kultura wiedzy*. Kraków: Wydawnictwo Uniwersytetu Jagiellońskiego.

Kubicki, P. (2012). Efekt ESK. *Kultura Enter. Miesięcznik Wymiany Idei* (43). [Online]. Available from: http://kulturaenter.pl/article/efekt-esk/ (Accessed 15 October 2018).

Landry, Ch. (2008). *The Creative City: A Toolkit for Urban Innovators*. London, Sterling: Earthscan.

Richards, G., & Palmer, R. (2010). *Eventful Cities: Cultural Management and Urban Revitalisation*. London and Burlington (MA): Elsevier.

Tucki, A. (2013). *Wizerunek i atrakcyjność turystyczna Lublina. Raport końcowy z badania przeprowadzonego na terenie Lublina w dniach 15.06–09.09.2013 r*. Lublin: City of Lublin, MCSU.

Tucki, A. (2014). *Wizerunek i atrakcyjność turystyczna Lublina. Raport końcowy z badania przeprowadzonego na terenie Lublina w dniach 5.06–30.08.2014 r*. Lublin: City of Lublin, MCSU.

6 Place branding through culture and arts events

Cases from Eastern Canada

Lee Jolliffe and Nancy Chesworth

Introduction

Destinations may employ a portfolio of events to contribute to the branding of their locations for tourism. Such events may include those that address a specific interest, such as culture, arts, sports or business, as well as major or hallmark events associated with the destination. Events can create a sense of place and an identity for destinations, contributing to a unique brand proposition that may serve in a competitive marketplace to differentiate one place from another. In some cases, events can become synonymous with place, contributing to a brand that attracts visitors: for example the Edinburgh Festival in Scotland or the Venice Biennale in Italy.

Culture and arts events in particular offer communities the opportunity to express their identity and convey a sense of place to visitors (Bowdin et al. 2012). These events may portray an image of the cultural and creative city (Richards 2011) that is attractive to tourists, especially those interested in and motivated by experiencing culture and the arts through festivals and events. Destinations thus host events that celebrate place. Cultural events may encompass a wide variety of cultural expressions, while arts events might focus on art forms including the visual arts, music, dance, theatre and literature. Arts events include festivals, fairs and expositions, temporary and travelling exhibitions, studio- and gallery-related events and community or arts education events (du Cros and Jolliffe 2014). However, festivals are the type of cultural and arts events most commonly featured by destinations, given that they bring together different forms of the arts with benefits to both organizers and communities. There is the possibility for destinations to bundle the smaller types of events into products that will enhance the destination image and identity for the arts, as in the case of studio and gallery visits (du Cros and Jolliffe 2011).

The advantages of using cultural and arts events as part of place branding strategies may include establishing an identity reflective of the creative city. Cities are increasingly using cultural events to improve or contribute to their image, as well as to attract visitors (Richards and Wilson 2004). One of the disadvantages of using culture and arts events for branding is consistency for they are very often run by not-for-profit community groups that depend on local volunteers with variable commitments from year to year. For place marketing communications, arts events such as festivals have visual appeal as they convey a strong sense of place, reflective of the destination's culture and creativity.

Destination management organizations (DMOs) involved in branding cities may work with partners. Joint endeavours with groups sponsoring culture and arts events can be used for branding. DMOs may support or contribute to existing events and can be proactive in attracting, sponsoring or operating such events. They may also participate in external programmes that designate cities as "creative": for example, in Canada (Cooke and Lazzeretti 2008), Europe (Waitt and Gibson 2009) and elsewhere. This is encouraged by organizations such as Canada's Creative Cities Network. The creative cities agenda (Landry and Bianchini 1995; Florida 2003) includes economic development through culture and the arts.

In Canada, cultural workers and artists have migrated to urban areas (Bain 2003), and arts and culture events have been stimulated by government programmes at the federal and provincial levels. In terms of tourism, arts and culture tourists are recognized as a visitor segment by many Canadian jurisdictions. Destinations are aware of the value of appealing to this segment through events. Investigating these issues and challenges surrounding place branding through culture and arts events, this chapter considers the case of two destinations in Eastern Canada.

Literature review

Destination place branding

There is a perceived need for destinations to engage in place branding, developing a unique identity in order to differentiate themselves from their competitors. A destination brand represents a unique combination of product characteristics and added values (Morgan et al. 2007) with a superior proposition above that of the competitors, imparting meaning beyond the functional aspects (Middleton et al. 2009). A brand or destination image is considered to be the sum of the beliefs and impressions people hold about place.

The public sector is often involved in destination branding as by building a brand, they can link the destination to a chosen set of attributes or benefits (Clare and Lyn 2012). The role of destination managers in branding is usually one of research, coordination and funding. This is most often accomplished through a destination management organization, that is either a part of government or operates at arm's length from it. Successful destination branding campaigns concentrate on delivering the essence or the spirit of the place. However, DMOs face numerous challenges in building a destination brand, including lack of product control, limited budgets and political interference (Fyall and Garrod 2005).

A study of 12 English cities concluded that destination managers saw branding as relevant but did not always understand effective implementation, citing particular factors of significance as organizational complexity and control, the management of partnerships, product diversity and measurement of success (Hankinson 2001). Another UK study examined the extent to which former industrial cities were able to overcome past images in their branding for tourism (Bradley et al. 2002). An additional study examining place branding strategies found initiatives hampered by an overemphasis on operational thinking among destination managers (de Noronha et al. 2017).

Marketing communications

Partnership and collaboration are important in any tourism branding initiative, as are integrated marketing communications (Pike 2007). Marketing communications through various forms of media and word of mouth maybe used to communicate destination brand. According to Morgan and Pritchard (2005), brand advantage is secured through marketing communication that highlights the specific benefits of a product. Methods of promotion and marketing communication include advertising, sales promotions, publicity and direct to the contact market through print and internet (Bowdin et al. 2012).

Events and place branding

Can events be employed in building a brand, and, if so, how? Events are acknowledged to be an important contributor to building a destination brand (Jago et al. 2003). Research has identified community involvement and support as well as a good strategic and cultural fit with the destination as the basis of building events into destination brands (Jago et al. 2003).

Events have become part of destination branding efforts, especially for urban areas (Bradley et al. 2002). Cudny (2016a) refers to this phenomenon as the festivalisation of urban spaces. This process normally involves leadership on the part of DMOs in cooperation with partners (Clare and Lyn 2012). Using events for branding includes the fact that they are seen as effective marketing tools that may also bring economic, social and cultural benefits to destination areas (Middleton et al. 2009). Most destinations have a portfolio of events. For events to be successful in branding their destinations in the marketplace, ideally, they are authentic and demonstrate a unique sense of place.

Culture and arts events

Do culture and arts events have a special value in contributing to the brand? They have the capacity to deliver in terms of conveying the identity of a destination as well as nurturing audiences and attracting new visitors. If scheduled throughout the year or in the shoulder seasons, such events also have the ability to tackle the issues of seasonality by spreading visitation beyond peak times. Culture and arts, through events, can contribute to developing the destination image and associated branding in particular, by the packaging and bundling of components into products (Pike 2007). Previous research has shown that the bundling of art experiences into a product contributes to urban tourism (du Cros and Jolliffe 2011). In some areas around the world, urban renewal has also led to the creation of shopping venues as festival marketplaces (Cudny 2016b).

Community festivals and arts events offer destinations an opportunity to celebrate their identity and presence while building a destination image (Bowdin et al. 2012). Given that events have their own media impact, they also serve as a showcase and media promotion tool for the destination. In addition, culture and arts events can contribute to changing the image of the destination for existing audiences as well as attracting new visitors for the destination (Bowdin et al. 2012).

While there has been literature on the role of arts and culture in the place branding of large cities and states – for example, in the cases of Berlin and Singapore (Ooi and Stöber 2010) and of European cities (Richards 2011) – there is a need to examine the issues faced by smaller cities, in particular with reference to branding using culture and arts through events. In addition, much of the research on events has focused on economic impact rather than on the ability of events to contribute to the destination brand (Jago et al. 2003).

Branding is seen as necessary in differentiating a given destination from competitors. Ashworth (2009) describes destination planning strategies used either separately or in combination to achieve this end. Three main categories are discussed. First, personality association, where a place attempts to relate its identity to a famous person, living, dead or mythological. Secondly, signature building and design, which Ashworth (2009) divides into three components: flagship building, signature design and signature districts. Third, he notes the contribution of event hallmarking. Ashworth's work speaks directly to events designed to aid in branding places.

Methods

A literature review on the branding of destination cities through events is considered as a background to the study. A multi-methods case study approach was chosen, as it is appropriate for tourism research. This is a technique whereby multiple methods are used to gather information, including interviews, participant observation and the use of secondary information (Beeton 2005). Jennings (2005) notes the value of using semi-structured conversation-like interview techniques. The benefit of using more than one case study is that it provides the opportunity for the comparative analysis of the results (Yin 1994). The use of two cases also allows for within-case and cross-case analysis (Brotherton 1999).

For this research, individual in-depth semi-structured interviews were scheduled with destination managers and guided by a common list of questions. The choice of study locations is one of convenience; the two authors are located in the region and are familiar with tourism here, especially in terms of the relationship of events to place branding. The assessment of marketing communications for events within the cases involved an examination of social media practices at both study locations.

Study context

The Canadian province of New Brunswick, located in Eastern Canada, borders the Atlantic Ocean. The region is situated northeast of the New England states (USA), southeast of Quebec (Canada) and southwest of Newfoundland (eastern Canada). The provincial economy is based on agriculture, fishing, forestry, mining and tourism. Tourism is the third-largest service sector in the province. Provincial product marketing is under the categories of festivals and events, outdoor adventure, cultural heritage and hunting and fishing (Tourism New Brunswick n.d.). As reflected by this product mix, events are an important part of the tourism portfolio employed by both the province and individual communities within New Brunswick in creating and marketing a destination image.

Case study: Fredericton

Location

The city of Fredericton is located in the south-central section of the province of New Brunswick in eastern Canada. The government of Canada classified Fredericton as a medium-size urban area in 2016 (Statistics Canada 2016). The city's population of 59,405 is augmented by nearby suburban areas and villages, effectively creating a population of 101,706.

Situated on the banks of the Saint John River, the city originally functioned as a military garrison whose well-preserved remains now serve as one of the main tourist attractions in the city. The changing of the guard and the artists' shops in the former barracks are popular with both local residents and tourists. Other attractions include the area around the Garrison District, the seasonal Boyce Farmers Market, the Beaverbrook Art Gallery, Gallery 78, the Beaverbrook Playhouse and several Victorian era public and private buildings.

Fredericton's economy is derived primarily from its role as capital of the province and, as such, home of the provincial legislature. The University of New Brunswick, New Brunswick College of Craft and Design and a growing technology sector are also major contributors to the economy. Tourism in general and events in particular, play an important role in the city's economy. Over time, the university and city populations have diversified, becoming more multicultural. Recent increases in immigrant numbers have added a new dynamic to the area as a whole. Events focused on culture provide an opportunity to create a more inclusive community.

Structure of the destination management organization

The DMO operates within Fredericton Tourism, funded by the city with some donations from the private sector. The organization also works in cooperation with the provincial Department of Tourism, Culture and Heritage to promote tourism in the province. The Destination Management Organization is led by a manager and nine full-time staff, supplemented in summer by up to thirty part-time employees.

In cooperation with the public and private interests noted earlier, the DMO is responsible for events taking place in the city, including outdoor events and large- and small-scale public events staged throughout the year. Sport, conferences, tourism and travel trade are handled by the provincial Department of Tourism, Culture and Heritage. The historic Garrison District is the focal point for many events in the downtown area, blending the relatively old with the new (Fredericton Tourism n.d.).

The authors interviewed the DMO manager regarding branding and the image of the city as a whole. He provided insight into the DMO's processes of branding the city for tourism and sees branding as an ongoing, evolving effort to differentiate Fredericton from competitors.

Branding policy

In the past, Fredericton has been viewed as a staid, conservative and stagnant destination. The main aim of the DMO is to create a cultural destination and change that perception to one of a contemporary, appealing place to visit. Events are seen as the optimal instruments to realize this goal. In the process of effecting this change, hallmark events are being used to develop, promote and manage the brand. Four categories of events are employed to achieve this aim. Described by the manager as reflecting the "pillars of the branding policy", they are cultural experience, heritage, nature and culinary, which are grounded in the city's resources for tourism. Together they form the basis of the cultural destination brand for Fredericton. This policy reflects the third of Ashworth's (2009) instruments of place branding: event hallmarking.

New event ideas may come from within the DMO or, more often, from individuals or groups in the community. The manager and staff provide consultation and guidance to those interested in developing an event. He maintained that new event proposals "must be based on an understanding of the market, research, and work with the psychology of the town" (Seabrook 2018) to be successful.

One of the aims of the DMO is to reflect the local culture by encouraging events that appeal to many demographic segments. Those events that reflect local mores and the evolving multicultural sensibilities of the area are more likely to succeed in terms of both support from the DMO and local participation. The city tourism manager stated that events developed by and for the resident population are seen as authentic by tourists and are therefore more attractive to visitors (Seabrook 2018). As well, those same events contribute to community building and a new perspective and sense of pride on the part of residents.

Types of events

A wide range of events is offered each year in Fredericton. Some, such as the New Brunswick Provincial Exhibition, the NB Highland Games Festival and the Harvest Blues and Jazz Festival are annual events. Other one-time events add differing experiences depending on the audience, venue and season. Aside from those held in the summer, numerous events are staged in other seasons, including those such as Shivering

Songs, musical performances of all genres including Christmas-themed experiences and Frostival, a winter festival held over three weekends in January. Stand-alone, one-time events, such as a performance by a well-known celebrity, add to the mix.

Table 6.1 illustrates the various kinds of events available in summer. Those listed draw the highest attendance and are staged from June to September. Note that two of these events, the NB Provincial Exhibition and the Night Market, are bundled, multifaceted experiences. For example, the Night Market is held on Thursday evenings from June to September next to the Garrison's grounds. A new event for Fredericton, this market location provides an opportunity for outdoor concerts; fresh, local farm produce; local and international street-food; fine art and craft items. Historic activities such as the changing of the guard and the use of the Garrison's Barrack Square for performances, display space and working artist's shops create a multifaceted experience for visitors. It should be noted that, with ungated events such as those examined here, it is difficult to measure visitation (Kelly et al. 2006).

Other events centre around fine arts, such as the edVentures Fredericton programme, which gives the public the opportunity to learn a new skill during one of many workshops; an art gallery open house event; performance arts, including Bard in the Barracks; the NB Summer Music Festival and arts and crafts festivals. Cultural events include St. Mary's Pow Wow, Acadian Day celebrations and Canada Day festivities. The growth of local craft beer breweries has encouraged the development of beer-tasting rooms and a Craft Beer Festival. Those interested in wine can explore locally produced and international wines at the Fredericton Wine Festival. A successful beverage event, the annual Whisky and Spirits Festival, the largest of its kind in Canada, is held in November.

Table 6.1 Fredericton cultural experience events

Event	Type	Estimated visitation (2017)	Message
New Brunswick Provincial Exhibition	Agricultural and entertainment	Estimated 5,000 to 20,000 visitors	Progress, competition, rural-urban interaction, family fun
Harvest Jazz and Blues Festival	Cultural music performance	Estimated 40,000 to 70,000 visitors	Signature event, niche market, contemporary culture
Rib Fest	Culinary culture	About 4,000 visitors	Urban experience
New Brunswick Highland Games Festival	Cultural	Estimated by organizers at 5,000	Living historic culture
Garrison Night Market	Street market, bundled event	Organizers estimated 8,000 at 2018 opening weekend, 2,000 to 4,000 other weekends, depending on weather	Engaging with contemporary culture

Source: Authors, Fredericton Tourism and media sources

Marketing communications

Discussing the DMO's marketing efforts, the manager stated that marketing is "focused on identified tourist consumers" (Seabrook 2018). To reach the target market, "emphasis is placed on the use of social media as the main marketing tool". In doing so, the goal is to employ cultural events to attract a younger demographic, creating excitement around the experiences offered, with the outcomes of developing the brand and changing the image of Fredericton as discussed earlier. To this end, a variety of social media platforms are used to engage the target demographic. Icons to connect with Facebook, Twitter, Instagram, YouTube and Flickr are featured on event and tourism websites. A staff member is tasked with keeping up with postings and reviewing comments; however, numbers of followers are not tracked. New Brunswick is the only province in Canada to recognize two official languages. Therefore, all publications are produced in English and French. This is reflected in both print and web promotional materials.

In addition, bloggers as well as the traditional press are courted by way of familiarization tours showcasing tourism options and events and/or direct contact. The advantage of engaging the blogging community is their influence with their established followers interested in the blogger's perspective and recommendations. This kind of word-of-mouth marketing along with postings on other social media platforms directly addresses and engages the demographic segments the DMO is targeting. According to a recent media report, success is evaluated by increases in hotel occupancy as well as the impact of events. "However, there's a lot of opportunity in the annual events, utilizing our local community groups and our facility sizes to ensure that we continuously have annual events that will create economic activity in the city" (Drost 2018). The city tourism manager in this interview also noted the success of the Garrison Night Market in terms of the number of vendors and visitors in 2018 as exceeding expectations.

When asked to comment on research regarding the impact of social media as a strategy, it was said that research involving primary data collection is problematic due to the lack of baseline data (Seabrook 2018). The complexity of the model put forth by the Conference Board of Canada makes it difficult to use. Consequently, the DMO uses estimated attendance numbers to gauge the effectiveness of the marketing plan.

Some events generate their own marketing by person-to-person word of mouth. An example of this is the Garrison Night Market, which drew an estimated 8,000 people on its first night and continued to draw between 2,000 and 4,000 visitors each time it was held during the season. Other events use websites and print media to reach their audience.

Conclusion

Fredericton's focus on culture makes it possible to use both the signature historic district and a variety of signature events to create the brand. This combination of Ashworth's (2009) instruments appeals to residents and visitors. In particular, the primary target market, a diverse, young audience with less exposure to the old staid reputation of the city, sees it increasingly as vibrant and attractive with interesting experiences in which to participate (Seabrook 2018). Ongoing events and the use of social media provide the opportunity to consolidate the positive changes that the DMO's branding efforts have brought about.

In the case of Fredericton, either by default or intentionally, the majority of events combine two or more aspects of the four pillars of the DMO's branding strategy. Many of these events integrate two of the branding instruments described by Ashworth (2009): signature district and event hallmarking. Integration of these instruments provides a stronger branding platform and more likely success, bringing historic districts alive through cultural and arts programming. While success using this approach is not guaranteed, for small-scale destinations, integrating two or possibly more branding instruments seems a more feasible path to effective branding.

Case study: Saint John

Location

Saint John is located in the southern part of the province of New Brunswick. The city, with a population of 58,341 (Statistics Canada 2016), is a medium-size population centre. It is a shipping and cruise port as well as an industrial centre with a developing information technology sector. The historic preservation district in the city centre reflects the city's status as the first incorporated city (1785) in British North America (now Canada) due to a population influx of Loyalists after the American Revolution.

Saint John has both long-established art galleries and museums, including Canada's first public museum (New Brunswick Museum) dating to 1842, and an emerging contemporary art scene as well as a number of small public and private galleries. The architecture of the historic City Market, Canada's oldest continually operating market, reflects the shipbuilding heritage of the city. Urban renewal in the 1980s led to the development of Brunswick Square shopping mall as a festival marketplace. The city is situated within the UNESCO-designated Stonehammer Geopark and is known for the Reversing Falls or Rapids where the Saint John River meets the Bay of Fundy, which has highest tides in the world.

Destination management organization

Discover Saint John is a not-for-profit public-private corporation established in partnership with the city of Saint John and the Saint John Hotel Association. Governed by a board of directors appointed in part by the city council, it is administered by an executive director and seven others year-round in addition to fifteen to twenty seasonal staff who operate several visitor information centres. This case is based on an interview by one of the authors with the executive director, secondary information and participant observation (Clarke 2018). Over 400 city tourism-related businesses are members of Discover Saint John. Funding comes from the Saint John Hotel Association (destination marketing tax collected by hotels), the city of Saint John, membership fees and special grants. The mandate of Discover Saint John stated in the 2017 annual report is to "increase tourism revenues in Saint John by marketing our unique and competitive experiences to high potential markets" (Discover Saint John 2018). The agency also works in cooperation with Tourism New Brunswick, the destination marketing agency of the Tourism, Heritage and Culture section of the provincial government in terms of the travel trade, allowing them to reach new markets.

Branding policy

The DMO's marketing objectives reflecting the resources for tourism experiences are embodied in the brand pillars of culinary, outdoors, history and urban, with the goal to "increase brand awareness, change perception and increase engagement with the four pillars" (Discover Saint John 2018). The involvement in events is seen as a vehicle for the telling of a unique story about the industrial port city that is exciting and dynamic. A positive change in brand awareness of Saint John was recorded between 2015 and 2017, altering the perception of the city from "old" to "friendly and welcoming", which was the number one answer to the question "if Saint John were a person which traits first come to mind" (Summus Insight Reports, 2105, and Urban Report 2017, quoted in Discover Saint John 2018). The executive director attributes the marketing success to long-standing relationships and partnerships, authenticity, good lead filtering, a best-practice familiarisation (FAM) programme for travel media and a team approach to winning, stating "we are closers" (Discover Saint John 2018). In 2017 the FAM programme had 80 travel media visitations.

Types of events employed in branding

Through cooperation between civic officials, the destination management organization, the business improvement association (Uptown Saint John) and other public and private stakeholders, culture and arts events and performances are staged. Events employed as destination branding include festivals, art performances and bundled culture and arts experiences. These efforts against the backdrop of the historic city differentiate the place from others. This also reflects the arts and cultural policy (City of Saint John 2005) that recognizes that participation in and appreciation of the arts enhances the lives of residents and contributes to the development of the community (Jolliffe 2017).

The vibrant arts and culture scene with a variety of events reflects the branding policies of the DMO (Table 6.2). The manager attributes success in innovation in part to having a small team. For example, a member of the team saw street art by Sean Yora (aka Hula) and came up with the idea to invite the artist to the city to create an art installation (mural) revitalizing an unused waterfront area. The availability of funding designated for events and the willingness to take risks allow the

Table 6.2 Saint John culture and art events examples and messages

Event	Type	Estimated visitation (2017)	Message
Area 506 Festival	New Brunswick culture festival	Ray Gracewood concert: 6,500 through gate; overall 45,000 visitors	Music, culture, goods in a shipping container village on a wharf in the port
Buskers on the Bay Festival	Street theatre festival	Organizers estimated 50,000 people attended	Signature event, nightlife
Hula	Mural	Not tracked	Urban area revitalization
Third Shift Festival of Public Contemporary Artworks	Contemporary arts festival and market	Not tracked	Engaging with the urban environment
Moonlight Bazaar	Night market	Organizers estimated 3,000 people attended	Recreating the urban scene
Saint John Gallery Hop	Gallery tour	Not tracked but reported at capacity	Bundled art experience
Tall Ships	Tall ship festival		Celebrates port city's maritime heritage

Source: Authors and Discover Saint John

DMO to play a variety of evolving roles in event establishment, sponsorship and implementation.

Discover Saint John was instrumental in encouraging the establishment in 2016 of the now-annual Area 506 Festival, using 50 to 60 borrowed shipping containers that reflect the working port city. In 2017 it sponsored the *Discover Saint John Cargo-Tecture Design Competition*, inviting creative entries for transforming the containers into new forms that were then displayed at the festival. It also raised the destination profile of the city through the art performance by the artist known as Hula in 2017 when a painting of a woman on a seawall demonstrated what Clarke referred to as "a marketing stunt" and "a piece of performance art demonstrating the urban experience of the highest tides on the planet" (Clarke 2018). In cooperation with the province of New Brunswick, a 2017 public sculpture competition, Salmon Run (Figure 6.1), also contributed to branding (Discover Saint John 2018).

The Saint John Gallery Hop is a long-running bundled art event targeted at locals and visitors and scheduled three times a year (du Cros and Jolliffe 2014). Recently, the Saint John Gallery Association and Discover Saint John have invested in a video about the event, designed to profile the galleries on a year-round basis. Another newly established event that celebrates the urban environment for one evening is the Moonlight Bazaar. Support of the Third Shift Festival

Figure 6.1 Salmon Run sculpture
Source: Lee Jolliffe

of Public Contemporary Artworks has allowed the free event to grow from being undersubscribed in 2015 to attracting larger crowds in 2016 and 2017. This event aims to inspire residents to reimagine their city, reclaiming vacant and underutilized areas while engaging with the surroundings of the built environment in the core of the city.

Marketing communications

Through partnerships, Discover Saint John extends its reach for marketing communications delivering the current slogan of "Saint Awesome" using traditional and social media. The slogan was developed to reflect the branding pillars mentioned earlier with the goal to "increase awareness, change perceptions and increase engagement with four brand pillars (culinary/outdoor/history/urban)" (Discover Saint John 2018). Locals using the "Saint Awesome" hashtag were recognized as brand ambassadors after the first year of the campaign. The executive director notes that the photographic and digital recording are as important as the events themselves, as the presence on social media contributes to the conversation about Saint John (Clarke 2018). The Saint Awesome theme plays into "Find Your Saint Awesome Adventure" on social media, promoting a combination of culture and arts, history and nature. In the last several years, new events have contributed directly to strengthening the cultural and arts scene and the urban branding message reflecting what Cudny (2016a) describes as the festivalisation of the urban space and a realisation of experience societies idea presented by Schulze (1992).

Discover Saint John measures the success of its marketing communications in branding the destination as reported for 2017 in the form of 1) unique visitors to the website, 2) followers on social media, 3) use of the hashtag "Saint Awesome" and 4) social media response to the Hula project (Discover Saint John 2018). Unique visitors to the website were reported as 418,415 for 2017 versus 295,695 for 2015. Also, awareness of the destination is reported to have increased from 16 percent in 2015 to 54 percent in 2017. In this way, the destination is able to monitor the effectiveness of its various marketing communication initiatives on the brand image.

It is evident that culture and arts events are key to conveying a lively image of their city as they support the tagline "Saint Awesome" and significantly contribute to the image of the place as a tourism brand. The investment in events, in sales to attract events to the city and contributing to the visitor experience through event support and creation form the major part of what is spent on programme investment in the brand (Discover Saint John 2018).

Conclusion

Branding efforts in Saint John reflect a combination of Ashworth's (2009) instruments of place branding, employing a signature historic district and hallmark events to convey a message that the destination can deliver a vibrant urban experience in a historic setting. The destination marketing agency has celebrated both the historic environment and the working port of the city through cultural and art events, creating an engaging conversation about the place that is appealing to locals and visitors alike and changes perceptions not only through event experiences but also via the event legacy communicated through social media.

Comparing the case studies

Branding policy

Both Fredericton and Saint John base their branding efforts on four pillars, with a slightly differentiated focus (Table 6.3). In this way, they are linking their

Table 6.3 Branding pillars of Fredericton and Saint John

	Fredericton	Saint John
Branding Pillar 1	Culture	Culinary
Branding Pillar 2	Heritage	Outdoors
Branding Pillar 3	Nature	History
Branding Pillar 4	Culinary	Urban

Source: Authors, Fredericton Tourism and Discover Saint John

destinations to a chosen set of attributes (Clare and Lyn 2012). The cities are promoting culinary experiences and heritage/history, with similarities in promoting nature and the outdoors. In Fredericton, culture is one of the pillars while Saint John offers an urban experience.

Fredericton and Saint John have many similarities in their approach to branding. Three points in common stand out. Both cities are committed to 1) using branding to create a new image in the eyes of both residents and tourists, 2) utilizing culture and the arts as vehicles for a substantial part of the branding effort and 3) using historical artifacts and buildings as a backdrop or focal point for many events.

Another factor is that the cultural and arts programming in both case study locations is both DMO initiated and independently organized or accomplished through partnerships. While culture is emphasized in Fredericton and the arts in Saint John, each reflects both in practice. Other similarities include events such as the gallery tours, annual agricultural exhibitions and performance venues.

Types of events employed

A variety of culture and arts events are staged in Fredericton and Saint John, against the backdrop of historic city centres. Both locales have signature or hallmark events, as well as smaller events that bundle experiences together such as the gallery tours (Downtown Gallery Hop and Saint John Gallery Hop). In addition, they are both taking advantage of festival and event venues to feature culture.

Rather than just promoting their locations, these destination management agencies are involved in creating experiences that deliver their branding messages with the support of restaurant week events (culinary) and urban events (culture and urban). In the last several years, the two agencies have taken a hands-on approach to delivering the cultural and urban messages: Fredericton through the organization of Garrison Night Market featuring food, arts, crafts and music in the historic district and Saint John in organizing art performances (Hula) and public art (Salmon Run) in the historic preservation district.

Fredericton does seem to be stronger in terms of major signature events with three festivals featured (Fredericton Frostival, Highland Games and Harvest Jazz and Blues Festival) by the provincial tourism website under "18 Festivals to Be

Excited for in 2018" and with Saint John's Buskers on the Bay Festival being the only featured event (Tourism New Brunswick n.d.).

Marketing communications

Both Fredericton and Saint John are using social media as their main marketing tool in an effort to change the image and brand of their destinations. They are employing an evolving combination of social media platforms including Facebook, Twitter, Instagram, YouTube and Flickr in order to change the conversation about their cities. Also, they are using familiarization (FAM) tours inviting bloggers and other influencers to create messages and content about their destinations. Different methods for measuring the effectiveness of marketing efforts are reported, with Fredericton judging success by estimated attendance at the cultural events and Saint John linking its success to the social media impact as reported in their 2017 Annual Report (Discover Saint John 2018). In addition to these DMO social media platforms, individual events may have their own websites and may use other media forms including newspaper, radio and, on occasion, television. The DMOs themselves place more emphasis on the use of social media but may print maps, brochures and guides for use at the destination and for tourism and events. These materials may also be distributed in electronic form.

Pike (2007) noted the valuable role of partnership and collaboration in tourism branding efforts. Fredericton Tourism and Discover Saint John regularly meet with parties who propose new events. If what is put forward fits into their city brand proposition, they are ready to partner, on occasion providing funding and in-kind assistance. In some cases, as with the Area 506 Festival in Saint John, the DMO will provide more support in foundation years until the event is more established. In both cities, volunteers are essential to delivering a rich palette of cultural and arts events, demonstrating the value of community involvement in building events into destination brand ambassadors. Furthermore, both DMOs have sought out events that provide what Jago et al. (2003) identify as a good cultural fit, reflecting brand pillars that can be employed to convey a unique sense of place.

These small-city DMOs, through the use of social media, are demonstrating the importance of integrated marketing communications noted by Pike (2007) as essential to any tourism branding initiative. For example, with Saint John's 2017 Hula event, the marketing communications included print, web, signage on site, Twitter and a live Facebook feed.

A formula

As the authors proceeded with the field work necessary in developing the cases related here it became apparent that Ashworth's (2009) branding instruments – personality association, three forms of signature design and hallmark events – fit the situations and events under study. Ashworth (2009) stated that his concepts ideally would be used in concert. An application of all branding instruments, provided all are an appropriate fit with the location and each other, would theoretically provide a strong branding tool and a globally recognized brand. Thus, personality association related to a flagship building or other flagship construction, featuring signature design in a signature district which provides a basis or venue for hallmark events, would fulfill all of Ashworth's criteria.

One example of all instruments working together is Shakespeare's Globe Theater in the Bankside district in London, England. In this case, the personality association of William Shakespeare, widely regarded as the best writer in the English language, serves as the focal point around which all Ashworth's (2009) instruments have been successfully combined. The theatre is a reconstruction of the original Globe Theater building (flagship) with, in these times, a signature design close to the original centuries' old location. The events staged include Shakespeare's works, modern interpretations of those works and new productions related to Shakespearian times. The recreated Shakespearian experience offered here gives residents and visitors as authentic an experience as is possible in modern times. Few examples of this sort of application can be found. Indeed, Ashworth (2009) pointed out that personality association in almost all instances is fraught with difficulties and risks. Among other drawbacks, celebrities or other famous people, living or deceased, historical or mythological can be controversial or not well known outside the boundaries of their influence. Thus, the use of personality association for branding purposes is not recommended.

Ashworth's second instrument, signature building, in the form of flagship building, signature design and signature districts, is a more accessible concept. Unfortunately, flagship building involving new construction is, for most communities, expensive, and there is no guarantee of success in creating a brand around the flagship creation, making this a less-desirable option. Signature design and signature districts can be cost effective, especially when visual appeal is incorporated into existing infrastructure in signature districts. Ashworth's third component, hallmark events, can be created and developed by most communities.

Combining these components and integrating them into "wider planning and management strategies" was recommended by Ashworth (2009) but not elaborated upon. He did, however, note that the combination of hallmark events with signature design would create a stronger brand with the opportunity to offer a unique selling proposition appealing to a wide audience.

It should be noted that application of all Ashworth's branding instruments is, for most places, not feasible. In most cases, two or three factors may be available. As noted, personality association and flagship building are fraught with potential difficulties and negative connotations. Therefore, the best option is in events coupled with signature building and/or signature districts. As seen in the studies of branding in Fredericton and Saint John, combining a signature district and event hallmarking, even though an unconscious choice, has fulfilled the main aim of both places. We have labelled this "historic district-event hallmarking". We believe, based on our comparative fieldwork with these two small cities, that this concept may be of use to other small cities, towns and historic areas. This approach to branding offers the opportunity to increase the chances of branding success.

In most situations, the most desirable instruments are hallmark events linked to signature districts or events combined with signature design. This is the case in Fredericton, Saint John and others included in the literature, where it is clear the application of two or, where possible, more branding instruments is more likely to result in success. Thus, events can be considered the keystone instrument in place branding practices. Branding efforts using this approach are found in many locations.

Further, historic districts are found all over the world. In the case where the signature district is a historic one, the combination of the historic district with events appears to be the optimal approach for places looking to brand using their built heritage. For this and other reasons, the use of the historic district-hallmark event formula will be of interest to other locations seeking to engage in brand development. Grounded in Ashworth (2009) and revealed by the field work, a simple formula adapted from Ashworth (2009) emerges as: Signature Historic District + Hallmark Events = Place Brand.

This formula supposes that positive connotations are inherent in the reputation of a recognised and/or revitalised historic district and that events are well conceived, appropriate, well executed and well managed. Careful use of social media is recommended in developing and maintaining the resulting brand.

Conclusion

Fredericton and Saint John have, albeit unconsciously, applied this "historic district-event hallmarking" formula in their branding practices. The net result is a noted change in the images and reputations of both cities as reflected by the interviews with the destination managers and observations made by the authors. Fredericton is now known not only for its hallmark event, the Harvest Blues and Jazz Festival, but also for other events, as well as quality culinary, wine, beer and spirits experiences, which appeal to key markets. The formerly predominant industrial image of Saint John has faded as new events and rehabilitation of its signature historic district have created a new visual and experiential image and positive reputation in a revitalized urban landscape.

The cases of two small-city DMOs in Eastern Canada have demonstrated the value of culture and arts events as part of destination branding initiatives, when paired with a signature historic district. For the DMOs involved, the events staged against the backdrop of historic city centres allows them to change brand impressions of their places. This policy contributes to positive conversations through social media, encouraging increased visitation.

For other cities with historic districts hosting cultural events, valuable lessons can thus be gained through the cases of Fredericton and Saint John. In particular, culture and arts events are essential to creating positive images and conversations that endure long beyond the events. The "historic district-event hallmarking" branding formula could be a practical tool for small-city DMOs in places with historic districts that desire to employ cultural events in branding and for academics who wish to investigate place branding in this context.

References

Ashworth, G. (2009). The instruments of place branding: How is it done? *European Spatial Research and Policy*, 16(1), 9–22.

Bain, A. L. (2003). Constructing contemporary artistic identities in Toronto neighborhoods. *Canadian Geographer*, 47(3), 303–317.

Beeton, S. (2005). The case study in tourism research: A multi-method case study approach. In B. W., Ritchie, P., Burns and C. Palmer (eds). *Tourism Research Methods: Integrating Theory with Practice* (pp. 37–48).

Bowdin, G., Allen, J., Harris, R., McDonnell, I., & O'Toole, W. (2012). *Events Management*. Oxon: Routledge.

Bradley, A., Hall, T., & Harrison, M. (2002). Selling cities: Promoting new images for meetings tourism. *Cities*, 19(1), 61–70.

Brotherton, B. (1999). Case study research. *The Handbook of Contemporary Hospitality Management Research* (pp. 115–142). Hoboken, NJ: John Wiley & Sons.

City of Saint John. (2005). Arts and Culture Policy. Retrieved from https://www.saintjohn.ca/site/media/SaintJohn/SJ%20Arts%20Policy-EN.pdf

Clare, I., & Lyn, M. (2012). *Tourism Management: An Introduction*. London, UK: Sage.

Clarke, V. (2018). Interview of Discover Saint John CEO with Lee Jolliffe October 23.

Cooke, P. N., & Lazzeretti, L. (eds). (2008). *Creative Cities, Cultural Clusters and Local Economic Development*. Cheltenham: Edward Elgar Publishing.

Cudny, W. (2016a). *Festivalisation of Urban Spaces: Factors, Processes and Effects*. Cham: Springer.

Cudny, W. (2016b). Manufaktura in Łódź, Poland: An example of a festival marketplace. *Norsk Geografisk Tidsskrift-Norwegian Journal of Geography*, 70(5), 276–291.

de Noronha, I., Coca-Stefaniak, J. A., & Morrison, A. M. (2017). Confused branding? An exploratory study of place branding practices among place management professionals. *Cities*, 66, 91–98.

Discover Saint John. (2018). Annual Report 2017. Retrieved from www.discoversaintjohn.com/

Drost, P. (2018). Fredericton Heads to Record Year in Tourism After Strong Summer. *CBC Posted* September 24. Retrieved from www.cbc.ca/news/canada/new-brunswick/fredericton-summer-tourism-1.4836387

du Cros, H., & Jolliffe, L. (2011). Bundling the arts for tourism to complement urban heritage tourist experiences in Asia. *Journal of Heritage Tourism*, 6(3), 181–195.

du Cros, H., & Jolliffe, L. (2014). *The Arts and Events*. London: Routledge.

Enterprise Saint John. (2018). 5 Questions on Innovation with Victoria Clarke. Retrieved from enterprisesj.com/wp-content/uploads/2018/04/5-Questions-with-Victoria-Clarke.pdf

Florida, R. (2003). Cities and the creative class. *City & Community*, 2(1), 3–19.

Fredericton Tourism (n.d.). Retrieved from www.tourismfredericton.ca/en

Fyall, A., & Garrod, B. (2005). *Tourism Marketing: A Collaborative Approach*. Clevedon: Channel View Publications.

Hankinson, G. (2001). Location branding: A study of the branding practices of 12 English cities. *Journal of Brand Management*, 9(2), 127–142.

Jago, L., Chalip, L., Brown, G., Mules, T., & Ali, S. (2003). Building events into destination branding: Insights from experts. *Event Management*, 8(1), 3–14.

Jennings, G. (2005). Interviewing: A focus on qualitative techniques. In B. W. Ritchie, P. Burns and C. Palmer (eds). *Tourism Research Methods: Integrating Theory with Practice* (pp. 99–117). Wallingford, Oxfordshire: CABI.

Jolliffe, L. (2017). Engaging new audiences by bundling art experiences. *Caribbean Museums*, 2, 1–12.

Kelly, J., Williams, P. W., Schieven, A., & Dunn, I. (2006). Toward a destination visitor attendance estimation model: Whistler, British Columbia, Canada. *Journal of Travel Research*, 44(4), 449–456.

Költringer, C., & Dickinger, A. (2015). Analyzing destination branding and image from online sources: A web content mining approach. *Journal of Business Research*, 68(9), 1836–1843.

Landry, C., & Bianchini, F. (1995). The creative city. *Demos*, 13, 12.

Middleton, V. T., Fyall, A., Morgan, M., & Ranchhod, A. (2009). *Marketing in Travel and Tourism*. London: Routledge.

Morgan, N., & Pritchard, A. (2005). On souvenirs and metonymy: Narratives of memory, metaphor and materiality. *Tourist Studies*, 5(1), 29–53.

Morgan, N., Pritchard, A., & Pride, R. (2007). *Destination Branding*. London: Routledge.

Ooi, C. S., & Stöber, B. (2010). Authenticity and place branding: The arts and culture in branding Berlin and Singapore, *Re-Investing Authenticity: Tourism, Places and Emotions* (pp. 66–79). Bristol: Channel View Publications.

Pike, S. (2007). *Destination Marketing Organisations*. London: Routledge.

Richards, G. (2011). Tourism development trajectories: From culture to creativity? *Tourism & Management Studies*, (6), 9–15.

Richards, G., & Wilson, J. (2004). The impact of cultural events on city image: Rotterdam, cultural capital of Europe 2001. *Urban Studies*, 41(10), 1931–1951.

Schulze, G. (1992). *Die erlebnis gesellschaft. Kultursoziologie der gegenwart*. Frankfurt, Germany: Campus.

Seabrook, D. (2018). Interview of Dave Seabrook, manager, Fredericton Tourism by Nancy Chesworth and Lee Jolliffe, July 30.

Statistics Canada. (2016). Population Centre and Rural Area Classification. Retrieved from www.statcan.gc.ca/eng/subjects/standard/pcrac/2016/introduction

Tourism New Brunswick. (n.d.). Retrieved from www.tourismnewbrunswick.ca/

Waitt, G., & Gibson, C. (2009). Creative small cities: Rethinking the creative economy in place. *Urban Studies*, 46(5–6), 1223–1246.

Yin, R. (1994). *Case Study Research: Design and Methods*. Beverly Hills: Sage.

7 Resisting Rio de Janeiro's event-led place promotion

From insurgent rebranding to festive counter-spectacle

Anne-Marie Broudehoux

Introduction

In his work on dramaturgy, Goffman (1976) defines "impression management" as the act of manipulating the perception others may have of us, using mechanisms called "sign vehicles". The image we impress onto each other, he claims, is always a compromise between an objective reality and a constructed, fictional ideal. Goffman identifies two simultaneous realities that coexist in the process of representation. The front stage is the official façade presented to the world, which seeks to convey a particular impression, however staged or fabricated. The back stage is where the more fragile, private, and authentic self is preserved and where the front stage identity is formed and reproduced. For Goffman, the disconnect between front and back stages carries a certain potential for alienation.

This chapter addresses the notion of city branding in the wider sense of urban image construction, as a composite of both promotional discourses and promotional events. It is concerned with the way cities consciously transform their images and manipulate "sign vehicles" in order to elicit expected reactions in ways that support their own agendas. The chapter is thus particularly interested in the politics of urban image construction and focuses on promotional practices used in the context of recent sporting mega-events in the city of Rio de Janeiro, host of the 2014 FIFA World Cup and the 2016 Olympic Games. The chapter argues that in Rio de Janeiro, top-down initiatives to transform the perception of the city to serve local political and economic elites were opposed by an insurgent counter-branding movement that sought to reverse the exclusive, hegemonic vision portrayed. The chapter results from nearly ten years of empirical research conducted in the city of Rio de Janeiro, before, during, and after both mega-events. It rests upon a multidisciplinary methodology, which combines ethnography and visual and spatial analysis with an analytical framework derived from critical human geography. Data was gathered through repeat, on-site observation; interviews with a broad range of actors; extensive press reviews; scholarly literature; media reports; official bid documents; event propaganda; planning documents; official websites; activist blogs; and other relevant secondary sources.

The chapter begins with a discussion of the highly political and exclusive character of event-led image construction. It then examines the construction of Rio de Janeiro's place image as an event city through an analysis of some of the discourses that have driven this process. The remainder of the chapter discusses the emergence of a subaltern counter–public sphere to counter the negative effects of event-led urban image construction. It details some of the strategies developed in Rio de Janeiro to oppose place promotional practices and resist the event-spectacle. The chapter concludes with a reflection on the impacts of these insurgent rebranding strategies and other acts of resistance to the city as spectacle on overall impression management in the construction of the event city.

City branding and the politics of place image promotion

Urban elites have always sought to project a favourable image that could attract visitors, residents, and businesses. Over time, they devised various strategies to reframe perceptions, emphasize distinctiveness, and promote their best assets. The urban crisis that marked the late 20th century city, following de-industrialization, falling tax bases, and declining public expenditures, has stimulated the resurgence of concerted practices of place promotion, as derelict cities sought to correct perceptual problems associated with their image (Hannigan 2003). The need for economic survival, anxieties about one's position in the dominant world order, and the fear of being upstaged by rivals on the national and international scene have driven cities to update ossified representations and redynamize their image.

Place promotion has become an essential part of the broad "entrepreneurial ethos" (Ward 1998) which now dominates neoliberal public policy. With the growing mobility of capital investment, the footloose quality of enterprises, and increased global connectivity, cities have had to become proactive in capturing mobile investment, attracting prospective firms and their workforce, enticing up-market tourists and conference organizers, and convincing high tax payers to settle there permanently (Hannigan 2003; Ashworth and Voogd 1990; Kearns and Philo 1993; Harvey 1989).

Urban imagineers and city marketers have helped cities market and advertise themselves by capitalizing upon an alluring urban iconography and enticing promotional campaigns. In recent decades, cities seeking a competitive advantage in the global economy have increasingly turned to global-scale events as key generators of symbolic capital (Judd 2003, Ashworth and Voogd 1990). With their vast media coverage and strong branding power, world-class sporting events such as international exhibitions and sporting competitions like the FIFA World Cup or the Olympic Games have come to be seen as exceptional moments for the production and consumption of urban images. Sporting mega-events represent unparalleled opportunities for cities to gain recognition and prestige and to advertise themselves to audiences of millions. They are perceived as a stamp of approval from the international community that will attest to a city's economic performance, organizational efficiency, and cultural sophistication.

The exclusionary nature of place promotion

Largely based on selectivity and discernment, place promotion is by nature an exclusionary practice, which also makes it highly political. The construction of an attractive place image is generally achieved by discursively reframing a city's representation through conscious omissions, manipulations, and the skewing of reality. Carter (2006, p. 156) views place promotion as a "highly contentious and problematic process that is rife with social divisions of all sorts". This is why so many social scientists regard city marketing with scepticism (Harvey 2001; Smith 2005; Healey 2002; Colomb 2012). They find the practice to be socially regressive, incompatible with the welfare objectives of public policy and thus deeply problematic from an ethical point of view (Healey 2002). For Rosalynd Deutsche (1996), the construction of a unified, coherent, and cohesive urban image is a highly exclusive process that can only be achieved by expelling differences and conflicts within. It entails the reduction of a rich, complex, heterogeneous urban reality into a simplified, homogenous, one-dimensional marketable commodity (Deutsche 1996). Healey (2002) views the creative projection of a fictional yet totalizing image of society as undermining more plural, multidimensional, and progressive visions of urban life.

For Vale and Bass Warner (2001), it always matters who devises urban representations, for whom, and for what purpose. Power is a determining factor deciding who and what are to be included in official urban representations (Powell and Marrero-Guillamón 2012). The urban image that is promoted often embodies elitist conceptualizations of what is deemed desirable, respectable, or attractive (Smith 2005; McCann 2009). Healey (2002) views the process of giving a city what elites believe is a respectable face as depending upon silencing the politically weak and making poverty – and the poor – purposely invisible. Usually left out of representations are the ordinary landscapes of the poor, considered to be "out of place" (Wright 1997) in the city's public image. Deutsche (1996, p. 173) talks of a "politics of erasure", in which the absence of undesirable groups is discursively inscribed in representations of the city.

Mega-events and city promotion in Rio de Janeiro

Rio de Janeiro is located in the southeastern part of Brazil on the Atlantic Gulf of Guanabara. It is the capital of the state of Rio de Janeiro and, with a population of 12 million inhabitants, is the second largest city in Brazil. In October 2009, Rio de Janeiro was selected to host the 2016 Olympic Games, just a few years after Brazil had been awarded the title of host country for the 2014 FIFA World Cup, with Rio hosting the finals. Rio de Janeiro thus became one of the rare cities in history to host the world's two top sporting mega-events within a two-year span. Then-President Lula Ignacio da Silva expressed with unusual clarity the historical significance of this recognition for his nation: "Brazil has left its second-class status behind and has joined the first class. Today we received respect. This is a victory for 190 million souls, a victory for Latin America, a victory for the Olympics . . . Brazil today won her international citizenship, we broke the last barrier of prejudice" (Redação Estadão 2009). This twin host status was both the result of intense city promotional efforts and a harbinger of more to come.

Rio de Janeiro's incursion into the realm of mega-events goes back to 1992, with the United Nations Conference on Environment and Development

(UNCED). Over the next decades, the city would firmly embrace mega-events as a core promotional strategy, under the leadership of Mayor Cezar Maia and Luiz Paulo Conde, governor of the state of Rio de Janeiro. This strategy was part of a new entrepreneurial mode of governance adopted by the city to strengthen its competitiveness as a tourist destination and a hub for global capital investment. During his first of three mandates, Cesar Maia elaborated Rio's first strategic plan, launched in 1996, in collaboration with Catalan consultant Jordi Borja, known for his key role in Barcelona's Olympic transformation. Hosting mega-events was seen as a unique opportunity to stimulate global interest and would be pursued as an "aggregator of value" (Gaffney 2016) that could help position Rio among the great world cities.

Over the first decade of the 21st century, Rio de Janeiro ran as a candidate for the 2004 Olympics and hosted, among others, the 2007 Pan American Games, the 2010 World Urban Forum, the 2011 Military World Games, the 2013 World Youth Day, the 2014 FIFA World Cup, and the 2016 Olympic Games. The Olympic dream would be achieved under the rule of mayor Eduardo Paes and state governor Sergio Cabral, who categorized the event as part of the "trophies" the city had been collecting to buttress its stature, consolidate the local brand, and elevate its position in the global hierarchy. Rio de Janeiro's winning Olympic candidacy file, deposited in 2009, stated that the games would "lift Brazil to a new level of international recognition and be an opportunity to accelerate the transformation of Rio de Janeiro into a real international city" (Rio 2016 Vol. 1, 2009, p. 18).

Geography of desire: nature and culture as strategies of seduction

Rio de Janeiro has long capitalized on its unique landscape to capture world attention and attract visitors. Endowed with a spectacular topography, an idyllic shoreline, and a rich urban culture, the city enjoyed a great reputation as Brazil's primary tourist destination and remains one of the most visited cities in the southern hemisphere. It was the French poet Jeanne Catulle Mendes, author of *Rio: La Ville Merveilleuse* (1912), who cornered what would become the city's most enduring slogan: *Cidade Maravilhosa*, the Marvelous City. Immortalized by André Filho in a 1935 carnival march, the phrase was later adopted as the city's official anthem. Over the 20th century, films, novels, and advertising campaigns helped impose *Cidade Maravilhosa* as a brand and played an important role in the diffusion of representations of the city that would support its claim to be the "most beautiful city in the world" (Machado 2004).

Rio de Janeiro's competitive advantages include unique natural assets, with beaches, mountains, lagoons, and tropical forests. It also boasts lively cultural traditions that range from architecture, samba, and Carnival to football and capoeira. Since the 1960s, promotional efforts have capitalized on the city's exotic tropical nature, cultural effervescence, and proverbial bohemian lifestyle, stereotypically expressed as sea, sex, and sand, to convey its easygoing, fun-loving and laid-back urban culture. More recent promotional campaigns led by the city's tourism bureau (Riotur)[1] in the 1990s and 2000s strove to maintain a consensual representation of the city as a light-hearted, easygoing tropical paradise of carefree excitement and leisure, in spite of rising drug-related violence and rampant social inequality. One of the city's most persistent promotional strategies thus largely relied on seduction, especially in the arousing of desire and attraction by appealing to natural beauty, sensuality, and exoticism.

Promotional material produced in 2009 for the city's Olympic candidacy drew heavily upon the same "culture and nature" repertoire, focusing on the beauty of the city's scenery and the fun-loving, body-conscious, outdoorsy "nature" of the true *Carioca* (Rio de Janeiro native). The festive dimension of *Carioca* culture was also emphasized, with suggestive allusions to pleasure, sensuality, and the exaltation of all senses. The bid file stated that "Celebration, partying and leisure have always been part of the life of Rio de Janeiro, Brazil's cultural capital. The city's natural beauty and climate provide a perfect setting for sports and other outdoor activities. Bistros, cafés, plazas and the coastline epitomize the city's life style, intense and passionate, with a diversity of rhythms and flavors" (Rio 2016 Vol. 1 2009, p. 15). To project this seductive image of the city, the candidacy file relied on a highly aestheticized visual discourse. The file juxtaposed images of Rio's sensual, curvaceous landscape with shots of the perfect bodies of local citizens engaged in a variety of sporting activities. This essentialist representation played a triple role, acting as a sensual titillation for potential visitors while naturalizing Rio's vocation as Olympic host and diverting attention from more sensitive urban issues (Broudehoux 2017).

Chris Gaffney (2016) qualifies such use of erotically loaded images of Rio de Janeiro's urban landscapes in the marketing of mega-events as *geoporn* – based on a definition of pornography as "the sensational depiction of acts so as to arouse a quick, intense emotional reaction". He denounces the manufacturing of consensus about the event city through the use of representational techniques of possession and domination that feed into consumer fetishes and act as an extension of the privileged masculine gaze. He sustains that the superficial and consensual narrative portrayed in these geopornographic images masks the violence, domination, perversity, and exploitation that are embedded in the landscape (Gaffney 2016). In many ways, these images recall 19th-century colonialists' depictions of faraway exotic lands that sought to arouse desire while inciting (forced) possession (Suleri 1992, pp. 16–17).

In Olympic and World Cup propaganda, caricatured representations of a "*Carioca* way of being", characterized by the everyday experience of pleasures and celebrations, promise potential visitors a life of non-stop partying. By drawing on long-established stereotypes, this depiction feeds into the fantasy and expectation of its targeted audience of middle-class European and North American men. Such representation not only appears to condone, even encourage, the most lewd behaviour among tourists; it also exacerbates the sexualization of the Brazilian (female) subject and implicitly portrays Rio de Janeiro as a sex tourism destination (De Lisio et al. 2019). But more than anything, such jovial, aestheticized representations divert attention from the main issues that lie hidden behind the city's picture-perfect image.

Harmony and cordiality as cultural smokescreens

A complement to the "nature and culture" discourse found in Rio de Janeiro's official branding for the 2014 FIFA World Cup and 2016 Olympic Games were the twin keywords of "harmony and cordiality", which also have deep roots in historical representations of Brazil and Rio de Janeiro. The notion of Brazilians living in harmony with one another in spite of their social and racial differences remains a powerful founding myth of modern Brazil, especially in the face of rampant race-based social inequality.

Since the 19th century, the notion of the "cordial man" has been invoked to describe the Brazilian elite's idealized self-representation, a myth widely documented by historian Sergio Buarque de Holanda. Under the presidencies of Luis Inacio Lula da Silva and Dilma Rousseff, a similar discourse that embraces cultural diversity and harmony was forged and proclaimed Brazil to be a country diverse and for all (with the slogan *"Brasil, um pais de todos"*). This vision emphasized the importance of local, traditional, and folkloric culture for the construction of a shared national identity that was a hybrid of all local influences and largely drew upon what Chauí (1994) called a "green-yellow mythology" to describe the incorporation of the popular into the national in Brazilian nation building.

This very same mythology would guide Olympic-related branding activities. Rio 2016's candidacy file repeated the same basic message of fraternal love and harmonious cultural diversity. The Olympic organizing committee's official discourse, which permeated widely distributed public relations packages, tourism brochures, and other propaganda material, focused on the two overarching notions of diversity and harmony, thereby reproducing the enduring, idealized image of the quintessential Brazilian, living in harmony with nature and with his ethnically diverse fellow citizens. The cultural coordinator for the games more specifically focused his vision on the three uplifting themes of festiveness, human warmth, and colour, which drew heavily on notions of rhythm, musicality, miscegenation, and unity. Such framing conveyed a vision of Brazilianness that fed upon the same repertoire long found in tourism advertising, thereby recycling stereotypes of an idyllic tropical Brazil, where diversity is harmonious and conflict inexistent.

The same message can be said to have permeated the 5 August, 2016 Olympic ceremonies, which widely featured Brazilian nature and culture in a celebration of harmonious diversity. Arts and culture were reduced to safe, folklorized versions of themselves, with dancers clad in emblematic white Bahia dresses and a few references to Brazilian natives. Contemporary artistic production was narrowly embodied by representatives of pop culture as singers, dancers, and fashion models. For many local critics, such rose-coloured depiction of Brazil as a postcard-perfect tropical paradise betrayed an inability to address the complexity

of contemporary society as well as its multiple challenges. By recycling enduring clichés and eclipsing references to race-based inequality, gang violence, and
environmental degradation, this idyllic representation felt like nothing more than
a clumsy attempt to camouflage rampant insecurity and other pressing issues
behind a green-yellow smokescreen.

The anti-poor discourse in the branding
of Rio de Janeiro's mega-events

The official discourse that permeated mega-event propaganda not only projected
an idealized image of the city, but also included important omissions that helped
divert attention away from issues that could tarnish Rio de Janeiro's global representation. One of the greatest perceived threats to the city's idyllic image in
preparation to host the 2014 and 2016 mega-events was the visibility of poverty,
especially the omnipresence of *favelas* in the urban landscape. The semantic association of these informal settlements with notions of violence, illegality, disor-
der, and environmental degradation meant that an overwhelming proportion of
beautification initiatives and promotional strategies devised by the city sought to
downplay their ubiquity.[2]

Concerted efforts to de-emphasize, even silence, the problems of poverty,
inequality, and violence that were tearing the city apart were legitimized by an
unspoken discourse that had long been hegemonic among the city's economic
elite. This anti-poor rhetoric can be traced back to the hygienist movement of the
early 20th century, whose racist undertones have roots in the city's slave past.
Having acquired a revanchist flavour with the rise of neoliberalism, it would
influence the city's pre-event branding efforts in more or less overt ways (Broudehoux 2017).

When Rio de Janeiro was awarded the status of Olympic host city in 2009,
local elites' long-established desire to eradicate the presence of *favelas* in visual
representations of the city gained momentum. In 2011, major Brazilian newspapers ran a full-page advertisement from Petrobras, Brazil's large oil conglomerate,
depicting an idealized birds-eye view of the city, in which all *favelas* had been
replaced by lush vegetation. In April 2013, a little over a year before the World
Cup, Rio de Janeiro's *favelas* also disappeared from Google Maps. The mayor's
office as well as the city's tourism bureau had since 2009 exerted pressure on
Google, even lodged a formal complaint against the company for giving *favelas*
too much visibility in its mapping services, especially by identifying illegal settlements that the city administration had long refused to include on formal maps.
Under renewed pressure, Google finally caved in and agreed to replace the word
favela with the euphemism *morro*, or hill, a decision that was widely contested by
citizens' groups for contributing to the symbolic erasure of these territories from
the virtual landscape (Broudehoux 2017).

Rio's Olympic candidacy file was another great exercise in image control, carefully avoiding urban realities that could negatively affect global perceptions and
suggest insecurity, instability, or underdevelopment. Of the 174 images published

in the candidacy file, an overwhelming proportion (45 percent) showed the city's littoral South Zone (Zona Sul), home of Rio's wealthiest residents and host to only two events. In spite of the fact that a quarter of the city's population lives in *favelas*, the entire file included a single representation of these neighbourhoods. In most propaganda clips and illustrations, *favelas* were airbrushed, cropped out, fast-forwarded, digitally erased, or conveniently washed out by powerful sunrays, mist, or haze. Venues located in Rio de Janeiro's poor Zona Norte were always depicted as isolated objects in close-up shots to avoid revealing the poor communities surrounding them. Representations of Rio's famous Maracanã stadium were always shown from the same angle, so that the nearby Mangueira *favela* would not be visible in the background (Broudehoux 2017).

Rio de Janeiro's Olympic opening ceremony, held on 5 August, 2016, similarly sought to curtail representations of the *favela*. Media around the world praised Brazil's openness in addressing so transparently some of the most problematic aspects of its history, from colonialization and slavery to the development of one of the modern world's most unequal societies. If the *favela* was omnipresent during the ceremonies, the difficult issues that underscore its existence, especially the discrimination, marginalization, economic exploitation, and state abandonment from which they suffer, were deproblematized behind an aestheticized representation as a happy, festive, colorful urban construct, used as a mere backstage for live performances. Like the problematic issues it embodies, the *favela* was pushed into the background as a disgraceful hurdle that should not stand in the way of this great global-scale celebration.

Apart from its symbolic erasure in the visual narrative of event-related propaganda, the expunging of the city's "poverty problem" also transpired in the verbal rhetoric used by prominent members of the event organization and their supporters. For example, when Brazilian Olympic committee president Carlos A. Nuzman declared, in reference to the major infrastructure projects that transformed the city for the games, "We can now host our guests in the living room", he inferred that without such projects, which caused the demolition of countless *favelas* and the displacement of their population to the far periphery (an estimated 70,000 in total), Brazil would have had to shamefully host foreign visitors in the kitchen.

Individual members of the power coalition behind the city's two mega-event candidacies have also contributed to this anti-poor discourse, sometimes with unusual candor. In 2015, real estate tycoon Carlos Carvalho, who would stand as one of the greatest beneficiaries of the privatization of public land for the Olympics, talked to journalists about the Olympic Athlete's Village he built in elite Barra da Tijuca. Explaining why the village's future transformation into a private luxury condominium – incidentally called *"Ilha Pura"* (or Pure Island) – would require the eviction of long-established poor residents, he sustained that Barra should be the exclusive realm of the elite. "Different segments of society should only live where they can afford to live. The 'right' to live somewhere should depend on one's capacity to pay" (Puff 2015). Carvalho argued that the elite belong in the city centre while the lower social classes should move to the periphery. "They should move to houses built to their standards. They have to go" (Watts 2015).

Counter-discourse and insurgent rebranding in the event city

Nancy Fraser (1990) has underlined the importance of marginalized and under-represented groups with limited access to the dominant public spheres (commercial media, local government meetings, academia) coming together and creating alternative spaces, which she calls subaltern counter-public spheres. In order to carve a space in the existing and increasingly closed commercial media, these groups have turned their attention to producing their own media, where they control the narrative and frame their own identities. The counter-discourses they invent and circulate allow them to formulate oppositional interpretations of their identities, interests, and needs. These alternative spheres are sustained by diverse communicative practices that include autonomous newspapers and websites, community networks, and other media strategies (Fraser 1990).

During preparations for the hosting of the 2007 Pan American Games in Rio de Janeiro, a vast coalition of social actors from various spheres, known as the *Comitê popular do Pan* (Popular committee of the Pan) was born. Made up of students, intellectuals, legal workers, activists, and citizens, the *comitê*'s main goal was to denounce unfair evictions and excessive policing; to document power abuses, corruption, and other wrongdoing; to organize people against unlawful evictions; and to help affected population groups by providing legal guidance, housing assistance, and moral support.

Following the same model, in the years leading up to the 2014 World Cup, social actors from across the country developed a vast, national network of " people's committees " (*comitês populares*) that similarly included activists, academics, and legal aid workers. Over the years, this coalition of social movements came to constitute a pan-Brazilian counter-public sphere and coordinated a series of civil society actions across the country. It helped local citizens groups develop resistance strategies, organize civil disobedience actions, and fight relocation and exclusion in the courts. Rio de Janeiro's own *comitê popular* would later broaden its focus to embrace Olympic-related causes (ANCOP 2011, 2014).

The strength of this vast solidarity movement came from the union of diverse social movements fighting for causes ranging from unlawful housing eviction and demolition to the criminalization of informal work. They were very vocal in condemning public service cuts, the privatization of public land, restrained access to collective resources, and the tightening of the social control apparatus. Together, they mobilized against real estate speculation, excessive public spending on ill-conceived projects, and the diversion of public funds from more pressing social issues. Far from the compliant, exotic bodies portrayed in event-related propaganda, these students, professors, activists, and citizens were intellectually sophisticated, highly articulate, and unabashedly cosmopolitan in their adhesion to globalized anti-neoliberal social movements.

Research and documentation were key tools in developing insurgent rebranding strategies against Rio de Janeiro's mega-event spectacle. Academic members of the *comitês populares* used their skills as researchers to scientifically document shady real estate transactions, to keep track of public spending and legalistic manoeuvrings, and to collect an impressive amount of information on rights violations, illegal transactions, and possible collusion. The national network released two reports, in 2011 and 2014, documenting various abuses and irregularities (ANCOP 2011, 2014). The group worked closely with local and international journalists to disseminate information, feeding them facts that had never been made public.

One of the great strengths of this subaltern counter–public sphere lay in its strategic understanding of the dominant pro-event discourse, essential to the development of a rich counter-discourse, and of various insurgent rebranding strategies. Members of the coalition strove to correct the distorted reality projected by event sponsors in their efforts to build consensus around the event-spectacle. While the city's branding machine strove to portray Rio de Janeiro as a peaceful, harmonious, and exciting city, inhabited by beautiful, exotic, happy-go-lucky individuals, this well-organized group methodically deconstructed the dominant discourse, revealing widespread misinformation and bringing to light the dark and sordid reality behind the construction of the Olympic city.

Their first weapon of choice was discursive, with the production of a counternarrative that symbolically mimicked the event's official sign vehicles and impression management strategies, while turning them on their heads. By modeling their rhetoric on the state's aestheticized discourse, they managed to deconstruct the mythology disseminated by pro-event propaganda, to ridicule its pretensions, and to unveil its false claims. This counter-discourse was neither cordial nor harmonious but blatantly pro-poor, openly denouncing racism, inequality, nepotism, and corruption. In their speeches, pamphlets, and publications, activists used the same vocabulary and symbolic strategies as event organizers but reflected them back as in a distorting mirror, so as to endow them a new meaning, in a way that revealed their absurdity, hypocrisy, and deceitful character.

In a creative, verbal form of *detournement*, they appropriated official megaevent parlance, redefining ubiquitous keywords such as *legacies* and *standards* in terms of loss: of social equality, civic rights, ethics, environmental quality, or public services. One popular slogan used in the resistance against Brazil's World Cup borrowed the idiom "FIFA standard" (*padrão FIFA*) to denounce pressing but neglected issues that should deserve the same quality standards required by FIFA in the construction of large, expensive football stadia. Chants, boards, and banners called for FIFA-grade schools, hospitals, and social services. Humour, wit, and irony were also widely deployed to symbolically challenge the prevailing consensus, unsettle the hegemonic discourse, and bring attention to its most preposterous claims. Popular slogans creatively merged social demands, mega-event criticism, and contempt of Rio's city branding initiatives. "Call me a stadium and invest in me!" "How many schools are worth one Maracanã?" (Rosner 2013).

Rio de Janeiro's expensive branding efforts were countered by effective campaigns of insurgent rebranding that sought to show the world the other side of the picture. Using propaganda vectors similar to those used by the World Cup and the Olympics, resistance movements printed banners, posters, T-shirts, and stickers bearing their slogans, which were sold at various events and widely disseminated on the web. They also called upon politicized members of the Brazilian star system to act as spokespersons in their social media campaigns.

One insurgent rebranding strategy relied upon the tactical utilization of urban space by graffiti artists and muralists to promote a visual counter-discourse, through practices of creative reworking that widely borrowed from *subvertizing* (Borghini et al. 2010) and *brandalism* (Goodson 2012). Many event billboards and sponsor advertising were subverted and vandalized with original artworks and clever commentaries that challenged the authority and legitimacy of event-related propaganda (Smith-Anthony and Groom 2015). Street artists were also extremely prolific in the production of giant murals that denounced the exclusion of the poor from the mega-event festival and exposed the greed and corruption of event leaders and organizers.[3] Rarely aggressive in tone, the murals were rather poetic and evocative – for example, featuring a child in tears at the sight of a football on his dinner plate – or satirical – depicting businessmen playing football with a money bag. Graffiti generally bore a more accusatory tone and repeated, at nauseam, the same slogans throughout the city: FIFA go home! World Cup for Whom? *Olimpiadas para quem?*

Organized resistance and the festive counter-spectacle

In Rio de Janeiro, the most effective way to counter the mega-event spectacle was through organized forms of resistance and active engagement in collective civic actions and other forms of civil disobedience. Street protests were common in Brazil in the run-up to the World Cup. Demonstrators used highly strategic and evocative territories as sites for the expression of discontent: it was around major stadia, in front of emblematic infrastructure, and near establishments of power that people came to voice their grievances.

In June 2013, over a two-week period which coincided with FIFA's Confederations Cup, Brazil was shaken by social conflicts on a scale rarely seen in recent history. Throughout the country, crowds in the tens of thousands, among which diverse sectors of civil society were represented, called for a radical transformation of Brazilian society and a deep reform of the exercise of political power (Badaró 2013). Recriminations ranged from rising costs of living and heavy-handed policing programmes to public transportation, education, health, and other pressing collective issues. Protests were also the product of widespread frustrations about public exclusion from the multi-billion-dollar World Cup bonanza. So deep was public anger that even the middle classes, usually less politically engaged, briefly joined the movement (Vainer 2013).

Many collective contestations mimicked mega-events' festive dimension and proposed their own participant-driven events, using genuine festivity as a counter-reaction to the highly formalized event-spectacle. The notion of genuine festivity draws from Debord and his colleagues, who distinguished between event festivity and genuine festivity, or the kind of festivity which is not driven by the interests of capital but by human creativity and sociability (Rojek 2013). In Rio, a city with a century-old carnival tradition and a taste for the dramatic and theatrical, many protests were highly carnivalesque in mood and drew their strength from Carnival's subversive power (DaMatta 1991). Literally fighting spectacle with spectacle, protesters used deception and disguise to denounce the masquerade of capitalist greed that had travestied their city and its most basic values (Rosner 2013). Many demonstrators wore masks and costumes, dressing up as superheroes or as Anonymous's Guy Fawkes. They turned protests into artful performances of urban citizenship, using the city as a stage to reconquer contested territories and to reconfigure urban space (Broudehoux 2017).

Another festive deployment of collective resistance organized by members of Rio de Janeiro's *comitês populares* consisted of informal and apparently innocuous gatherings, convened on the web and through social media, to bring attention to a particular cause. Their innovative, non-confrontational approach and highly inclusive, friendly outlook played the double role of boosting the morale of participants and attracting sympathy and solidarity. Many took advantage of the global spotlight linked to the mega-event spectacle to make their recriminations heard. For example, on several weekends in 2014 and 2015, a series of picnics convened on Facebook encouraged people from the poor North Zone to congregate on the elite beach of Ipanema for a family-friendly day out to denounce widespread discrimination. Ironically called *faroferos*, these events adopted a deprecatory moniker commonly used by elite *Carioca* to deride poor, black, unsophisticated beachgoers who bring their own lunch to the beach. (*Farofa* is grilled manioc flour.) These events were held to protest the pre-mega-event police expulsion of underprivileged black youth from public buses connecting the periphery to the littoral on weekends on suspicion of criminal intent. These families symbolically reclaimed their right to the city's beaches, too often monopolized by the white, rich elite and foreign tourists.

Another playful act of collective resistance organized by Rio de Janeiro's *Comitê popular da Copa* to denounce the exclusionary nature of mega-events was the *Copa dos excluidos* (Cup of the excluded). Held just before the 2014 World Cup, this festive daylong gathering took the form of an informal football tournament, where families shared drinks and food and played football in a highly convivial act of resistance, whose harmless, light-hearted, and highly symbolic nature could only attract public sympathy for their cause.

Insurgent rebranding 2.0: web-based strategies of resistance

If many protests took to the streets, other acts of dissidence were organized on the internet, which became an important tactical tool for resistance movements and a crucial weapon in the battle against the event-spectacle. As a cheap, accessible, and democratic means of mass communication, the internet was used as an instrument of recruitment and outreach, as a forum for discussion and organization, and as a vector to disseminate information and share strategies.

In June 2013, a widely successful web-based campaign against the World Cup emerged in Brazil during the protests that rocked the Confederations Cup. Known by its bold slogan, *Não Vai Ter Copa* (There Will Be No Cup), the movement reached millions around the globe, thanks to the wide reach of social media. You could find *Não Vai Ter Copa* groups on Facebook and the hashtag #NaoVaiTerCopa on Twitter, often in conjunction with another popular slogan, #CopaPraQuem (Cup For Whom). *Não Vai Ter Copa* was also adopted by the hacker group Anonymous, which used the phrase in the hacking of several government sites and social media accounts in Brazil (Nunes 2014).

This social media campaign allowed the June 2013 protest movement to reach beyond Brazil's borders. The movement had itself been catalyzed by social media and spread across the country using these networks. The web campaign informed the world that the most expensive edition in the history of FIFA's tournament would be held at the cost of widespread corruption, rampant property speculation, police brutality, lack of political accountability, and the failure to complete even 50 percent of its promised infrastructure projects. Although it remains difficult to measure its full impact, the campaign certainly affected the image of the World Cup and helped turn it into a toxic brand, temporarily curbing the extent to which the sporting event could be exploited commercially and politically. It dampened Brazilians' enthusiasm for the cup and turned what should have been a festive year into a year of protest and denunciations. It also clearly stated that the World Cup was not going to be another public display of "cordiality" when Brazilians set grievances aside and put on a show of national unity (Broudehoux 2017).

Brazil's government attempted to discredit the campaign and to revamp the image of the cup by launching its own counter-slogan, with the hashtag #VaiTerCopa, (There Will Be a Cup). But the state's harsh denunciation of anti–World Cup sentiment as international jealousy, national defeatism, leftist agitation, and right-wing destabilization only added fuel to the fire and antagonized protesters. The scathing, authoritarian tone of the rebuke proved to be counter-productive, forcing the state to replace its motto with the more neutral #CopadasCopas (The Cup of Cups), widely used on President Dilma's Twitter feed and Facebook pages. It was also circulated on other government social media profiles to share positive messages about the cup and declare that the tournament would benefit all Brazilians (Nunes 2014). As 2014 went by and the World Cup took place, other copycat slogans emerged to contest other issues, including *Não Vai Ter Tarifa* (There Will Be No [public transportation] Fare Hike) and *Não Vai Ter Final* (There Will Be No Final). These campaigns expressed a sentiment shared by many Brazilians: that their collective hopes for a long-awaited tournament, meant to bring football back to its symbolic home, had been dashed by greed, waste, and corruption. For many, there was, indeed, no real World Cup, and the way the final ultimately played out for Brazil confirmed this failure in a spectacular way (Broudehoux 2017).

Conclusion: assessing the real impacts of branding and counter-branding

The chapter sought to highlight some of the mechanisms of city marketing in the context of hosting sporting mega-events. The case of Rio de Janeiro's mega-event-driven place promotion initiatives exemplified the complex politics of event-led impression management. The chapter demonstrated some of the social and cultural costs of the manipulation of "sign vehicles" in the construction of an idealized, fictional vision of the city. It detailed the projection of a fabricated, seductive, and highly exclusive place image that emphasized some aspects of the city's image while carefully omitting others, generally deemed to be less palatable. It also showed how such top-down initiatives to transform the perception of the city to serve local political and economic elites were opposed by an insurgent rebranding movement that sought to reverse the hegemonic vision portrayed. The chapter documented various ingenious strategies to counter the event-spectacle, which allowed those affected by this exclusive vision to regain part of their dignity, of their right to representation as part of their city's image, and of their right to participate in urban life.

Barely two years after the closing of the 2016 Olympic Games, as the world's eyes were once again turned towards Brazil on the occasion of the 2018 elections, one could not help but wonder about the actual impacts of Rio de Janeiro's expensive rebranding efforts. The city had spent almost ten years preparing to host the world's two most important sporting mega-events within a two-year span, a historical first. Had Rio de Janeiro really become more "marvelous" as a result of such costly promotional initiatives? Did those costly projects, expensive public relations campaigns, and marketing strategies really pay off?

There should be no contest to affirm that the answer to these questions is a resounding no. The day after the closing of the events, the festive city woke up with a tremendous hangover. Brazil's economic and political systems had begun to crumble. Within weeks, the glossy façade of order, prosperity, and harmony that had been erected for the city's global coming out was shattered. Even before the two events came to a close, the state of Rio de Janeiro had declared bankruptcy, and the nation's president was impeached in what many denounced as a "coup d'état". Few to none of the events' legacies were realized, as most stadia were left to rot.

However, members of various resistance movements who had spent years denouncing irrational spending and social welfare cuts could not rejoice and say "We told you so". They were too busy picking up the pieces to try to rebuild a life in the rubble of the event city. Undeniably, the greatest winners in this image-construction process were international sports federations, event sponsors, local organizers, and their allies in the broadcasting, construction, and real estate sectors. But the city itself, especially its vast impoverished masses, gained little from such an expensive rebranding and promotional campaign.

Assessing the real impacts of the insurgent rebranding strategies deployed during this ten-year period is no easy task. Gains in terms of eviction delays and project re-evaluations were notable, if incidental. But it is clear that the work accomplished by the *comitê populares* and other members of the vast resistance movement to the city as spectacle was not carried out in vain. Their relentless campaigns, festive actions, and activities played a significant part in raising public awareness to the hardships posed by event-led image construction. It was thanks to the hard work of different actions from the *comitês* that these issues entered the public debate. They can also be credited with having brought to international attention the dark side of the hosting of mega-events, as testified by the unprecedented critical coverage of the negative impacts of these events by foreign journalists. Finally, they have played an important role in strengthening local civil society and inspiring others in future host cities to replicate their strategies. That alone could stand as one of the greatest legacies of Rio de Janeiro's hosting of the 2014 Football World Cup and the 2016 Olympic Games.

Notes

1 These include Riotur's *Rio.Incomparavel* in 1997 and *Rio Maravilha* in 2002, as well as civic pride campaigns like *Orgulho de Ser Carioca* (Pride of Being *Carioca*) in the 1990s.
2 Ironically, city marketers had to work against the foreign community's growing fascination for the *favela* and its recognition as a trademark of the city's image abroad (Zeiderman 2006).
3 Many examples can be seen here: www.jornaldiademanews.com.br/exposicao-de-artes-veja-copa-dos-excluidos-na-visao-de-artistas-no-rio-de-janeiro/.

References

ANCOP (Articulaçao National dos Comitês Populares da Copa). (2011). *Dossiê Megaeventos e Violações de Direitos Humanos no Brasil: Dossiê da articulação nacional dos comitês populares da copa*. Rio de Janeiro: ETTERN/Fundação Heinrich Böll.
ANCOP (Articulaçao National dos Comitês Populares da Copa). (2014). *Dossiê Megaeventos e Violações de Direitos Humanos no Brasil*. Rio de Janeiro: ETTERN/ Fundação Heinrich Böll.
Ashworth, G., & Voogd, H. (1990). *Selling the City: Marketing Approaches in Public Sector Urban Planning*. London: Belhaven Press.
Badaró, M. B. (2013). 'A multidão nas ruas: construir a saída para a crise política' [The multitude on the streets: building an exit for a political crisis]. Unpublished text. History department, Federal Fluminense University.
Borghini, S., Visconti, L., Anderson, L., & Sherry, J. (2010). Symbiotic postures of commercial advertising and street art. *Journal of Advertising*, 39(3), 113–126.
Broudehoux, A. M. (2017). *Mega-Events and Urban Image Construction: Beijing and Rio de Janeiro*. London: Routledge.
Carter, T. F. (2006). Introduction: The sport of cities spectacle and the economy of appearances. *City & Society*, 18, 151–158.
Chauí, M. (1994). *Conformismo e resistência: aspectos da cultura popular no Brasil* (6a ed). São Paulo: Brasiliense.
Colomb, C. (2012). *Staging the New Berlin: Place Marketing and the Politics of Urban Reinvention Post-1989*. London: Routledge.
Comitê Popular da Copa e Olimpíadas do Rio de Janeiro. (2013). 'Megaeventos e Violações dos Direitos Humanos no Rio de Janeiro'. Available at: https:// comitepopulario.files.wordpress.com/2013/05/dossie_comitepopularcoparj_2013.pdf (Accessed 7 October 2018).
DaMatta, R. (1991). *Carnivals, Rogues, and Heroes: An Interpretation of the Brazilian Dilemma*. Notre Dame, IN: University of Notre Dame Press.

De Lisio, A., Hubbard, P., & Silk, M. (2019). Economies of (alleged) deviance: Sex work and the sport mega-event. *Sexuality Research and Social Policy*, 16(2), 1–11. https://doi.org/10.1007/s13178-018-0319-z (Accessed 6 August 2019).

Deutsche, R. (1996). *Evictions: Art and Spatial Politics*. Cambridge, MA: MIT Press.

Fraser, N. (1990). Rethinking the public sphere: A contribution to the critique of actually existing democracy. *Social Text*, 25–26, 56–80.

Gaffney, C. (2016). 'Geo-porn: Selling the City Through Mediated Spectacle', *Urban Transformation Processes: The Role of Flagship Architecture as Urban Generator (American Association of Geographers Conference)*. San Francisco.

Goffman, E. (1976). *Gender Advertisements*. New York: Harper & Row.

Goodson, S. (8 August 2012). 'Brandalism at the London Olympics', Forbes. Available at: www.forbes.com/sites/marketshare/2012/08/08/brandalism-at-the-london-olympics/#23f20703c37d (Accessed 7 October 2018).

Hannigan, J. (2003). Symposium on branding, the entertainment economy and Urban place building: Introduction. *International Journal of Urban and Regional Research*, 27(2), 352–360.

Harvey, D. (2001). *Spaces of Capital: Towards a Critical Geography*. New York: Routledge.

Harvey, D. (1989). From managerialism to entrepreneurialism: The transformation in Urban governance in late capitalism. *Geografiska Annaler, Human Geography*, 71, 3–17.

Healey, P. (2002). On creating the "City" as a collective resource. *Urban Studies*, 39, 177–179.

Judd, D. (2003). *The Infrastructure of Play: Building the Tourist City*. New York: M.E. Sharpe.

Kearns, G., & Philo, C. (1993). *Selling Places: The City as Cultural Capital, Past and Present*. Oxford: Pergamon.

Machado, R. T. (2004). *Para a "Cidade Maravilhosa", um "Plano Maravilha": uma análise crítica sobre produção da imagem turística e marketing urbano no Rio de Janeiro*. Rio de Janeiro: Universidade Federal do Rio de Janeiro.

McCann, E. J. (2009). 'City Marketing'. In R. Kitchin and N. Thrift (eds). *International Encyclopedia of Human Geography* (pp. 119–124). London: Elsevier.

Nunes, R. (30 May 2014) 'There Will Have Been No World Cup', *Aljazeera*. Available at: www.aljazeera.com/indepth/opinion/2014/05/brazil-world-cup-protests-201452910299437439.html (Accessed 7 October 2018).

Powell, H., & Marrero-Guillamón, I. (2012). *The Art of Dissent: Adventures in London's Olympic State*. London: Marshgate Press.

Puff, J. (2015). 'Como é que você vai botar o pobre ali?', diz bilionário 'dono da Barra da Tijuca', BBC Brasil, Aug. 10, 2015.

Redação Estadão. (2009). Lula exalta vitória do povo brasileiro com a escolha do Rio 2016. *Estadão*. Available at: www.estadao.com.br/noticias/esportes,lula-exalta-vitoria-do-povo-brasileiro-com-a-escolha-do-rio-2016, 444826,0.htm (Accessed 7 October 2018).

Rio 2016 Bid Committee. (2009). Candidature File for Rio de Janeiro to Host the 2016. *Olympic and Paralympic Games*, 1–3.

Rojek, C. (2013). *Event Power: How Global Events Manage and Manipulate*. London: SAGE.

Rosner, N. (2013, 7 July). 'Tinker Research Reports, Summer 2013: Masking Urban Marginality', Center for Latin American Studies. Available at: http://clas.berkeley.edu/research/problematizing-socio-spatial-development-margins-rio-de-janeiro (Accessed 7 October 2018).

Smith, A. (2005). Reimaging the city: The value of sport initiatives. *Annals of Tourism Research*, 32, 217–236.

Smith, A., & Groom, J. (2015). Brandalism and subvertising: Hoisting brands with their Own Petard? *Journal of Intellectual Property Law & Practice*, 10(1), 29–34.

Suleri, S. (1992). *The Rhetoric of English India*. Chicago: University of Chicago Press.

Vainer, C. B. (2013). Megaeventos, meganegócios, megaprotestos. Available at: www.ettern. ippur.ufrj.br/ultimas-noticias/196/mega-eventos-mega-negocios (Accessed 7 October 2018).

Vale, L. J., & Bass Warner, S. (2001). *Imaging the City: Continuing Struggles and New Directions*. New Brunswick, NJ: Rutgers University Center for Urban Policy Research.

Ward, S. V. (1998). *Selling Places: The Marketing and Promotion of Towns and Cities, 1850–2000*. London: Routledge.

Watts, J. (2015). The Rio Property Developer Hoping for a $1bn Olympic Legacy of his Own The *Guardian*, 4 Aug.

Wright, T. (1997). *Out of Place Homeless Mobilizations, Subcities, and Contested Landscapes*. Albany, NY: State University of New York Press.

Zeiderman, A. (2006). *The Fetish and the Favela: Notes on Tourism and the Commodification of Place in Rio de Janeiro, Brazil*. Stanford, CA: Stanford University Press.

8 Geographies and branding impacts of non-metropolitan music festivals in the Western Cape province of South Africa

Ronnie Donaldson and Henry Duckitt

Introduction: let's get festive

The social, economic and cultural impacts (both negative and positive) of festivals and events on non-metropolitan areas are well known (Arcodia and Whitford 2006; Connell and Gibson 2004; Curtis 2011; Davies 2015; De Bres and Davis 2001; Derrett 2003; Duffy 2000; Duxbury and Campbell 2011; Gibson 2007; Gibson and Connell 2005; Gibson et al. 2009, 2011; Ma and Lew 2012; O'Sullivan and Jackson 2002; Sharpe 2008; Waterman 1998). In a South African context, Donaldson (2018) provided a comprehensive literature review of academic research into festivals and events outside the big cities and metropolitan areas in the country. The bulk of the studies reviewed focused on the economic impacts on both town and regional scales. Other studies have looked at market segmentations and the management issues of organising festivals. Furthermore, there have been investigations of motives for attending festivals as well as the experiences and viewpoints of festival attendees, the socio-demographic characteristics of attendees and their visiting patterns and who spends what at the events. Issues of the greening of festivals (e.g. recycling waste, limiting use of energy) have received little attention. Some research has paid attention to the contribution of the transformational nature of art festivals as platforms for debating the goals and values of society. A single study has investigated the VICE model (visitors, industry, community and environment) as a crucial success factor in the sustainable development of any tourism destination. Festivals do have a tendency to quickly and efficiently build an image for the destination and, as a result, can put it on the proverbial map as a tourist destination (Gibson et al. 2011). However, with the exception of Donaldson (2018), there has been a paucity of research into aspects pertaining to branding and place identity through events and festivals. The aim of the chapter is thus twofold. First, to map the nature and extent of music festivals in the Western Cape province of South Africa. Second, to provide a brief qualitative review of how the small town of Oudtshoorn hosts an annual classical music festival to counter the image and brand the town is associated with: namely, the hosting of an annual, mainly Afrikaans-speaking national arts festival.

Preparing for the festival: a literature review

A significant growth and variation in music tourism was observed towards the end of the last century. Indicative of this was an apparent growth in a new phase of popular music. The renewed interest in folk or community music and the continuation of classical music were key attraction points for many "sophisticated" destinations (Gibson and Connell 2007). Literature shows that an increased interest in festivals within tourism geography and cultural studies may be due to the growth in pursuits of novel pleasures and experiences in a materialistic and leisure-driven society (Davies 2015; Connell and Gibson 2004; Gibson and Connell 2005, 2007). These novel pleasures and experiences may oftentimes be found within the sensuous constructions of tourist destinations (Duffy 2000). Music tourism arguably forms the quintessence of the sensuous. Music has become a new motivating factor for travel, rather than simply being a supplementary part thereof (Gibson and Connell 2007). Thus, music tourism takes place when people are motivated to travel, at least in part, for the pursuit of music, be it to concerts, opera houses or festivals (Gibson and Connell 2007). Together with an increase in mobility and leisure time, these new types of travel have become ever more viable. Furthermore, the growth in affluence in the 1990s resulted in the expansion of the tourist market from being purely for the elite to one of mass consumption. Music tourism no longer fills only one significant niche (classical music) but now incorporates numerous types and genres (Gibson and Connell 2005). It becomes apparent, then, that music forms a crucial part in the new cultural turn in tourism geography upon referring to Gibson and Connell's (2005, p. 14) statement that "music is both a key cultural industry, and a text through which places are known and represented, providing new sources of images and sounds for tourism promotion". Music tourism will always be a social construct which cannot clearly be separated from other types of tourism, and it is evident that music tourism is related to various industries, such as entertainment, events management and hospitality (Gibson and Connell 2005).

According to Wynn and Yetis-Bayraktar (2016, p. 204), "mayors and other place marketers in recent years have embraced music festivals as a fast, temporary, and affordable way to promote the image of a city – a less expensive alternative to investing in costly and permanent cultural infrastructure." Getz (2014) identified five attributes of the successful development of a planned event. Firstly, they can attract tourists in the off-peak season, extend the tourist season or create one where there is a lack of tourists but the potential for tourism. Secondly, they can play an important role in the creation or promotion of a certain place's image or otherwise be branded as a festive place. Thirdly, they can act as a catalyst for development. Fourthly, they have the potential to animate attractions as well as venues and spaces which tourists are attracted to through the duration of the event. Lastly, they can assist greatly in the marketing of a specific place. There are also those who argue that economic growth and place promotion are not necessarily the primary functions of festivals (Visser 2005). On the other hand, socio-cultural aspects are shown to play a vital role in conceptualizing the nature of festival tourism. According to Ma and Lew (2012, p. 13), "participation or attendance at a festival, in comparison to a non-festival event, is more likely to be a liminal experience that takes people out of their mundane workaday world, while also offering opportunities for socio-cultural affirmation and personal transformation." Historically, major festivals were associated with uncommon sights and experiences with an emphasis on the sensual, drawing on the plethora of sounds, colours and sights different to those of ordinary urban life (Davies 2015). Consequently, they added to the range and character of experiences otherwise not encountered within everyday life. It is in this context that the seminal work of Schulze (1995) and subsequently Cudny (2016) argue that experience value is replacing use and monetary values. In Western societies, therefore, to live and experience mean basically the same thing.

Table 8.1 differentiates between three types of music festivals on the basis of the genesis, demographic and symbolic significance attached to a festival and displays the spatial tendencies of each festival type. The beginning of *youth music festivals* (around the 1960s) provided the audience not only with music, but also with spaces where identities could be acknowledged and strengthened (Curtis 2011). Instead of an economic imperative, these festivals arose out of the new social practices of contemporary times with the emphasis on transgressive behaviour and the challenge to orthodoxy generally exhibited by the youth of the time. According to Gibson and Connell (2005, p. 217), these festivals provide the opportunity to "get away with more risqué behaviour than in other spheres of life – drug consumption, public nudity, protest and performance – an expressiveness not permitted in domestic and public spaces". This alternative space acts as the tourism product for some. *Classic music festivals* are, to a large degree, typically considered an elitist activity. However, there is evidence that the middle classes are showing more interest in these types of events, arguably due to the ambition of these classes to progress in social status. The symbolic significance of these types of festivals is used by promoters to attract the "right" type of demographic, such as older professionals and tourists with higher disposable incomes. It is this attached symbolism that instils the destination with an element of sophistication (Gibson and Connell 2005). *Community music festivals* are smaller events aimed at specific audiences from a domestic tourist market or at enhancing the cultural awareness and experiences of local populations. These festivals are less concerned with economic imperatives and focus more on the celebration of community and tradition (Gibson and Connell 2005). As a result, their "ideal tourist" originates from the region and has the tendency to promote their tourism product through offerings celebrating local or traditional culture.

Placemaking is a concept "that transcends the boundaries of potential effects of cultural urban policies on space" (Rota and Salone 2014, p. 92). According to Sevin (2013), it is no longer possible to separate destination marketers and public authorities as the sole producers of brand images and the public as consumers, although the public does not incorporate formal brand elements into their destination accounts; destination branding is now a negotiation process among various stakeholders and audiences that generate a diversity of images. Events

Table 8.1 Typology of music festivals

	Youth music festivals	Classical music festivals	Community music festivals
Genesis	In the counterculture of 1960s, these types of festivals emerged out of the challenge to orthodoxy.	The Grand Tour in the 18th century saw a rise in the visitation to musical destinations such as Italy. Out of this, classical music festivals evolved with regards to music skill acquisition and enhancing the "high" culture sought after on the Grand Tour.	Community festivals have been hosted since antiquity. Although music does not play a big part therein, it has always been an accompanying part.
Demographic and attached symbolic significance	Younger crowd in pursuit of liminal experiences, usually associated with an alternative space for social and sexual interaction, drug consumption and musical expression.	Originally, these were the pursuit of an older, elite and more educated crowd, but they have become more popular among the middle classes and those with ambitions to upward social mobility in contemporary times.	Mixed crowd. Family orientated. Usually aimed at a domestic market as opposed to the liminal experiences sought after at youth music festivals, they tend to emphasize heritage and tradition.
Spatial tendencies	A strong tendency towards "placelessness", i.e. there is a trend that these festivals occur more frequently outside of towns than in the towns themselves.	A tendency towards place-specific festivals; however, the trend is for these types of festivals to occur outside towns (at event venues, for example).	A strong tendency towards place-specific festivals; however, it is not uncommon for these festivals to occur outside towns.

Source: Adapted from Curtis (2011), Davies (2015), Gibson and Connell (2005), Gibson et al. (2011) and Ma and Lew (2012)

are therefore seen as part of the placemaking process comprising three important elements: "the physical city itself, the lived experience of place that is shared among the stakeholders or users of the city and the symbolic imaginings of the city that are projected through city images and brands" (Richards 2017, p. 10). The arts have much to offer the reinvention of places, as Gibson (2010, pp. 66–67) remarked:

> Filtering artistic attempts to re-make places are three key competing pressures: first, the demands of regional development managers, treasury bureaucrats and council general managers for accountability, 'hard data' and measurable outcomes; second, desires of local residents, non-profit organisations and community development specialists to use the arts as a means to promote social inclusion and recognition of social difference; and third, professional concerns of artists themselves to produce creative expressions that advance practice, experiment, and/or challenge prevailing norms. Often, these pressures are thought of as irreconcilable or incorrigible.

Placemaking is a complex phenomenon, a process of actions and an "open-ended process of complex interactions between physical spaces (themselves a generating process) and the people inhabiting/producing those spaces/places. It is about the never-ending dynamism of physical environments, the behaviours of people, the subjective and somatic experiences of the body-in-place where perception, memory, language, the senses, representations, beliefs, values, spirituality, ritual (and so forth) are invested with the symbolic in a process of continuous enactment and articulation" (Staiff and Bushel 2017, p. 57). In contemporary times, music festivals connect the audience and the performers within a unique setting of marvel and wonder where the "festival space itself creates a dialogue of musical communication and emotional and affective responses" (Curtis 2011, p. 280). It is, therefore, this sensuous construction of place as part of the place-making process which provides the tourist with a "soundscape" to interact with. It is the soundscape that allows the listener to create a musical identity and, in relation to others sharing the space, make sense of it in a collective manner. However, the musical identity of the listener and, by extension, the capacity to construct collective meaning out of it, like that of culture in contemporary times, are more brief and more involved with one another than in the past due to the global/local nexus to be relational rather than contrasting (Connell and Gibson 2004). An authentic soundscape for all should, therefore, not be sought as this is highly improbable.

Getting there – on route to the festival: methodology and study area

Whereas previous research on festivals in South Africa focused mainly on their social and economic impacts, our focus is on a spatiality approach: namely to generate an overall picture of the prevalence of non-metropolitan festivals in one of South Africa's nine provinces, the Western Cape. Mapping festivals enable spatial analysis of their distribution, regional clusterings and differentiation. As a starting point, a comprehensive database had to be constructed on annual music festival events in the non-metropolitan areas of the province. For this an extensive web search, combined with emailing regional tourism offices in the province for information, was conducted to create the database. The festivals were then segmented into three categories: youth music festivals, classical music festivals, and community music festivals (see Table 8.1). The relevant information was geocoded and mapped in ArcGIS accordingly. One classical music festival was selected as case study. In the remaining section of the chapter, a brief qualitative review of the festival's contribution in the placemaking process in Oudtshoorn is presented. Classical music was initially part of the annual national arts festival, the Klein Karoo Kunstefees (KKNK), but the decision was made to create a unique short event that runs over a weekend to attract visitors to the town during the winter. Personal interviews were conducted with the festival organizer and the town's tourism manager to get a better understanding of the festival's characteristics (funding, promotion, marketing), its connections to the broader region and the future prospects of the festival and the territory in terms of branding.

Geographies of non-metropolitan music festivals: Western Cape province

Cudny (2014, p. 141) remarked that, from a geographical point of view, an often-neglected yet important focus of festival research is the time-space analysis aspects. Further to his call, and for the purpose of this section, location maps were created to reflect on the spatial distribution of festivals in non-metropolitan Western Cape.

Generally, music festivals have been accepted to be the most common as well as the oldest type of destination for music tourism. The Three Choirs Festival of England claims the label of Europe's oldest festival and dates back to 1724 (Gibson and Connell 2005). Musicians (often tourists themselves) were regularly part of festivals celebrating community values around important turning points of the season or celebrating traditional heritage. These heritage and seasonal aspects revolved around the celebrations of equinoxes, harvests, village fairs and gatherings of a social nature. Musical performances provided the opportune breakaway from the routine of day-to-day activities (Gibson and Connell 2005).

A total of 139 music festival events were identified to have taken place in the province outside the Cape Town metropolitan area in 2015 (which served as the base year for this investigation). Music festivals that are adding most value to place branding in the province are those that appeal to festival attendees attracted from outside the province. These include the popular music festival Rocking the Daisies in Darling in the spring, as well as the two music festivals in Stellenbosch: the Stellenbosch International Chamber Music Festival in the winter and the Oude Libertas Summer Season. All three of these events are within easy reach of Cape Town and also attract international performers. The festival outside the small town of Darling has become the "opposition" festival to the internationally recognized Oppikopi Festival (Kruger and Saayman 2009) held in the Limpopo province on the complete opposite side of the country.

Of the three broad types investigated (see Table 8.1), youth music festivals (48 percent) made up almost half of music festivals, with classical music festivals being the fewest (19 percent). Seasonality is crucial in the event tourism industry. According to Getz (2008, 2014), the peaking of events usually take place in the summer months, with a decrease in winter months. Figure 8.1 depicts the monthly spread of music festivals in the province. A peaking of events in the summer months is evident, with spring (September marks the beginning of spring season) showing a sudden increase in the number of events hosted. The celebratory aspect attached to this seasonality can be traced to antiquity. Certain events celebrate the passing of the seasons and acknowledge the "rhythms and mysteries" of life (Davies 2015, p. 544). It is further revealed that festivals occurring during spring have a greater tendency to brand their events as turning of the season festivities and celebrations, such as the iPotsoyi Spring Festival, Sprung and Wolfkop

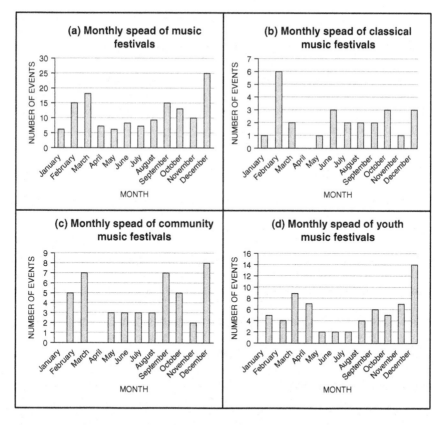

Figure 8.1 (a–d) Monthly spread of music festivals in the Western Cape in 2015
Source: Author's elaboration

Weekender: Power Flower Picnic, which indicate the celebratory symbolism attached to these festivals according to season.

Classical music festivals have a partially consistent monthly spread but with an outlier month in the summer (February) hosting twice as many events as any other month. More classical music festivals are, indeed, hosted in summer than in any other season, yet they display fewer events during the summer than the other two categories. In this regard, Gibson and Connell's (2005) remarked that classical music festivals receive increasing competition from other types and genres of music festivals. However, it should be considered that these festivals complement each other, in that they provide different spaces for differing socio-cultural groups (Sharpe 2008). This seasonality of demand might warn against the intermittency of the benefits accrued on annual basis from individual festivals. Nevertheless, the potential for year-round planning work exists.

Although seasonality of demand plays a vital role in the motivational aspects of hosting events at certain locations, other spatial tendencies have been shown to play a much larger role. For example, Rofe and Winchester (2011) argue that localities positioned within a day-trip distance to metropolitan areas are ideally situated to attract an increased number of tourists, in comparison to areas which are farther away and, consequently, less accessible. This spatial tendency is further endorsed by considering that tourist hubs within the pleasure periphery have increasingly been promoting their peripheral areas as an alternative to sun, sea and sand tourism (Scott 2000). It is the pleasure periphery, therefore, that has the potential to successfully host desired events and attractions for an expanding urban clientele. This spatial trend is noticeable in Figure 8.2. An agglomeration of music festivals near the metropole is observable, with the Winelands District municipal region forming the largest clustering of events. Gibson et al. (2011) assert that where larger towns had numerous festivals, potential existed for sustained annual employment across a broad range of industries which play a supporting function, such as hospitality and events management. This could arguably be the case for the Winelands District municipal region, as can be seen in Figure 8.2, since an agglomeration of festivals occurs in that specific area. According to Visser (2003), the dominant pattern of tourism development in South Africa has occurred in a spatially uneven manner with few positive tourism knock-on effects reaching areas outside the main tourism centres. This observation is evident in Figures 8.3 and 8.4. Music festivals are less prevalent the farther one travels from the Cape Town metropole. In addition to the metropole playing such a fundamental role in the spatial manifestation of festivals, certain other factors have been identified. By drawing on Australian examples, (Gibson et al. 2011, p. 6) "places with the most festivals tended to be large regional towns outside capital cities, regions reliant upon tourism industries or coastal lifestyle regions with mixes of tourism and retiree in-migration." Such places usually have populations large enough to validate a festival tourism industry with a lower risk of failure (Gibson et al. 2011; Rofe and Winchester 2011; Scott 2000; Visser 2003). As for regions reliant on tourism industries, it can be argued that Knysna, Plettenberg Bay and Greyton represent such tendencies. Lastly, places such as Hermanus and places

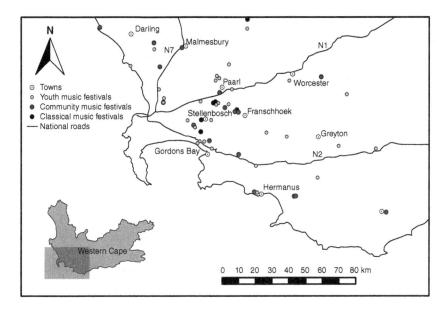

Figure 8.2 Festivals occurring at the southern extent of the Western Cape province

Source: Author's elaboration

Note: For each category, the size and the colour of the points indicating the spatial properties is different (for example, the youth music festivals are indicated in light grey and are 14 pp, the community music festivals are indicated in dark grey and are 18 pp, and the classical music festivals are indicated in black and are 22 pp). Furthermore, the largest category (youth music festivals) is represented by the smallest points. This is done to avoid cluttering the figures with data from the largest category, as well as to clearly indicate the smallest category. A further rationale for the differing sizes of the three categories indicated on the maps in Figures 8.2–8.4 is that certain festivals from different categories may happen in the same setting but at a different time, so data may be lost due to the stratified nature of the GIS software used. Thus, the points are made different sizes to show whether a setting hosts more than one category of festivals.

near Mosselbay, which also hosts numerous festivals annually, represent regions with a growing retiree population situated near the coast. The potential for tourism development in the Karoo and the West coast interior is far less significant (Ferreira 2007).

Music festivals are places where the social routines of ordinary life are transformed by people who would otherwise not gather in such a fashion (Gibson et al. 2011). As such, festivals are sites where daily life gets animated for the period of the festival event. The unusual gathering of people and the animation of place in the promotion of the tourism product are depicted in one of the investigated music festivals' promotional strategies as follows:

> Escape to the River Republic. A place where time slows and feet are moved by the rhythm of the river and the movements of the sun. Where

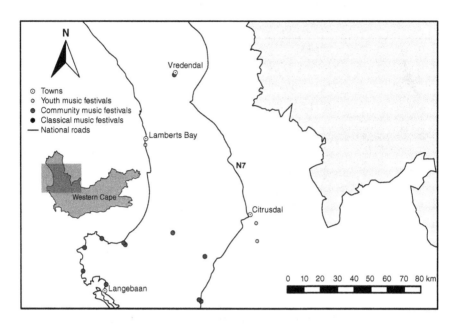

Figure 8.3 Festivals occurring at the northwestern extent of the Western Cape province

Source: Author's elaboration

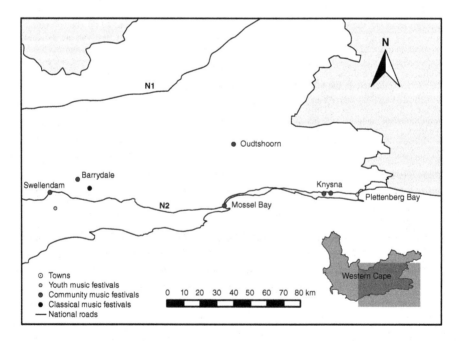

Figure 8.4 Festivals occurring at the eastern extent of the Western Cape province

Source: Author's elaboration

people laugh and scream and dance and dream, and there's no hate or sadness or horror or badness, just joy and electro, and light and delight. Catch your most loved local musicians, both DJs and bands, and play chess on a dance floor quite chequered and grand. Meet new people and make friends for life, and for a while forget your city strife. Let the music keep playing with a shake and a shiver, and you'll be ever so grateful you escaped to the river.

(River Republic 2016)

This animation of place arguably relies heavily on commodification to attract the "ideal tourist". It has been argued that commodification first occurs primarily through the promotion of the destination, making use of the media and travel brochures and, secondly, through the processes by which the cultural and natural artefacts of the destination are personally experienced upon visitation (Williams 2009).

In the categories of youth music festivals and classical music festivals, it is shown that aspects of the natural landscape are heavily drawn from as part of the tourism promotional strategies. With the necessary environmental qualities at its disposal, the Western Cape province is ideally suited to develop its alternative tourism industry in rural locations (Viljoen and Tlabela 2007). Through enabling the celebration of nature, seasonal transitions and culture, music festivals are uniquely equipped to draw on rural commodification for tourism promotion (Gibson et al. 2011). This is, in part, evident in the rising number of organizers marketing their festivals under the "outdoor events" section on websites aimed at promoting local tourism and for organizers to promote their events with an emphasis on *outdoor* in the name of the event. For example, Sunflower Outdoor Music Festival, Spilt Milk Presents: Tech-It Outside, Musiek Oppie Lande, Ultranoize: Outdoor Festival, Eden Experience: State of Happiness and Into the Wild: The Awakening. Festivals enable the celebration of nature (Gibson et al. 2011). Here, reference is made to the perceived strategies involved in the creation of the tourism product for one of the event organizing companies: namely, Vortex Trance Adventures. They have posted the following on their festival website:

This realm exudes harmony, beauty and peace – it echoes the magic of the trees, hidden forest creatures and the mysteries of the ancients. With its idyllic mountain views, it is completely secluded and sacred, making it an ideal sanctuary for river parties, gatherings and psychedelic adventures. Located at the Endless River beneath the mystical mountain ranges, one can hear the cry of the African Fish Eagle, admire the sounds of the forest and marvel the oak trees which have been worshipped by travellers for decades. Shaded camping for every tent and a beautiful river to cool off in are just a few of the attractions hidden inside this magical venue.

(Vortex Trance Adventures 2016)

To conclude, music may be a way in which tourist spaces are conceptualized and controlled in numerous ways:

- The capacity of the festival to attract certain people and deter others is a process in which it is established who belongs and who does not. For example, residents may cringe at the styles of music being hosted in their near vicinity as it may represent symbolic narratives that they are not comfortable with (Gibson and Connell 2007).
- On the other hand, intricate relations between locals and visitors can facilitate the tourist experience and subtly shape musical spaces (Saldanha 2002).
- If local events are mainly community driven, a good argument is put forth for not exploiting them (Getz 2008).
- Too many music festivals in the Western Cape are celebrating, instead of emphasising community values.

Oudtshoorn case study: contrasting placemaking through festivals

The "ostrich capital of the world", the small town of Oudtshoorn, with just over 60,000 inhabitants, is located in the Western Cape province (see Figure 8.4). The town is synonymous with the ostrich industry, the Cango Caves and the Klein Karoo Nasionale Kunstefees/the Little Karoo National Arts Festival (KKNK). The town's ostrich industry dates back to 1864 when ostrich feathers became fashionable accessories among European nobility. The feather boom era has long passed, but has since 1994 (a significant year in South African history – the year in which the first democratic elections were held after centuries of colonial and apartheid white rule) the town again has become "famous". Now, it is famous for hosting one of the two biggest national arts festivals in the country, the KKNK, which takes place annually in the month of Easter. In addition to the KKNK, the town also host one other national festival: namely, the Klein Karoo Klassique (KKK).

Cultural activities such as repeater festivals create "meaning as they are concerned with expression, celebration and achievement. They thus embody the identity and values of a place. They express local distinctiveness" (Landry 2004, p. 12). Hence, placemaking is generally contextualized at three different scales. First is how governments and organizations attempt to present places to the wider world to attract inward investment and regeneration. In this regard, as host of one of the premier national art festivals in the country (KKNK), it is therefore not surprising that one of the seven strategic objectives of the Oudtshoorn municipality is the promotion of the town as an arts and culture economic town creating economic and social opportunities through the arts and heritage. As the festival has become such a well-known brand, the promotion and association of arts and culture with Oudtshoorn have become synonymous. The second pertains to how architects and planners attempt to create meaningful and authentic places through urban design. The third is how local community groups (such as residents' associations, heritage associations and social media) shape the places they live in.

Coghlan et al. (2017, p. 66) stated that "the act of placemaking through strategies such as events depends upon the attitudes and actions of precinct managers and event organisations."

There is a range of role players in the placemaking process, which includes governments, corporate bodies, non-profit organizations (NPOs) and community groups (AS and A LEVEL Delivery Guide 2016). One such NPO, *Kunste Onbeperk*, is the organization that annually offers the KKNK, the Klein Karoo Klassique and several workshops and programmes as part of the Klein Karoo Arts Academy. The purpose of the company is the promotion, encouragement and conservation of arts, culture and habits, mainly through Afrikaans. The company's vision is to be a leader in and through the arts. They are based in Oudtshoorn. In creating a unique event such as the KKK, major corporations and donors are eager to sponsor official events (Wynn and Yetis-Bayraktar 2016). It is thus not surprising that the KKK's main sponsor is the Rupert Music Foundation. The chairperson of the foundation is Hanneli Rupert, who performed in orchestras around the world and is the daughter of the later Anton Rupert, a South African billionaire businessman, philanthropist and conservationist. Insofar as the municipality's contribution is concerned, a budget of R20,000 has been set aside to advertise both the KKNK and the KKK in 2019 (Oudtshoorn Municipality 2018). It is interesting to note that there is no mention of either of these two events in the current Spatial Development Framework or the two most recent Integrated Development Plans of the municipality, indicating that the marketing, promoting and stakeholder inputs at the start of the KKNK have now completely shifted to the organizers. Typically, a strategic vision is needed to ensure that the event programme gains and maintains meaning for all the stakeholders in the town.

The KKNK is an Afrikaans language arts festival. The festival includes both the visual and the performing arts and is officially recognized by the South African government as a national arts festival. In 2019 the town will host the 25th annual festival. The festival includes visual and performing arts such as cabaret, musical theatre, classical music, jazz and popular music, bringing more than 250 productions to the stage and including more than 1,000 artists. Public streets are closed in the centre of town, and public and private buildings and facilities are used as venues. The KKNK, however, has a specific brand and image and is not really reflective of South African society as a whole. Local businessman Nic Barrow and a former public relations manager for the South African publishing firm Naspers, Andrew Marais, conceived the festival. From the start, the festival's primary target audience has been the country's Afrikaans-speaking community. Available statistics on the KKNK for 2015 show that the total economic impact on the town was R64,693,485, which is by far the biggest impact of a national festival on any city or town in the country, attracting festival goers from the province (Western Cape 53 percent); neighbouring Eastern Cape (16 percent) and the economic heartland of the country, Gauteng province (14 percent). The festival specifically appeals to an educated audience (72 percent have a post-school qualification) and to those in the age groups 18 to 25 (28 percent), 26 to 35 (22 percent) and 36 to 50 (25 percent). The town hosted, on average, 33,278 visitors per day for the duration of the event, and festivals goers would stay on average 5.6 days at the event (https://diehoorn.com/mening/lyk-die-invloed-van-die-kknk-syfers/).

In view of criticism of the festival as merely an "Afrikaner bazaar" and not a cultural festival, Hauptfleisch (2003, p. 274) remarked that

> it was abundantly clear that Oudtshoorn was almost brazenly and stereotypi-
> cally declaring itself to be a vast and sprawling fête or bazaar. A place for
> speakers of Afrikaans to feel at home, to interact, laugh, argue, philosophise,
> eat, drink, be merry and engage with each other across their variety.

Although the KKNK's identity is strongly linked to the geographic region the Little Karoo, "a relatively small part of what makes up the arts festival is pro-
duced or procured locally" and this "is in line with observations internationally that festivals, as they grow in size are becoming standardized, often because of a focus on economic success, and usually at the cost of local needs and products" (Stander et al. 2018, p. 235). They argue that "the sense of place is more elusive than anticipated, because the standardization and duplication act against the local flavour and content which is supposed to characterize the festival" (Stander et al. 2018, p. 235). Notwithstanding these critiques of the KKNK, the study of Pretorius, Viviers and Botha (2014) tested the actual general perception of festival attendees of the KKNK and found that festival attendees have become "accus-
tomed to what an arts festival offers, perhaps by seeing or by experiencing the artistic products, activities and performances repeatedly" (Pretorius et al. 2014, p. 177). Despite the finding that the festival provides for a quality arts experi-
ence, they claim that the event also serves a purpose for socialization and that "some festival visitors barely attend the festival shows and productions, only attending the festival for its stalls, restaurants and pubs" (Pretorius et al. 2014, p. 160). Despite the somewhat negative social constructions to public space and the reworking of rules (Van Heerden 2011), the KKNK's attendees can, according to Saayman et al. (2012), be categorized into three clusters – escapists, festi-
val junkies and culture seekers – each cluster having their own tastes and needs. The KKNK communication channels vary from their Facebook page (32,000 followers), Twitter (18,000 followers) and their dedicated website to receiving wide publicity on the dedicated Afrikaans television channel on satellite (Kyk-
Net) throughout the year (but particularly a month or so leading up to the event and then during and immediately after the event).

Unlike the mother festival (the KKNK), the annual Klein Karoo Klassique (KKK) music festival has been running since 2009 over a weekend in August (coinciding with a national public holiday), which is the town's dead tourist sea-
son (midwinter). Although there is no consensus between the organizers of the event and the local tourism office regarding the actual impact of the event on the town during the winter, it does add to the inflow of visitors during an otherwise low period. Major promotion outlets are popular regional- and national-focused travel websites such as Traveller 24, Winelandsweb and the very popular Cape Town Magazine website.[1] One of the founding members of the KKNK decided

that the town needed another festival, one specifically focusing on classical music. They did not conceive the festival to attach a different meaning to the placemaking process of the town. It is the type of event that contributes to the formation of a different image of the town than that formed via the KKNK. The primary purpose is to attract visitors to the town during winter. However, the branding of the festival deliberately steers away from the KKNK image and brand, calling it a festival

> with world class classical music, delectable cuisine, blue ribbon wines and local art. The programme offers a divine medley of chamber music and symphonic music performed by several ensembles and soloists. We are very privileged in that we are able to welcome several internationally known and (in most instances) also celebrated soloists in Oudtshoorn.
>
> (www.oudtshoorn.com/default.php?ipkCat=63&sid=63)

Marketing of the festival in the Cape Town Magazine sees an emphasis on the natural environment of the Little Karoo and the stylishness associated with the event itself:

> With its beautiful Swartberg Mountains and evergreen fynbos-fragrant landscape, the wintry Karoo is the ideal location for this festival; the uncomplicated beauty of the area complements the simple pleasure that comes from listening to superb music. The Klassique is not just about the music though, it also offers a feast for the senses, including beautiful fine art for the eyes and delicious delights for the tongue. So, prepare for a wonderful weekend of culture in the colourful Klein Karoo.
>
> (www.capetownmagazine.com/klein-karoo-klassique)

Similarly, the Traveller 24 website states that

> The Klein Karoo Klassique (not the Klein Karoo National Kunstefuus) focuses more on the finer things to be found in South African art. The event is a celebration of classical music, food, wine and art.
>
> (www.traveller24.com/Explore/Family/
> Take-a-road-trip-to-the-Klein-Karoo-Klassique-20150804)

In addition, the Winelandsweb promotes the festival as follows:

> Classical music, wine, food and art – If art and music are to bring a message, it should be the mirror of gifted personalities who, by virtue of their originality of vision and style, show us how much richer life is than it seems to the ordinary citizen.
>
> (www.winelandsweb.co.za/klein-karoo-klassique-in-oudtshoorn/)

These examples of marketing material emphasize the deliberate attempt to portray the event as "classy". It is not about the festival venue and music only; great emphasis is also placed on the immediate region, its cuisine and ambience. These marketing sources deliberately try to lure the rich to visit the town in the winter. One can even speculate that they are trying to attract those who would not normally attend the bigger KKNK festival. Successful brands can create strong, positive and lasting impressions to identify quality and satisfaction, which can create trust in the brand among attendees. The result will be repeater purchasing or visiting of the tourism product or brand. In a different setting, Dobson (2010, p. 111) observed that "classical music audience research at a chamber music festival has in fact demonstrated a close relationship between social and musical enjoyment with this particular audience valuing a sense of collectivity and community in their listening experiences, but also feeling valued themselves as 'active participants' in a socio-musical event." Such attitudes have similarly been developed at the KKK festival through a number of specific factors such as the concert venue's intimate setting (a historic sandstone church) and the presence of a core group of loyal audience members who have attended since the festival's inception. It is thus not about attracting large numbers of attendees. The event has just over 2,000 Facebook followers. The event website is largely inactive. There are only around ten performances, and attendees come from across the country (mainly from Johannesburg, Cape Town and Pretoria) (personal interview, Theart 2018). In the absence of statistical data, according to the tourism manager of the town, the event is specifically promoted nationally and not only regionally; however, the bulk of the attendees are from the region and province (personal interview, Barnard 2018).

Conclusion: cleaning up the site

Branding is considered to create added value and meaning to a place (Andersson 2014). In addition, it promotes both tangible and intangible attributes to compete for a share of consumers, tourists, businesses, investments and skilled workers. Place branding differentiates one tourism spot from similar tourism experiences in other locales. It furthermore promotes cultural distinctiveness and uniqueness of experience. The branding of festival places and regional destinations can be a more intricate and challenging process than the branding of services and goods. Places are "often more multidimensional in nature than products and services; the stakeholders involved are typically more heterogeneous than consumer segments; the branding process may be fraught with politics; brand equity and brand loyalty are more difficult to achieve and measure; and funding and marketing budgets may especially be limited" (Pike 2005, p. 259). Creating a brand identity – such as the major Afrikaans cultural festival town in the country – is more likely to be sustainable if place identities are affected, represented and/or contested (Donaldson 2018).

In terms of the geography of music festivals in the province, it was seen that the majority of all types of music festivals take place within easy reach of the province's capital (Cape Town houses almost three quarters of residents in the province). December (peak summer season), the end of summer and beginning of autumn see the most music festivals taking place in the province. Tourist commodification is an important consideration in the creation of a positive identity (De Bres and Davis 2001) and, consequently, has the capacity to build a positive image of rural tourism in the Western Cape. Through music events, rural spaces thus have the potential to use a "soundscape" to attract a diverse range of tourists.

An important value of successful festivals is that they make a strong impact through the media, as they are often presented on TV, in newspapers and magazines, on the Internet, on social media and so on. Although organizing and sponsoring events creates an opportunity to appear in different media (traditional and social) it also lends itself to being branded through these mediums in a specific way. In terms of Anholt's (2008) innovative ideas about place branding or competitive identity, Oudtshoorn has a clear and coordinated communication system in place to influence public opinion – the KKNK receives maximum exposure in all forms of the media every year, especially prior to and during the event. On the other hand, the KKK is a comparatively low-key event that receives exposure mainly in the regional media. Festivals have the potential for positive social and cultural impacts on communities and the branding of small towns in which they are able to quickly and efficiently build an image for the destination (Gibson et al. 2011).

According to estimates, the traditional sources of tourism in Oudtshoorn – namely, the Cango caves and other natural attractions – contribute almost 76 percent of the total income from tourism, followed by the KKNK (22 percent) and 2 percent mainly contributed by sports tourism (www.oudtshoorn.gov.za/sites/default/files/documents/oudtshoorn_economic_profile.pdf). Considering that the festival spans just more than a week, it is safe to argue that one of the key brands associated with the town, the arts, is a central feature of the town's cultural identity. In an attempt to expand this cultural identity, a small-scale music festival was started in the winter season.

The KKNK has been branded as a festival dedicated to Afrikaner (white) culture. However, in the past, numerous attempts have been made by the organizers to break this image (for example, the introduction of English plays, black African artists as main festival fine artists, non-white Afrikaans-speaking people as anchors in debating shows etc.). The hosting of a "classy" event in the winter, around the theme of classical music, is an attempt to break the stereotype associated with the KKNK as a middle-class white Afrikaner festival only. However, the marketing strategies and exposure to media of the two events are very different.

The idea of capitalizing on place marketing using one of the largest national festivals, the KKNK, as a selling point to brand the town as a place for festivals did create an awareness that there is more to the town culturally, than just the KKNK. The KKK festival, albeit very small in comparison, annually has sell-out packages and has established a loyal following, perhaps similar to the KKNK. It does, however, take years to establish a brand and grow a festival. The KKK has been running for ten years but persists in not having parallel events running during the long weekend. The organizers deliberately want to "sell" the event as intimate and classy.

In the case study of Oudtshoorn, it was seen that the town meets six of the geographical perspectives on place branding postulated by Andersson (2014):

- Place branding can be considered a "means to create, change, preserve or regain place identities and place images" (KKNK contributed to a renewed interest in Oudtshoorn as the former ostrich capital of the world) or can be seen as a "window of opportunity" (in the case of KKK) (Andersson 2014, p. 143).
- A second principle relates to a growing urban entrepreneurialism within public administration and urban governance where the seminal work of Harvey (1989) introduced the concept of the neoliberal turn. Local governments and public-private partnerships are commonly the initiators of place branding, while the minority of projects are mainly run by private agents (Andersson 2014). Although the local government provides support in terms of policy and regulations to make the festivals possible, the direct control and overall branding of both festivals have been successfully accomplished by a non-profit organization based in the town. Therefore, it is neither political organizations nor local authorities, but rather private companies, that try to create positive place images.
- There is a theoretical relationship between branding and geography, i.e. how the concept can be understood in geographical terms. As one of the first nationally established arts festivals, the KKNK has established a powerful brand. Since the establishment of this festival, there has been a surge in Afrikaans-orientated arts festivals in the country (e.g. in Bloemfontein, Mbombela, Potchefstroom, Stellenbosch). However, the established KKNK and Oudtshoorn brand provides a meaningful competitive advantage that competitors find it difficult to duplicate or improve on. One can also question the uniqueness of all the subsequent festivals.
- Active participation in and attendance of festivals are usually geared towards the middle classes. Invariably, such events are promoted among the social elites, and the less powerful groups in society are systematically marginalized. The Oudtshoorn festivals are by no means different.
- The role of the creative class (in this case, the NPO *Kunste Onbeperk*) in making the festivals a success should be seen as key factor in successful branding.
- Finally, place branding is also discussed in the "relationship between products and the place-bound symbolic qualities of a geographic region where a product is produced" (Andersson 2014, p. 143). In this regard, in the case of Oudtshoorn, the place (the town) and the brand (KKNK) have become synonymous.

Note

1 Traveller News 24 provides daily updates on travel alerts for travel and medical advisories, flight delays and airport closures as well as the latest events or trends and is linked

to the News24 website of South Africa. Winelands Web promotes events in the Cape Winelands. CapeTownMagazine.com is Cape Town's major online magazine. With almost two thirds of the Western Cape province living in Cape Town, many of its readers see the source as a "trusted friend" that enables them to make exciting discoveries in the region.

References

Andersson, I. (2014). Placing place branding: An analysis of an emerging research field in human geography. *Geografisk Tidsskrift-Danish Journal of Geography*, 114(2), 143–155.

Anholt, S. (2008). Place branding? Is it marketing, or isn't it? *Place Branding and Public Diplomacy*, 4, 1–6.

Arcodia, C., & Whitford, M. (2006). Festival attendance and the development of social capital. *Journal of Convention and Event Tourism*, 8(2), 1–18.

AS and A LEVEL Delivery Guide. (2016). Changing Spaces; *Making Places*. file:///F:/urban%20SA%20city%202018/308342-changing-places-making-spaces-delivery-guide.pdf. www.ocr.org.uk/geography.

Barnard, C. (2018). Personal Interview Conducted with the Tourism Manager, Oudtshoorn and De Rust, 15 October 2018.

Coghlan, A., Sparks, B., Liu, W., & Winlaw, M. (2017). Reconnecting with place through events: Collaborating with precinct managers in the placemaking agenda. *International Journal of Event and Festival Management*, 8(1), 66–83.

Connell, J., & Gibson, C. (2004). World music: Deterritorializing place and identity. *Progress in Human Geography*, 28(3), 342–361.

Cudny, W. (2014). Festivals as a subject for geographical research. *Geografisk Tidsskrift-Danish Journal of Geography*, 114(2), 132–142.

Cudny, W. (2016). *Festivalisation of Urban Spaces. Factors, Processes and Effects*. Cham, Switzerland: Springer.

Curtis, R. (2011). What is Wangaratta to Jazz? The (re)creation of place, music and community at the Wangaratta Jazz festival. In C. Gibson and J. Connell (eds). *Festival Places: Revitalising Rural Australia*. Bristol: Channel View Publications.

Davies, W. K. D. (2015). Festive cities: Multi-dimensional perspectives. In W. K. D. Davies (ed). *Theme Cities: Solutions for Urban Problems*. Calgary: Springer Science.

De Bres, K., & Davis, J. (2001). Celebrating group and place identity: A case study of a new regional festival. *Tourism Geographies*, 3(3), 326–337.

Derrett, R. (2003). Festival and regional destinations: How festivals demonstrate a sense of community and place. *Rural Society*, 13(1), 35–53.

Dobson, M. C. (2010). New audiences for classical music: The experiences of non-attenders at live orchestral concerts. *Journal of New Music Research*, 39(2), 111–124.

Donaldson, R. (2018). *Small Town Tourism in South Africa*. Cham, Switzerland: Springer.

Duffy, M. (2000). Lines of drift: Festival participation and performing a sense of place. *Popular Music*, 19(1), 51–64.

Duxbury, N., & Campbell, H. (2011). Developing and revitalizing rural communities through arts and culture. *Small Cities Imprint*, 3(1), 111–122.

Ferreira, S. (2007). Role of tourism and place identity in the development of small towns in the Western Cape, South Africa. *Urban Forum*, 18, 191–209.

Getz, D. (2008). Event tourism: Definition, evolution, and research. *Tourism Management*, 29, 403–428.

Getz, D. (2014). Timing tourism: MICE, events, and mega-events. In A. Lew, M. Hall and A. M. Williams (eds). *The Wiley Blackwell Companion to Tourism*. West Sussex: John Wiley & Sons Ltd.

Gibson, C. (2007). Music festivals: Transformations in non-metropolitan places, and in creative work. *Media International Australia Incorporating Culture and Policy*, 123, 65–81.

Gibson, C. (2010). Place making: Mapping culture, creating places: Collisions of science and art. *Local-Global: Identity, Security, Community*, 7, 66–83.

Gibson, C., & Connell, J. (2005). *Music and Tourism: On the Road Again*. Clevedon: Channel View Publications.

Gibson, C., & Connell, J. (2007). Music, tourism and the transformation of Memphis. *Tourism Geographies*, 9(2), 160–190.

Gibson, C., Waitt, G., Walmsley, J., & Connell, J. (2009). Cultural festivals and economic development in nonmetropolitan Australia. *Journal of Planning Education and Research*, 20(10), 1–14.

Gibson, C., Connell, J., Waitt, G., & Walmsley, J. (2011). The extent and significance of rural festivals. In C. Gibson and J. Connell (eds). *Festival Places: Revitalising Rural Australia*. Bristol: Channel View Publications.

Harvey, D. (1989). *The Condition of Postmodernity: An Enquiry into the Origins of Cultural Change*. Oxford: Blackwell.

Hauptfleisch, T. (2003). The cultural bazaar: Thoughts on festival culture after a visit to the 2003 Klein Karoo Nasionale Kunstefees (KKNK)in Oudtshoorn. *South African Theatre Journal*, 17, 258–275.

Kruger, M., & Saayman, M. (2009). Travel motives of visitors attending Oppikoppi music festival. *Acta Academica*, 41(1), 56–73.

Landry, C. (2004). *Imagination and Regeneration: Cultural Policy and the Future of Cities*. www.comedia.org.uk.

Ma, L., & Lew, A. A. (2012). Historical and geographical context in festival tourism development. *Journal of Heritage Tourism*, 7(1), 13–31.

O'Sullivan, D., & Jackson, M. (2002). Festival tourism: A contributor to local economic development? *Journal of Sustainable Tourism*, 10(4), 325–342.

Oudtshoorn Municipality. (2018). *Draft IDP Review, 2018–2019*. Oudtshoorn: Oudtshoorn Municipality.

Pike, S. (2005). Tourism destination branding complexity. *Journal of Product and Brand Management*, 14(4), 258–259.

Pretorius, S. C., Viviers, P., & Botha, K. (2014). Is it still about the arts? The perceived contribution of KKNK to the arts. *South African Theatre Journal*, 27(3), 159–182.

Richardson, G. (2017). From place branding to placemaking: The role of events. *International Journal of Event and Festival Management*, 8(1), 8–23.

River Republic. (2016). Escape the City [online]. Available form: www.riverrepublic. co.za/ (Accessed 17 July 2016).

Rofe, M. W., & Winchester, H. P. M. (2011). Marketing a sustainable rural utopia: The evolution of a community festival. In C. Gibson and J. Connell (eds). *Festival Places: Revitalising Rural Australia*. Bristol: Channel View Publications.

Rota, F. S., & Salone, C. (2014). Place-making processes in unconventional cultural practices. The case of Turin's contemporary art festival Paratissima. *Cities*, 40, 90–98.

Saayman, M., Kruger, M., & Erasmus, J. (2012). Finding the key to success: A visitors' perspective at a national arts festival. *Acta Commercii*, 12(1), 150–172.

Saldanha, A. (2002). Music tourism and factions of bodies in Goa. *Tourist Studies*, 2, 43–62.

Schulze, G. (1995). *The Experience Society*. London: Sage.

Scott, J. (2000). Peripheries, artificial peripheries and centres. In F. Brown and D. Hall (eds). *Tourism in Peripheral Areas*. Clevedon: Channel View Publications.

Sevin, E. (2013). Places going viral: Twitter usage patterns in destination marketing and place branding. *Journal of Place Management and Development*, 6(3), 227–239.

Sharpe, E. (2008). Festivals and social change: Intersections of pleasure and politics at a community music festival. *Leisure Sciences*, 30(3), 217–234.

Staiff, R., & Bushel, R. (2017). The "old" and the "new": Events and placemaking in Luang Prabang, Laos. *International Journal of Event and Festival Management*, 8(1), 55–56.

Stander, J. H., Sandham, L. A., & Visser, G. E. (1–5 October 2018). The geographies of arts festivals: Exploring the KKNK (pp. 225–238). In A. Van der Walt, N. Kotze, C. Barker and E. Kruger (eds). *Proceedings of the Biennial Conference of the Society of South African Geographers*. Bloemfontein: University of the Free State.

Theart, H. (19 October 2018). Personal Interview Conducted with the CEO (Acting) of Kunste Onbeperk, Oudtshoorn.

Van Heerden, E. (2011). The social and spatial construction of two South African arts festivals as liminal events. *South African Theatre Journal*, 25(1), 54–71.

Viljoen, J., & Tlabela, K. (2007). *Rural Tourism Development in South Africa: Trends and Challenges*. Cape Town: HSRC Press.

Visser, G. (2003). South African tourism and its role in the perpetuation of an uneven tourism space economy. *Africa Insight*, 33(1), 116–123.

Visser, G. (2005). Let's be festive: Exploratory notes on festival tourism in South Africa. *Urban Forum*, 16, 155–175.

Vortex Trance Adventures (2016). Circle of Dreams [online]. Available from: http://vortex-tranceadventures.co.za/the-venue/ (Accessed 23 June 2016).

Waterman, S. (1998). Carnival for elites? The cultural politics of arts festivals. *Progress in Human Geography*, 22(1), 54–74.

Williams, S. (2009). *Tourism Geography: A New Synthesis*. London: Routledge.

Wynn, J.R. and Yetis-Bayraktar, A. (2016) The sites and sounds of placemaking: Branding, festivalization, and the contemporary city, *Journal of Popular Music Studies*, 28(2), pp. 204–223.

Online sources

www.capetownmagazine.com/klein-karoo-klassique (Accessed 10 November 2018).

https://diehoorn.com/mening/lyk-die-invloed-van-die-kknk-syfers/ [Accessed 10 November 2018].

www.oudtshoorn.com/default.php?ipkCat=63&sid=63 – Oudsthoorn & De Rust Tourism. (Accessed 10 November 2018).

www.traveller24.com/Explore/Family/Take-a-road-trip-to-the-Klein-Karoo-Klassique-20150804 (Accessed 10 November 2018).

www.winelandsweb.co.za/klein-karoo-klassique-in-oudtshoorn/ (Accessed 10 November 2018).

9 Enhancing Macao's tourist destination brand image through cultural festivals

Xu Ye

Introduction

Located on the southern coast of China, Macao Special Administrative Region (SAR) is on the tip of the peninsula formed by the Pearl River estuary on the east and the West River on the west. It is 60 kilometres west of Hong Kong and 145 kilometres southwest of Guangzhou, the capital of Guangdong province. Known as the "Oriental Monte Carlo", Macao is one of the most visited tourism destinations in Asia. This city-state has grown from a modest Portuguese colony into a thriving metropolis that rivals well-established gaming centres like Las Vegas. But in the comparisons with six other gambling destinations on five continents by (Loi and Pearce 2012), it is suggested that consumers perceive Macao as sharing many similarities in terms of entertainment offerings with Genting, Atlantic City, Monte Carlo, Gold Coast and Sun City. However, Macao is regarded as a secondary gambling centre that is somewhat overshadowed by these gambling destinations. In fact, Macao overtook Las Vegas in terms of revenue derived from gambling in 2006 (Zeng 2006). Gaming is clearly important to both the image and the economy of Macao, but the casino image is incomplete as Macao is a much more diverse destination, and there is a need to draw attention to its other attractions and experiences so that a diversified image of Macao can be created (Pacific Asia Travel Association, PATA/Macau Task Force 2012). As Gao (2009) mentioned, reshaping an image is the inevitable way to further develop a destination with the changing of environment and times. Thus, constructing multiple brand images and changing stereotypical views are important considerations to push forward Macao's tourism industry for the long term.

According to the PATA/Macau Task Force (2012), the Macao SAR government is determined to position five branded images with the sequences of historic, leisure tourism and business events, gaming and transport, indicating the significance of non-gaming entertainment (Loi and Pearce 2012). Cultural event tourism combines the features of leisure tourism and business events, jointly representing the two kinds of destination images. On one hand, numerous scholars have realized the effective impacts of special events on destination image marketing (Richards and Wilson 2004; Kaplanidou 2007; Lee and Taylor 2005; Hede 2005; Boo and Busser 2005; Smith 2005; Hallmann and Breuer 2011). On the other hand, tourism stakeholders in Macao share the view that diversified entertainment is desirable for Macao's overall destination brand and image. Providing more diversified tourist entertainment will assist in promoting Macao to the world because of appeal to multiple segments (Loi and Pearce 2012).

Multicultural Macao

The complexity of Macao culture is necessarily related to its history. When the Portuguese started ruling Macao, the Portuguese culture was naturally rooted in its coastal cities and its rural hinterland, and even by the standards of the time, it was a relatively small European power. However, through its seaborne empire, it was able to project its wealth and power and was not only the first European country to have a colony in Asia, but it was also the last. Macao is widely said to be the longest European settlement in Asia, and by the 16th century, Macao had become one of the most important trading ports connecting the East and the West. Thereby, different cultures were brought into Macao as people from Europe, America, the East, Africa and the South and Southeast Asia began to reside here, forming a special situation coexisting with and combining various cultures. Since many distinct cultures can be found in Macao, it is a complicated place from the culture viewpoint: one cannot tell exactly one or two cultures from them all (Yuan 1995).

From the 16th century to its return to China in 1999, Macao has continued as the communication bridgehead between the East and the West. The city attracts people from all over the world, bringing different cultures to this small place: for example, the cultures of the Chinese South of the Five Ridges, western Portugal, East Asia, Latin America, the Portuguese colonies in Africa, Malays from Malacca and East Timor etc. Although the various cultures are blended and crossed, they live together in harmony, keeping their own features and boundaries. This kind of culture image is the one and only in the world, a model of the East-West cultural blend, which is the most prominent characteristic of Macao, different from the surrounding areas. Macao culture has a profound historical value, which can greatly enhance the image of Macao City, making it a world-class city (Zeng 2006). Among the many cultures, three represent the most citizens. These are Chinese traditional culture specializing in the South of the Five Ridges, Portuguese marine culture and Macanese culture, which finally become the mainstream.

The South of the Five Ridges culture

Macao is located on the southeast coast, with the closest connection to Canton. Thus, Macao is more embodied in the culture of South of the Five Ridges (Gao 2012). In the Southern Song Dynasty, there were residents living by fishing in Long Tian and Long Huan, two small fishing villages in Macao. After the middle of Ming Jiajing period, along with the development of foreign trades, the population immigrating to Macao grew continuously (Hao 2011). To date, Chinese residents account for 97 percent of the population, but when taking the ethnic or dialect groups into account, the Fujian and Shanghai people both make up big shares of the new Chinese immigrants in Macao. The Cantonese are the largest subgroup, and they share their customs and living habits with their fellow language speakers along the Pearl River Delta (Wu and Yang 1999).

In geographical terms, South of the Five Ridges refers to Guangdong, Guangxi and Hainan provinces and some places in Hunan and Jiangxi provinces generally. Because of its distance from the capital cities of the different dynasties, the culture of these areas formed unique characteristics that are from the mainstream Chinese culture. For instance, people worship the Heavenly Queen on lunar March 23rd and perform the lion dance on lunar April 8th. Every year when Macao City Fridge Festival is held, tourists from every corner of Pearl River Delta join in the celebrations and all kinds of activities. On the other hand, the four massive population migrations in dynasties brought to the South of the Five Ridges the cultures of the Central Plains and Yangtze River, instilling new characteristics into the original culture (Liang 2003).

Portuguese marine culture

The second representative culture of Macao is Portuguese. The Portuguese established Macao as the Catholic missionary centre in the Far East, as well as the base in East Asia to spread Christianity culture, and it was once known as the "Oriental Vatican" (Hao 2011). Another manifestation is its construction and custom. Many buildings in Macao have a strong feature of southern Europe. The life etiquettes, customs, habits, cuisines and festivals of the local residents also have a typical Portuguese style, branded with the Portuguese imprint (Hao 2011). In the Macao Arts Festival, typical music includes operas and symphonies with Western cultural features, which are provided to tourists and local residents.

Macanese culture

The other representative culture comes from the Macanese, an ethnic group which originated in Macao in the 16th century, consisting mostly of people with Portuguese ancestry combined with Chinese and possibly other ethnic groups. Violent clashes and fierce conflicts can be a feature of societies made up of different ethnic groups living together but not invariably so. The emergence of the Macanese community seems to indicate that people did get along. Most of the time, life was peaceful, but the interaction among different groups is no guarantee for interracial harmony. As the result, the Macanese have become a more or less distinct group, with its own political, social and economic interests to protect (Hao 2011). That sets them apart from both the Portuguese and the Chinese. The Macanese, with the closest relation with Macao history, have the most prominent characteristics. The Macanese culture is a combination derived from the mutual communications with and influence of China, Europe and even Southeast Asia through several centuries. Macanese people can speak fluent Portuguese and Cantonese; they follow diversified customs and celebrate both Portuguese and Chinese festivals.

Macanese people have their unique blended cuisine, which now is also an attraction for many culinary tourists (Hou 2011).

These three cultures are regarded as the cultural backbones of Macao (Zhou 2012). Except for the aforementioned groups, the multicultural variety of Macau is formed by immigrants from Malaysia, Philippine, India, Britain etc. They brought to the city their ethnic cultures as well. For example, the British were also a small but important group in Macao. For instance, the renowned British artist George Chinnery based himself in Macao from 1825 until his death in 1852 and is buried in the Protestant Cemetery in the city (Chinadaily 2018). Although people of different civilizations have different views and beliefs, such differences do not necessarily mean conflict, and conflict does not invariably lead to violence. In a diversified world, different cultures coexist and develop in the same area, forming a multicultural system.

Manifestations of multiculturalism

The multidimensional Macao culture has manifested in many aspects, including the complicated linguistic situation, special architectural features combining the East and the West, various religions in harmony, eclectic Chinese and Western festivals and a unique synthesized gastronomy. All these are regarded as valuable tourism features, which present Macao to visitors with a vivid and attractive image.

Languages

Chinese and Portuguese have been the official languages since the 16th century. When the Portuguese negotiated the handover of Macao to the People's Republic of China, they insisted that Portuguese remain as one of the official languages, the other being Cantonese (Wu and Yang 1999). Macao thus remains part of the Portuguese-speaking or Lusophonia world, and the city remains a point of contact for the Chinese world and a very diverse group of countries that continue to use Portuguese, the largest and most economically dominant being Brazil. The point is that Macao is much more than a simple meeting point of East and West, as it is the hub of a variety of connections to Asia, Latin America and Africa. However, the language in daily use is complicated, with people from different areas speaking different dialects. Cantonese is the most popular spoken language because the majority of the local residents came from the Pearl River Triangle (Hao 2011). Cantonese is spoken in radio programmes, on the television news and in school teaching. According to the demographic survey in 2006, 85.7 percent of the Macao population regarded it as their first language (DSEC 2018). After Cantonese, Mandarin is the second most widely used language after Macao's return and the promotion of communication with mainland China. Besides these, Fujian, Shanghai and Hakka dialects are used frequently in everyday life. Portuguese was the only official language before 1992, widely used in administration, legislation and justice. The aforementioned survey revealed that only 1.5 percent of the population used Portuguese (DSEC 2018). In addition, English is now widely used in social lives and education and, indeed, is spoken by many Portuguese and Macanese inhabitants of Macao. Tagalog (the national language of the Philippines), Vietnamese and Indonesian are used too because there is an increasing demand for household nannies who are mostly from these countries.

Architecture

Architecture, the first image of a place for tourists, represents the local cultural background and exhibits the appeal of a city. Macao is a museum of modern architectures of varied types, combining Portuguese and the South of the Five Ridges styles. Meanwhile, there are many contemporary buildings representing a blend of the East and West through the coexistence of pattern and the extremely high aesthetic and cultural value.

Macao historical buildings are mainly divided into three kinds: one is the South of the Five Ridges–style Chinese buildings, another is Southwestern-style buildings, and the third is a blend of East and West constructions. Under the first category, there are palace-like temples, courtyards and folk houses, A-Ma Temple, Lu Lim Iok Park and Mandarin House. The second category are the buildings of Baroque style in cultural renaissance. Some of the typical examples include provisional municipal council building, the post office, the ruins of Saint Paul's and the government headquarter of Macao. But Macao is a complex place, and even an outstanding piece of European architecture such as the ruins of Saint Paul's has Chinese elements in its façade (Chung 2009). Saint Augustine's Square, the Moorish Barracks and Sun Yat-sen Memorial Hall combine the East and the West constructions, which are reflections of blended cultures. The Historic Centre was approved to be a UNESCO World Heritage Site in 2005. This was important from a marketing point of view and allowed the common recognition of the city in the international scene (UNESCO 2018). Moreover, Portuguese architecture contains North African and Malay elements in Macao and thus differs from the architecture in the European metropolis.

In addition to the historic cultural heritage architecture, modern constructions can be found everywhere. Alongside the Golden Avenue of Taipa, the first-class luxury hotels with modern constructive features stand grandly. They include the Venetian, the Sands Centre, the Four Seasons etc. They have become the second-most visited places for tourists. If the Historic Centre is said to be the reflection of Macao's profound and rich culture, the modern construction group is undoubtedly the symbol of Chinese reform and its opening-up policies, indicating success cooperating with the world.

Religions

The diversified religious culture is a potential tourism asset, attracting tourists of different religious backgrounds. They may take part in the religious ceremonies or join in the festival celebrations. Since the residents have different roots and origins, the religions appear to be different, represented by Taoism, Buddhism, Islam, Catholicism and Protestantism. According to Berlie (2000) 49 percent of Chinese people worshiped various divinities, 37 percent had no religion, 11 percent were Buddhist and 3 percent Christian. More than two thirds of the Chinese population went to temples occasionally. The belief in Mazu (A-Ma) in Macao is viewed as a kind of Taoism, advocating disengaging with the political and social world and returning to a natural state of affairs. Coming from India, Buddhism in Macao began with the establishment of the Pou Tai Un, in the way of enlightenment through prayer and good deeds in the 17th century (Hao 2011). Besides Taoism and Buddhism, Catholicism is another religion with a large number of believers. Catholicism, the official religion of Portugal, was introduced to Macao three years after its occupation by the Portuguese in 1555 (Hao 2011). Thereafter, Macao became the missionary base for spreading Catholicism to China as well as elsewhere in East and Southeast Asia. The large number of churches indicates the success of Christianity in Macao. Huang (2007) mentioned that there were 40,000 Christians in Macao by 1644, mostly Chinese. Compared with the four biggest religions, Bahai, Islam and Mormonism are all relatively small and have been exerting less influence in Macao in particular and in China in general (Zhou and Huang 1994). To sum up, it is striking for so many religions to exist in such a small place. Even with the dual tracks in religion, they seemed to have lived alongside each other largely in harmony, but separately, most of the time (Jin and Wu 2001).

Cuisines

Because more than 90 percent of Macao's population is Chinese, the eight well-known cuisines from the different regions of China can be easily found. The eight culinary traditions of China are divided by region, which are Guangdong cuisine, Sichuan cuisine, Anhui cuisine, Shandong cuisine, Fujian cuisine, Jiangsu cuisine, Hunan cuisine and Zhejiang cuisine. Furthermore, Portuguese and Macanese cuisine, continental food and dishes from other countries attract a lot of consumers too. From the research of individual blogs, pop chop buns, egg tarts, African chicken, double-layer steamed milk and crab porridge are the specialties recommended by a great number of tourists, whether they are the first-time or repeat customers. Based on a survey carried out by the Macao Government Tourism Office (2012), 4.1 percent of mainland tourists and 16.4 percent of Hong Kong tourists came to Macao for the main purpose of tasting food, second after gaming. In other words, "to have special food" is in first place during their stay in Macao. Therefore, the gastronomy is one of the precious heritages loved by all nations and needs a joint effort to develop and promote so as to be another expectation for tourists.

Cultural festivals in Macao

Festivals are often seen as events presenting different cultures and, in the case of multicultural festivals, as emanation of multiculturalism (see Dawson 1991;

Lee et al. 2012b; Cudny and Maiava 2016). As one of the instruments of the development and inculcation of successful multiculturalism, with a combination of features from the Eastern and Western cultures, festivals (of both China and the West) are celebrated and commemorated in Macao. They present local folk and religious feasts and are great international events and activities (Lee et al. 2012a). Undoubtedly, the most important festival is the Chinese Spring Festival, which brings family members together to sit around the table and share a big meal. People squeeze into festive flower markets and buy flowers, decorating their houses in hope of bringing good luck in the next year. Pious prayers bless a good fortune and better life in A-Ma Temple and Kun Iam Temple. The glowing lanterns, fiery dragons, dancing lions, wafts of incense, art performances and fireworks displays turn the streets into a sea of joy. When meeting on the first day of the New Year, people greet one another by speaking lucky words. And children are extremely happy because they can get new clothes, gifts and red envelopes from parents and relatives. Besides the Spring Festival, the Lantern Festival, the Qing Ming Festival, the Dragon Boat Festival, the Double Ninth Festival and the Mid-Autumn Festival are of great significance and meaning. Since 97 percent of the population is Chinese, with many immigrants from Guangdong and Fujian provinces, celebrating Chinese traditional festivals is a way of maintaining the traditions and folk customs of the two provinces. As one of the most representative events, the annual A-Ma Cultural & Tourism Festival gets tens of thousands of tourists' attention and satisfies them with various religious celebrations. Some religious festivals – the Births of the Land God on 2 February, the Heaven Queen on 23 March and Kun Iam on 19 June – which are scarcely known in mainland China are celebrated in Macao (Gao 2012). In addition to the traditional festivals, events with Macao symbols such as the Lotus Flower Festival, the City Fringe Festival, the Food Festival etc. are recurring and booming.

Christmas is as significant to Westerners as the Spring Festival is to the Chinese. When it is the Christmas season, a unique continental European atmosphere fills the whole city, bringing a feeling of staying in Europe. Many bakeries and hotels sell traditional Portuguese Christmas cakes. The streets and even the lanes are decorated with various lamps; churches, whether big or small, are full of followers who recite prayers and sing special Christmas songs. Although it is a Western festival, the Chinese join the celebrations with Western friends. Besides, on Easter, All Soul's Day and the Feast of the Immaculate Conception, traditional Western ceremonies and celebrations are held annually. Since a few rituals are seldom organized in the places nearby, a large number of believers come all the way from Hong Kong, Guangdong or other places to participate in the activities.

Lusofonia Festival: presentation of the event

Lusofonia is a cultural festival. It is a unique combination of exciting delights that immerse residents and tourists in the unique Portuguese culture and Macao people's life while entertaining them with the picturesque setting of the Portuguese-style architectural compounds (IACM 2018). The first Lusofonia Festival was held in 1998, integrated into the programme of activities celebrating the Portuguese National Day on 10 June, honouring the Portuguese-speaking community residents in Macao for their contribution to Macao's development. In Portugal, June is considered to be festival season, with many celebrations held in cities and towns throughout the country. But the weather in Macao during that month is unpredictable – hot and humid, with frequent rainfall. So Lusofonia was moved to autumn, when the weather is cooler, drier and more likely to cooperate.

Organized by the Cultural Affairs Bureau and co-organized by the Macao Government Tourism Office and the Civic and Municipal Affairs Bureau, the festival offers a diversified programme of activities: gastronomy, music and dance shows and games. Every year, more than 150,000 residents and tourists participate in the event and experience the joyful, cheerful and harmonious atmosphere and the multiculturalism of the Macao Special Administrative Region (Macaodaily 2018). Meanwhile, the Portuguese will rally in the Camões Garden in memory of Luis de Camoes, who is regarded as Portugal's national poet and whose works include his masterpiece, *Os Lusíadas* (Moser 1996). At the Taipa House, where the festival takes place, Macao Portuguese-speaking communities from ten countries and regions (including Angola, Brazil, Cape Verde, Guinea-Bissau, Goa etc.) set up booths.

The festival's stakeholders introduce their countries' or regions' traditional music, photographs, arts and crafts, costumes, literature and gastronomy. The festival participants inject vitality in the event, allowing visitors to get to know the Portuguese-speaking countries' and regions' rich cultures in depth. Visitors of all ages can participate in traditional Portuguese games and table football tournaments, as well as experiencing the sensations of the Guia Circuit through a Macau Grand Prix Simulator. Children can take photographs and ride ponies, as well as participating in various children's games. Although Lusofonia has been a recurring event for 30 years, the publicity and its marketing communication is not enough. There is only a radio station installed on site to interact with visitors by broadcasting Portuguese music throughout the day (Macau ICM 2017). People who want to get updated information need to go to the spot or search for information on Facebook. No official website of the event but that of the organizer can be found.

Research methodology

The methodologies of image study can be identified as follows: (1) in the format of collecting information (multidimensional scales, semantic differential or Likert items, free proposal of adjectives and repertory-grid technique) and (2) in the attributes used to assess destination image. Many of these scales are the result of exploratory qualitative studies which identified the important attributes and determinants of the tourist destination image perceived by individuals. These qualitative studies, based on unstructured interviews and focus groups, focus on both the general public and professionals from the tourism sector. But these research reveals a lack of homogeneity among the attributes defining individuals' perceptions. At the same time, it can be observed that, in several instances, the validity and reliability of the scales was not established, casting doubt on their psychometric properties.

Additionally, in examining the methodologies used to measure destination image, it becomes evident that the majority of these studies are conceptualizing destination image in terms of lists of attributes and not in terms of abstract impressions (Echtner and Ritchie 1991). Um and Crompton (1990) once mentioned the importance of the holistic component of destination image in the tourism literature, describing destination image as a gestalt or holistic construct. Reilly (1990) emphasizes the total impression a place makes on the minds of others. Pearce (1988) points out the strong visual component, indicating that each individual can have a unique mental picture of a destination. Moreover, a publicly held common mental picture of a given destination, or stereotype, also exists. Based on Echtner and Ritchie (1991), Choi and Chan (1999) did a qualitative and quantitative assessment of Hong Kong's image as a tourist destination by requiring guests to describe the unique aspects of Hong Kong in their own words presented in a survey.

In any mixed-methods study, the purpose of mixing qualitative and quantitative methods should be clear. This allows the researcher to determine how the analytic techniques relate to one another and how the findings should be integrated (O'Cathain et al. 2008; Onwuegbuzie and Teddlie 2003). For example, standardized scales are adopted to measure the perceptions of functional and psychological attributes, in conjunction with open-ended questions to determine holistic impressions and to capture unique features and auras (Echtner and Ritchie 1991). In addition, there have been many studies on destination image that employed both qualitative and quantitative methods. For instance, Ramkissoon et al. (2011) discovered the relationship between destination image and behavioural intentions of tourists by using semi-structured interviews and a structured approach survey questionnaire. Lai and Li (2012) collected their data for quantitative testing by questionnaire survey. First, they conducted a pilot survey to validate the questionnaire, and later on, they carried out the qualitative test by semi-structured interview. Choi et al. (2007) used both qualitative (text mining and expert judgment) and quantitative approaches (correspondence analysis) to content analyze the narrative and visual information on the sampled websites. In addition, Chen and Tsai (2007), Assaker (2011), Jalilvand (2012), Cakmak (2012) and Huang (2013) made contributions in the same field.

The research presented in this chapter aims to explore the complex branding impacts of cultural events on the destination image. Thus, in order to figure out a comprehensive and dynamic Macao image through the Lusofonia Festival, the methodologies used cannot be exclusively structured or unstructured (Ostlund et al. 2010). The most complete measurement of destination image should include both types of methodologies, which is regarded as mixed-methods research (Pluye et al. 2009). In other words, the destination image can be considered in terms of both an attribute-based component and a holistic component. Mixed-methods research is defined as a combination of qualitative and quantitative methods conducted by a researcher or researcher team for the broad purpose of gaining breadth and depth of understanding or corroboration within a single study or closely related studies (Johnson et al. 2007).

The first research method used for the purposes of this chapter was the repertory-grid technique, in which the respondents could freely propose adjectives describing Macao as a destination. The author interviewed 100 visitors to Macao's scenic spots (the ruins of Saint Paul's, the A-Ma Temple, Senado Square, the Golden Lotus Square, Macao Fisherman's Wharf and the Venetian). The second research method employed a written survey, constructing four variables and 33 questions on the basis of literature review. After the pilot study showed satisfactory reliability and validity, it was distributed from 19 October to 21 October in the Taipa House, where the 21st Lusofonia was taking place, employing random sampling. Finally, 320 tourists were asked to do the questionnaire; 312 were valid.

Research results

The repertory-grid technique

The respondents taking part in the repertory-grid technique were asked to offer one to three keywords to describe their impressions of Macao. Finally, 422 keywords, including words with similar meanings, were collected. *Casino* or *gambling*, mentioned 152 times, ranks the first. Totaling 36 percent of the whole world bank were such terms as *capitalism*, *Portugal*, *Macao SAR government* and *colony* (Figure 9.1). These were elements relevant to politics and history and were

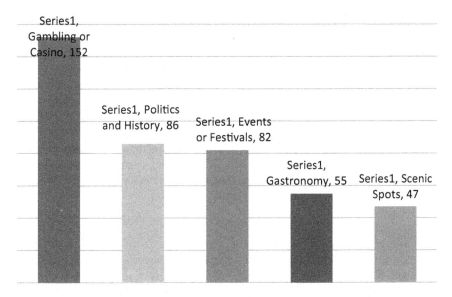

Figure 9.1 Structure of the keywords representing respondents' impressions on Macao
Source: Author's elaboration on the basis of the research

mentioned 86 times. Event fields, such as *fireworks, dragon boat competition, Grand Prix racing, light festival* etc. were mentioned 82 times, while *gastronomy* was mentioned 55 times, and scenic spots were referred to 47 times.

The rankings of the keywords (Figure 9.1) reveal that the gaming industry is inevitably the most impressive image of Macao, indicating there is still a long run to change its stereotypical old image. However, it is comforting that "events and festivals" has approximately the same frequency as the runner-up, gradually occupying an important position in visitors' perception. This sheds a light on how to promote Macao's brand image and enrich visitors' experience through events.

Questionnaire

As mentioned before, the second research technique used for the purposes of this article was the questionnaire taken during the Lusofonia Festival. Among all the respondents who filled in the 312 valid questionnaires, 47 percent were female visitors, and 53 percent were male visitors. In terms of age groups, 18 to 24 (51.8 percent) ranked first; the second group was between the ages of 25 and 34 (27.7 percent); the third group was ages 35 through 44 (18.1 percent) and the fourth group was those between 45 and 54 (2.4 percent). That is probably because the event has a very lively atmosphere; young tourists are much easier to get involved. In terms of education, the majority of respondents had university back-grounds, accounting for 72.3 percent, which means that the visitors had a good understanding of the background and culture of the event. In terms of the tourists' monthly discretionary earnings in RMB (Chinese yuan), 22.9% of the researched population earned RMB 13,000 or more. Those earning between RMB 2,000 and 3,999 and RMB 4,000 and 6,999 accounted for 20.5 percent respectively (64 people) of the overall attendance, followed by those who earned less than RMB 2,000 (14.5 percent), those earning between RMB 10,000 and 13,000 (12 percent) and those who earned between RMB 7,000 and 9,999 (9.6 percent).

The main target attracted by Lusofonia is students (49.4 percent), followed by the staff (15.7 percent). The majority of Macao visitors in the sample were from mainland China – up to 56.6 percent. The rest of the respondents were from Hong Kong (28.9 percent), Taiwan (6 percent) and other places (4.8 percent); 3.7 percent did not respond to this question. When asked their purpose for visiting Macao, it was good to find that sightseeing and attending events were the first two, outnumbering the others and revealing that seeking leisure experience is becoming more and important for tourists (Table 9.1).

Hypothesis testing

After using the bootstrap method of SPSS24.0 software to perform 5,000 times (Hatcher 1994), the model is analyzed to obtain the results in the Table 9.2.

In order to verify the effect of event perception (EP) on cognitive destination image (CI), as shown in model 1 in Table 9.2, $R^2 = 0.247$, $p<0.001$, the degree of model interpretation is good, and the EP coefficient is 0.5017***, indicating that

Table 9.1 Main purpose for visiting Macao

Measures	Frequency	Percentage
Sightseeing	150	48.1
VFR*	26	8.3
Business	22	7.1
Gambling	0	0.0
Events	114	36.5
Total	312	100

Source: Author's elaboration on the basis of fieldwork

Note: *VFR: visit friends and relatives

Table 9.2 Moderating effect of CI between EP and AI

	model1 (CI)		model2 (AI)		model3 (AI)	
outcome	coeff	R-sq	AI	R-sq	AI	R-sq
constant	1.9085***		1.4707***		−0.0863	
EP	0.5017***	.247***	0.606***	0.2905***	0.1975***	
CI					0.8159***	0.6935***

Source: Author's elaboration on the basis of fieldwork

Notes: * Significant at the p < 0.05 level (two-tailed)
** Significant at the p < 0.01 level (two-tailed)
*** Significant at the p < 0.001 level (two-tailed)
CI: cognitive destination image
AI: affective destination image

EP has significance for CI. The most obvious part of the cultural characteristics is the event activities in various regions. When visitors participate in these events, they can learn about local cultural customs. When people are more aware of the festival events in a tourist city, tourists will naturally show better perception to the city image.

In order to verify the effect of cognitive destination image (CI) on affective destination image (AI), as shown in model 2 in Table 9.2, R2=0.290***, p < 0.001, the EP coefficient is 0.606***, p < 0.001. It shows that CI has a significant positive impact on AI. The better the perceived image of the tourist city, the more the tourists know about it, and for the tourists, the better the perception of the situation with the locals, the more positive their feelings are. The city's love and intimacy are among the emotional perceptions.

In order to verify the influence of CI and EP on AI, as shown in model 3 in Table 9.2, R2 = 0.6935***, p < 0.001. The EP coefficient was 0.1975***, p < 0.001, indicating that EP had a significant positive effect on AI; the CI coefficient was 0.8159***, p < 0.001, indicating that CI had a significant positive effect on AI. It can be easily found that for every tourist location, local festival activities are often the most touching. Every time people travel, they hope to bring a new touch

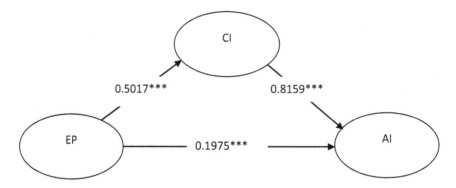

Figure 9.2 Model effect
Source: Author's elaboration on the basis of fieldwork

of colour to their lives and experience scenes that are different from their daily lives. These are all special events for the daily lives of local people. For tourists, it is to let them better understand the characteristics of local culture and to meet their needs. In this way, the event, as one of the city's labels, will allow people to transfer their awareness of the event to the overall impression of the city (see Figure 9.2).

Conclusion

In summarizing, it must be stressed that hosting events such as Lusofonia is very helpful for Macao's tourism development. The emphasis on such events can significantly improve visitors' cognitive image (CI) of the city. Thanks to such events, people can better understand that Macao is not a merely gaming centre, but also a colorful leisure centre, which, in turn, should attract more tourists to Macao. According to the research results, the first three purposes that participants attend events are "rest/relaxation" (42 percent), "novelty" (20 percent) and "education" (14 percent). This reveals that tourists not only want to relax, but also look forward to seeking new experience and accepting knowledge when attending events. For the tourists, events have become an important attraction. For the city, every hallmark event taking place here will become part of the city label, regardless of its origin. It is these unique events that display the city's versatile culture, establish the brand and satisfy tourists' diverse needs. Perhaps Lusofonia started up initially for the Portuguese and Macanese people in Macao. But, in fact, it has become a fantastic festival that every tourist and resident cannot miss. It is believed that enriching programmes and increasing event awareness will be solutions to better developing the sustainably of such events.

Events and festivals, originally local celebrations, can become international attractions for a destination (Arcodia and Whitford 2007). A distinct path of outward or inward internationalization may emerge as the festival increases engagement with external markets. How to cater to diversified visitors' needs while retaining the authenticity of the events will be a challenge for the event organizers. Meanwhile, the destination must provide appropriate infrastructure and an opportunity to create and promote tourist attractions, broaden media coverage and strengthen collaborative efforts among national, regional and local tourism organizations (Kim and Chalip 2004). Understanding the roles of festivals for different groups of attendees helps all key stakeholders to guide festival management to organize festivals (Lee et al. 2012b). Finding the key appeal of the festival and the culture backing it up and associating it with tourists' needs is definitely the way to facilitate harmony between cultures and enhance community cohesion as well as to successfully establish a destination brand image.

References

Arcodia, C., & Whitford, M. (2007). Festival attendance and the development of social capital. *Journal of Convention and Event Tourism*, 8(2), 1–18.

Assaker, G., Vinzi, V. E., & O'Connor, P. (2011). Examining the effect of novelty seeking, satisfaction, and destination image on tourists' return pattern: A two factor, non-linear latent growth model. *Tourism Management*, 32, 890–901.

Berlie, J. A. (2000). Macau's overview at the turn of the century. *American Asian Review*, XVIII(4), 25–68.

Boo, S. Y., & Busser, J. (2005). Impact analysis of a tourism festival on tourism destination images. *Event Management*, 9(4), 223–237.

Cakmak, E., & Isaac, R. K. (2012). What destination marketers can learn from their visitors' blogs: An image analysis of Bethlehem, Palestine. *Journal of Destination Marketing & Management*, 1, 124–133.

Chen, C., & Tsai, D. (2007). How destination image and evaluative factors affect behavioural intentions? *Tourism Management*, 28, 1115–1122.

Chinadaily. (2018). http://www.chinadaily.com.cn/cityguide/2009-03/17/content_7585933. htm (Accessed 2018).

Choi, S., Lehto, X. Y., & Morrison, A. M. (2007). Destination image representation on the web: Content analysis of Macau travel related websites. *Tourism Management*, 28(1), 118–129.

Choi, W. M., & Chan, A. (1999). A qualitative assessment of Hong Kong's image as a tourist destination. *Tourism Management*, 20, 361–365.

Chung, T. (2009). Valuing heritage in Macau: On contexts and processes of urban conservation. *Journal of Current Chinese Affairs*, 38(1), 129–160

Cudny, W., & Maiava, O. (2016). Auckland's Pasifika Festival and the łódź of Four Cultures Festival as elements of preserving and promoting multicultural heritage in the cities. *Annales Universitatis Marie Curie Skłodowska*, LXXI(2), 61–77.

Dawson, D. (1991). Panem et circenses? A critical analysis of ethnic and multicultural festivals. *Journal of Applied Recreation Research*, 16(1), 35–52.

DSEC. (2018). http://www.dsec.gov.mo (Accessed 2018).

Echtner, C. M., & Ritchie, J. R. B. (1991). The meaning and measurement of destination image. *The Journal of Tourism Studies*, 2(2), 2–12.

Gao, J. (2009). A destination image, positioning and branding: The conceptual analysis and relationship model. *Journals of Tourism*, 4, 25–30.

Gao, P. Y. (2012). *The Strategic Research on Promoting Macao to Be a Leisure Center* (Report). Macao, China: Research Center of Development and Strategy. http://www. chnlib.com/wenhuadongtai/2017-10/356022.html

Hallmann, K., & Breuer, C. (2011). Images of rural destinations hosting small-scale sport vents. *International Journal of Event and Festival Management*, 2, 218–244.

Hao, Z. D. (2011). *Macau History and Society*. Hong Kong: Hong Kong University Press.

Hatcher, L. (1994). *A Step-by-step Approach to Using the SAS(R) System for Factor Analysis and Structural Equation Modeling*. Cary, NC: SAS Institute.

Hede, A. M. (2005). Sports-event, tourism and destination marketing strategies: An Australian case study of Athens 2004 and its media telecast. *Journal of Sports Tourism*, 10(3), 187–200.

Hou, W. H. (2011). Macao event and festival development and its industrializations. *Executive*, 1, 5–16. http://www.macautourism.gov.mo

Huang, W. J., Chen, C. C., & Lin, Y. H. (2013). Cultural proximity and intention to visit: Destination image of Tai Wan as perceived by Mainland Chinese visitors. *Journal of Destination Marketing & Management*, 2(3), 176–184.

Huang, Y. (2007). *A Research on Macao Linguistics*. Beijing: Peking Business Printing.

IACM. (2018). www.iacm.gov.mo (Accessed 2018).

Jalilvand, M. R., Samiei, N., & Manzari, P. Y. (2012). Examining the structural relationships of electronic word of mouth, destination image, tourist attitude toward destination and travel intention: An integrated approach. *Journal of Destination Marketing & Management*, 1(2012), 134–143.

Jin, G. P., & Wu, Z. L. (2001). *The Misty Macau History*. Macao, China: Adult Education Association.

Johnson, R. B., Onwuegbuzie, A. J., Turner, L. A. (2007). Toward a definition of mixed methods research. *Journal of Mixed Methods Research*, 1(2), 112–133.

Joreskog, K., Kim, N. S., & Chalip, L. (2004). Why travel to the FIFA world cup? Effects of motives, background, interest, and constraints. *Tourism management*, 25(6), 695–707.

Kaplanidou, K. (2007). Affective event and destination image: Their influence on Olympic travelers' behavioral intentions. *Event Management*, 10(2), 159–173.

Lai, K., & Li, Y. (2012). Core-periphery structure of destination image concept, evidence and implication. *Annals of Tourism Research*, 39(3), 1359–1379.

Lee, C., & Taylor, T. (2005). Critical reflections on the economic impact assessment of a mega-event: The case of 2002 FIFA World Cup. *Tourism Management*, 26(4), 595–603.

Lee, I., Arcodia, C., & Lee, T. J. (2012a). Benefits of visiting a multicultural festival: The case of South Korea. *Tourism Management*, 33(2), 334–340.

Lee, I. S., Arcodia, C., & Lee, T. J. (2012b). Key characteristics of multicultural festivals: A critical review of the literature. *Event Management*, 16(1), 93–101.

Liang, F. L. (2003). The history and reality of the culture in the South of the five ridges. *Journal of Jinan University*, 2, 11–16.

Loi, K., & Pearce, P. L. (2012). Powerful stakeholders' views of entertainment in Macao's future. *Journal of Business Research*, 65(1), 4–12.

Macaodaily. (2018). http://macaodaily.com.mo (Accessed 2018).

Moser, N. (1996). Camões as a romantic hero: "Os Lusíadas" as an example of patriotism in the Netherlands between 1766 and 1880. *Portuguese Studies*, 55–67.

O'Cathain, A., Murphy, E., & Nicholl, J. (2008). The quality of mixed methods studies in health services research. *Journal of Health Services Research & Policy*, 13(2), 92–98.

Onwuegbuzie, A. J., & Teddlie, C. (2003). A framework for analyzing data in mixed methods research. *Handbook of Mixed Methods in Social and Behavioral Research*, 2, 397–430.

Ostlund, U., Kidd, L., Wengstro"m, Y., & Dewar, N. (2010). Combining qualitative and quantitative research within mixed method research designs: A methodological review. *International Journal of Nursing Studies*, 48(3), 369–383.

PATA (Pacific Asia Travel Association). (2012). *Macau: Projected and Real Destination Image*. PATA Task Force Report, 10–15.

Pearce, D. G. (1988). Tourist time-budget. *Annals of Tourism Research*, 15(1), 106–121.

Pluye, P., Gagnon, M. P., Griffiths, F., & Johnsonlafleur, J. (2009). A scoring system for appraising mixed methods research, and concomitantly appraising qualitative, quantitative and mixed methods primary studies in mixed studies reviews. *International Journal of Nursing Studies*, 46(4), 529–546.

Ramkissoon, H., Uysal, M., & Brown, K. (2011). Relationship between destination image and behavioral intentions of tourists to consume cultural attractions. *Journal of Hospitality Marketing & Management*, 20, 575–595.

Reilly, M. D. (1990). Free elicitation of descriptive adjectives for tourism image assessment. *Journal of Travel Research*, 28(4), 21–26.

Richards, G., & Wilson, J. (2004). The impact of cultural events on city image: Rotterdam, cultural capital of Europe 2001. *Urban Studies*, 41(10), 1931–1951.

Smith, A. (2005). Reimaging the city: The value of sport initiatives. *Annals of Tourism Research*, 32(1), 217–236.

Um, S., & Crompton, J. L. (1990). Attitude determinants in tourism destination choice. *Annals of Tourism Research*, 17(3), 432–448.

UNESCO. (2018). https://en.unesco.org (Accessed 2018).

Wu, Z. L., & Yang, Y. Z. (1999). *Macao Encyclopedia*. Beijing: Chinese Encyclopedia Press. www.icm.gov.mo

Yuan, J. (1995). *Macanese in Motion*. Macao: Macao Culture Bureau.

Zeng, Z. L. (2006). A comparison between Macao and Las Vegas. *Journal of Macao Gaming Association*, 1(1), 53–54.

Zhou, W. M., & Huang, Q. C. (1994). *Macao Religions*. Macao: Macao Foundation Press.

Zhou, X. H. (2012). *The Role of Guanxi Assets in Mediating Relationship Marketing Investments and Customer Loyalty in Chinese B2B Context*. Doctoral Paper of Macao University of Science and Techonology, Macao.

10 Brand Hong Kong

Art hub for China's Belt and Road Initiative

Hilary du Cros and Lee Jolliffe

Introduction

"Hong Kong's success as an art hub in Asia and in the Belt and Road Initiative includes 'perfect' logistics, a proliferation of arts venues and international trade connections", gushes Kevin Ching of the well-known auction house Sotheby's in a YouTube video. With Hong Kong being Sotheby's headquarters for Asia, he believes that the auction house is seeing the emergence of Chinese and Southeast Asian art in global markets, and these are being joined by the work of other artists from Belt and Road areas west of China (Kevin Ching on YouTube 25 June 2017; HKTDC 2017).

This YouTube video inspired this exploration of the role international contemporary art fairs (ICAFs) held in Hong Kong are playing in the creation of an arts event portfolio that uses Hong Kong Art Week/Month's arts events chiefly in furthering this vision because of the large number of collectors/art tourists they collectively attract. The galleries, auction houses and event organisers have set the Hong Kong Art Week at the end of March (HKAGA 2018), while the government includes it with the city performing arts festival, Hong Kong Art Festival, that runs throughout the month and a number of free public arts events to promote a Hong Kong Arts Month (HKTB 2019; Brand 2019). Either way, it is a draw card for art tourists, collectors, curators and critics from around the region and beyond as it includes Basel HK, which attracts art from all over the world with a strong global brand of its own (McDonald 2018a).

China's Belt and Road Initiative (BRI) also known as One Belt, One Road (OBOR),[1] has yet to find a clear arts/cultural role for Hong Kong, despite being in place for the last five years. At the end of 2013, People's Republic of China's President Xi Jinping announced one of China's most aspirational foreign policy and economic initiatives. The vision was for the construction of a "Silk Road" economic belt and a 21st-century "Maritime Silk" Road, drawing on these historic routes' cultural cache to be collectively referred to as One Belt, One Road (OBOR). It's now more commonly referred to as the Belt and Road Initiative. Hong Kong sits most comfortably within the Maritime Silk Road aspect.

Xi's vision is a comprehensive programme of infrastructure building to connect China's less-developed border regions with neighbouring countries. On land, Beijing aims to connect the country's underdeveloped hinterland to Europe through Central Asia. This route has been labelled the Silk Road Economic Belt. The second part of Xi's plan is to construct a 21st-century Maritime Silk Road, connecting the fast-growing Southeast Asia region to China's southern provinces through ports and railways (Cai 2017).

Literature review

The most relevant aspects of strategic event marketing that relate to the case study fall within two main categories:

1   Event portfolios and regional development for tourism
2   Place branding and public diplomacy: implications for events management

Event portfolios

The development of strategies to capitalize on event portfolios may seek to bundle peripheral small-scale events with larger, more broadly appealing ones. This can complement and enhance regional strategies for events. The development of strategies, led by either the public or private sector organisations, to capitalize on event portfolios can assist eventful cities being branded as such (Richards and Palmer 2010).

Eventful cities that are also branded as art hubs/cities require a healthy arts ecology to support this effort locally and global linkages with major auction houses, event organisers, museums and galleries with international reputations and the arts media. Such cities are usually also recognized as world-class cities (Richards and Palmer 2010) and are attractive to collectors and art tourists as places to visit generally. Whether it develops out of initiatives by the public or the private sector, an event portfolio is crucial to maintaining this recognition.

Currently, the art world recognizes at least 300 events as international contemporary art fairs, with around 100 of these being top-tier events (such as those organized by Basel, Frieze and Maastricht (McDonald 2018a; Artnet 2018). Within this category, it would be fair to say that only a small number of this 100 would also be what Getz (2008) calls periodic hallmark or signature events that are both high tourist demand and high value for a destination to benchmark itself as an event capital or a world-class city. This kind of event is what an event portfolio would need at its core around which to base all other activities for the greatest impact.

Accordingly, a crucial aspect of event portfolio management is that event planners of signature events need to take into account global and local art event calendars because poor coordination can impact negatively on event portfolios. It is likely that the private sector has the most influence in scheduling events, as ICAFs are usually also commercial art fairs (du Cros and Jolliffe 2014). However, this still needs careful negotiation between different signature event organisers to work best for each city on the global art calendar, as well as the organisers' events.

A well-positioned signature arts event has great value in that it can make a strong impact through the media as such ICAFs are quite attractive to film/photograph and are often presented on TV, in newspapers and magazines, on the Internet and so on. Therefore, organising and sponsoring events creates an opportunity to appear in different media (Gerritsen and Olderen 2014). This is a good way to promote a place, which could be measured by using the advertising value equivalent (AVE). For instance, Venice Biennale is a periodic signature arts event that is reported upon regionally and internationally.

Place branding and public diplomacy

These two related but distinct practices seem at odds; however, they are being scrutinized together more often in academic discourse. "Place branding" relates brand strategy and associated techniques to enhancing the economic, social, political and cultural development of cities, regions and countries, particularly in regard to tourism. "Public diplomacy" describes the practices by which a nation, a region or a city carries out foreign policy by directly engaging with foreign entities. Recently, this has become such a popular topic for researchers that it has spawned its own journal to look at how nations, regions and cities pursue reputation management and the nature of influence of external audiences, often involving interdisciplinary studies (Govers and Cull 2018).

Events that have been studied in detail in respect to this area are more likely sports or popular arts events such as the Beijing Olympics and the Eurovision Song Contest (Berkowitz et al. 2007; Manzenreiter 2010; Bodet and Lacassagne 2012; Vuletic 2018). Nevertheless, such events are also branding tools for nations and cities.

Methodology

This chapter uses a case study approach (Beeton 2005) to look at the implications this strategy and its outcomes have for place event marketing by the use of events, such as Hong Kong's ICAFs, in strategic marketing communications and the branding of the city. Brief interviews were also conducted face to face and by email with city destination management organizations' (DMOs) officials, event organisers, galleries, art collectors, art critics and artists between March and November 2018.

Due to funding issues, the face-to-face interviews were conducted with Australian-based art world experts who had recently participated in Hong Kong ICAFs and do so on a regular basis (three gallery owners, one art critic and one collector). The email interviews were conducted by sending questions to Hong Kong–based DMO officials and event organisers (two DMO officials and two event organisers). News reports and reviews by art critics were analysed for references to key issues such as the influence of BRI and how Hong Kong is maintaining its reputation as an art hub. Issues suggested in the interviews were also checked against information available from online sources from the art world, commerce and local news reports. Hence, the case study took an exploratory approach to the topic (Beeton 2005).

This research should also be considered a stage in a longitudinal study of Hong Kong ICAFs, as the authors have been following the impacts of the Hong Kong Art Festival being taken over/remixed as Basel HK since 2012 (du Cros and Jolliffe 2014; du Cros 2017). Further study is envisaged in the next few years to track how Hong Kong ICAFs are starting to influence the nature of other ICAFs in the region.

Hong Kong as an arts hub/Asia's world city

Hong Kong is populated by 7.4 million people and is located in southern China. The city is surrounded by the South China Sea. Since 1 July 1997, Hong Kong has been a special administrative region (SAR) of China. Even so, it has retained many legal and cultural aspects of the former British colonial administration. The rationale behind engaging closely with the BRI is that Hong Kong is already an efficient and popular logistics hub and has developed complex international trade connections. Since 2014, the city has seen a proliferation of arts venues and international contemporary art fairs (ICAFs), with the jewel in the crown being Art Basel HK. The evolution of these arts event initiatives discussed next is illustrated by Figure 10.1.

Hong Kong as an arts hub

Art critics and others note that Asia has enormous potential for art sales but not a particularly long history of public and private galleries, and visiting is not

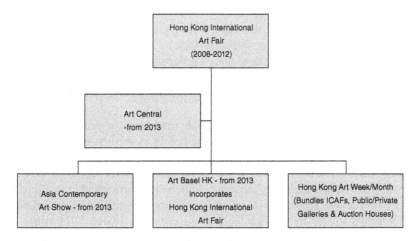

Figure 10.1 Hong Kong arts events development chronology

Source: Authors

considered an everyday activity for the public (Seno 2013). Increasingly, there has been a steady movement of private galleries to Hong Kong, as a result of the ICAFs' success (Lau 2016). Even so, the Hong Kong Tourism Board (HKTB) critiqued Hong Kong as a "cultural desert" in the late 1990s, which then spurred a massive capital works programme to create new public arts facilities for the cultural district at West Kowloon (du Cros and Leong 2011). Hong Kong has organically developed as a commercial arts sales hub (Wang 2012) without much government promotion until recently. In comparison with other countries in the region, it is exporting more than might be expected given its general and arts population. It is trusted as a place for making art purchases away from the source at internationally recognized galleries and auction houses by art dealers, collectors and curators (du Cros 2017).

Art Basel HK has provided a massive boost and focused attention on HK as an art hub. Art Basel began in the Swiss city of the same name in June 1970 and reached its current event size of 300 participating galleries in 1975, being highly selective and closely curated ever since. Miami Beach was added as the US edition, after the first successful event in December 2002. Hong Kong was added in 2013 in response to a "desire to build a cultural bridge between the long-established Western art world and the vibrant new scenes of the entire (Asian) region" (Art Basel 2018a). Art Basel still largely controls its name and branding from Switzerland and only takes on partners as sponsors after close vetting (du Cros 2017).

Art Central was established by one of the founders (and his partners) of the Hong Kong International Art Fair, which sold out to Art Basel in 2011. Their more recently founded event is aimed at highlighting galleries from the Asia Pacific region, featuring edgier works from emerging artists and is less tightly curated than Art Basel HK (Simon Chan personal communication). Both Art Basel HK and Art Central now feature as central attractions of Hong Kong Art Week in the last week of March each year and are reported on internationally (McDonald 2018b). Hong Kong Art Week, therefore, is a tag given by the art world to a group of bundled events that are put on over one week by local private and public sector organisations and one international one (Art Basel). The tag was first developed in 2013 (HKAGA 2018) and then became more popular in marketing after Art Basel HK was moved from May to March in the Hong Kong arts events calendar in 2015 (du Cros 2017).

The Asia Contemporary Art Fair, which runs twice a year (October and March), is not often mentioned in the same breath as the first two events, even though it also has one event during Art Week. It is not as well regarded as Art Basel HK and Art Central because it uses the Conrad Hotel rooms for galleries to exhibit and seems to mainly attract the galleries that are not able to afford the other two venues, according to art gallery interviewees. The latest estimated and/or actual visitor figures for these three events in March 2018 were: Art Basel HK (80,000 over five days), Art Central (39,041 over five days) and Asia Contemporary Art Fair (30,000 over four days) (Art Basel 2018b; Art Central HK 2019; Asia Contemporary Art 2018a). Art Basel HK, as the most significant event for the art world, featured 248 premier galleries from 32 countries, with 28 galleries selected by organizers to participate in the show for the first time (Art Basel HK 2018b).

Even so, with the plethora of art events described here, Hong Kong still lacks public contemporary art galleries. The M+ or Museum+ is still under construction in the West Kowloon Cultural District (WKCD), though it is staffed and holds temporary exhibitions in other spaces around Hong Kong. M+ will be situated within the WKCD as the first publicly funded contemporary art gallery in Hong Kong and one of the public cultural institutions expected to boost Hong Kong's status as a world-class city with facilities and activities that will appeal to both tourists and the creative class. The West Kowloon Cultural District Authority was established in 2008 and given HKD 21.6 billion by the Hong Kong government to develop 14 core arts and cultural facilities for WKCD on 40 hectares near the harbour in West Kowloon (du Cros and Leong 2011). When completed, M+ will collect, exhibit and interpret visual art, design and architecture and moving images from around the region and Hong Kong (du Cros 2017). A number of new gallery spaces have sprung up around HK in recent years with government support. These include two converted historic building complexes associated with Hong Kong's justice sector: the former central police station (Tai Kwun Centre for Heritage and Arts) and the married police staff quarters, both within easy walking distance of street-based private art galleries (HKTB 2018).

Figure 10.2 WKCD temporary exhibition of inflatable art

Source: Hilary du Cros

Meanwhile, the continued inflation of the Hong Kong art scene has inspired privately supported building projects while waiting for Museum + to open. The two best examples of Hong Kong entrepreneurship in relation to purpose-built spaces are the K-11 Art Mall in Kowloon and H Queens Tower in Central, a shopping mall and high-rise tower art gallery, respectively, in grand Hong Kong style. The latter has attracted international galleries such as the David Zwirner Gallery and Hauser & Wirth (two floors each) as well as smaller Hong Kong galleries in the centrally located tower. The building is specially designed to accommodate big artworks with its strong floor loadings, larger-than-normal lifts (which can accommodate artworks weighing up to 1.5 tonnes) and extra ceiling height (4.5 metres) (Shaw 2017; McDonald 2018b). All these gallery complexes and galleries plan to coordinate the opening of new exhibitions and other events with Hong Kong Art Week and the arrival of ICAF attendees (du Cros 2017).

Figure 10.3 K11 Art Mall temporary toast wall mural

Source: Hilary du Cros

Hong Kong as "Asia's world city"

Hong Kong has actively sought to brand its image as "Asia's world city" since the Chief Executive's Commission on Strategic Development in 2000. It recommended in its report that "Hong Kong needs to promote its unique position as one of the most cosmopolitan and vibrant cities in Asia to a wide range of international audiences." This led directly to the establishment by the Hong Kong SAR government of the Brand Hong Kong programme that bears the mission "to provide a greater focus to the international promotion of Hong Kong as 'Asia's world city'" (Chu 2010, p. 47; Brand HK 2018). Brand HK and the Hong Kong Tourism Board (HKTB) both work towards building and promoting Hong Kong's brand as "Asia's world city". Arts and culture have become an increasingly important part of that, given the public commitment to WKDC and the government's wish to benchmark the city firmly within the region (Brand HK 2018). Neither organisation is able to generate cultural activities on its own; however, they actively publicise any that are organised by other entities in Hong Kong online, through social media, in pamphlets and even in annual reports available from their websites (both) and information centres (HKTB).

Later, the Donald Tsang administration became keen on developing Hong Kong into a hub of Asian creative industries but not a base for local creative industries to grow in. Chu (2010) has argued that the Brand Hong Kong programme's failure to recognise that the distinguishing characteristic of Hong Kong was its emergent arts community where genuine cosmopolitanisms found the space to emerge. However, ICAFs still feature local content, and Hong Kong event organisers are more sophisticated than Chow feared and recognize that the brand of Hong Kong is not inevitably the property of the state-capital nexus because it is still deeply rooted in Hong Kong's complex cultural identity.

BRI, business and the arts

As a SAR of China, Hong Kong is both expected to be in a good position to make the most of the opportunities for trade that the BRI offers. The Hong Kong Trade Development Council (HKTDC) is ground zero for investment facilitation in BRI through Hong Kong. As such, it is not surprising that it is trying to leverage Hong Kong's advantages (HKTB 2018) in promoting key art fairs in relation to the government's branding of Hong Kong as an arts hub. The HKTDC is a statutory body established in 1966 and follows Hong Kong SAR government policies regarding Beijing initiatives, particularly when these benefit Hong Kong's trade position (HKTDC 2019).

It was not unexpected that HKTDC joined major auction houses in Hong Kong in promoting the city as the central art hub for China's Belt and Road Initiative (see quote at beginning). The earliest mention of business and arts combining on the BRI over an arts exhibition was through HK/Macau tycoon Pansy Ho's 2016 exhibition of female artists aimed squarely at attracting the attention of both the HK government and the central government in Beijing. The Hong Kong government had made numerous policy addresses regarding the BRI and trade; however, local arts commentators and others are just realizing that it has a role to play with regard to the arts. This awareness is evident in Ho's exhibition and two arts conferences facilitated by Zuni Icosahedron using BRI for greater cultural exchange. However, awareness about how arts events might interact with international relations is not as developed in Hong Kong as it is in other parts of the world, particularly with regard to travelling blockbuster art exhibitions put on by large art museums and galleries (Sylvestor 2016).

Ho described its potential public relations role in her comment, "the Belt and Road Initiative is not just about economic development, but was also an avenue for Beijing to showcase its soft power by taking the lead in bringing arts and culture from countries and regions along the 2,000-year-old exchange route" (Pansy Ho Chiu-king in Chow 2013).

Arts Week or Month?

Meanwhile, Brand Hong Kong and the Hong Kong Tourism Board are running with the ICAFs being the basis of not just an Art Week in March but a whole month in their place promotions (HKTB 2018). For instance, this year Hong Kong Art Week ran between 26 March to 1 April 2018, according to visual arts commentators/galleries/event organisers. Hong Kong Art Month ran all March, according to HKTB's destination marketing, and included the city performing arts festival, the Hong Kong Arts Festival, free outdoor public art events along the harbour and street arts festivals along with the art fairs, auctions, private gallery openings and so on from the Art Week (HKTB 2018). Later in the year, another Art Week looks like it is starting to develop in September, close to the mid-autumn festival with the Asian Contemporary Arts Fair and several other related events starting to cluster around that part of the calendar.

What is also curious is that, although this may seem organic or ad hoc in organization, it may not be as several art events focused on local collectors have been affected by the art event calendar changes. The Hong Kong Arts Walk was moved from March to later in the year so as not to clash with the ICAFs and then disappeared altogether as it was retired by its organizer, John Batten of the Hong Kong Art Galleries Association (HKAGA). Also, the Affordable Art Fair (Hong Kong) first started in March then was moved to May so as not to compete with larger ICAFs (John Batten personal communication 2014).[2] It is likely that market forces, rather than the government, are directing this scheduling and the branding of Hong Kong as more of a global entrant in the international arts events calendar, where collectors from outside are more important than those within the city.

Brand HK has also taken a hands-off approach to attracting global art fair brands to be part of the event portfolio for Hong Kong. They prefer to see market forces and commercial interests direct its management, rather than government policy. For instance, when asked if the government, through Brand Hong Kong, would do anything to attract the other major ICAF event brand, Frieze (Brett Free personal communication 2018).[3]

Finally, further investigations into HK Art Week/Month and its setting may also find a home within discourse about festivalisation spaces (Cudny 2016). These are urban spaces which festivals influence either by permanent festivalisation or by occupying them temporarily for festival purposes. Hong Kong's private galleries linked to the art fairs also show work in their usual spaces during that period, hoping to attract collectors/art tourists. The Hong Kong SAR government also ensures that there are arts events in public squares and arts facilities to showcase the city's arts (HKTB 2018), adding to the feeling of a temporary festivalisation of Hong Kong's urban cultural spaces.

BRI and ICAFs: a few observations

At this stage, there do not seem to be any major changes to gallery offerings to indicate that BRI is changing the arts mix at Hong Kong ICAFs to include more artists from Central Asia and Caucasus. There are still many more works by Chinese and Southeast Asian artists along with those from major art-producing centres in Europe and North America. This year, some artists from the Middle East were promoted but mainly in the Asia Contemporary Art Fair (ACAF 2018b).

The gallery owners and art critics interviewed all considered Art Basel HK a top-tier show, with others in the region offering no comparison for slickness and professionalism. It also provides an experience for VIP collectors and others, which have seen their numbers increase from 100 to 300 over the last two editions (McDonald 2018a). Other authorities have observed that Hong Kong, more than Singapore, is considered to be the gateway to Asia for regional artists.

Several other galleries with branches in other cities (e.g. Sunaram Tagore from Singapore and Chelsea in New York) were showing at Basel Miami this year as well as Hong Kong and consider Art Basel HK to be one of the fairs that all Asian galleries most want to participate in, if selected. They also thought that galleries and artworks from BRI countries would need to be of very high quality to be selected. Hence, Hong Kong is regarded as the art hub of Asia at present, due to a number of factors that have been building up over the past decade and will accelerate in the years ahead, according to most interviewees.

One Beijing gallery owner observed that, while BRI has these grand ambitions for cultural soft power, it should not force the issue in Hong Kong. On a trip to a country in Central Asia, he saw bulldozers coming over the border from China building the infrastructure for BRI but thinks that arts development is different and needs more finesse to accomplish the right style of relationship.

Even so, it is a work that could or should be slow to progress. Danny Yung (Yung and Zuni 2018), a founding member and co-artistic director of Zuni Icosahedron, has stated, "We in Hong Kong lack the foundation for collaboration because this issue has been discussed merely on the conceptual level. Hong Kong has yet to produce a long-term master plan and commit itself to a blueprint for setting up a Belt-Road cultural think tank."

A long-term government critic, Yung cites the city government's preference for "quick fixes" and "speedy solutions" as affecting how the BRI will affect the

Hong Kong art world. So far, he notes that governance on arts development "has been plagued by a lack of vision and long-term planning based on professional research as well as in-depth review and analysis. Instead, our impatient, blind rush to achieve and accomplish has led us to churn out an endless stream of slogans, activities and programmes that have markedly failed to produce a lasting legacy" (Yung and Zuni 2018).

Opportunities and challenges presented by BRI

A number of opportunities and challenges exist for Hong Kong retaining its significant art hub status in terms of enhancing its connectivity whilst staring down competition in the region. While discussing this project with some knowledgeable art world figures and Asian collectors recently, the following issues were revealed for ICAFs in regard to the BRI.

Opportunities

The construction of a 21st-century Maritime Silk Road connecting the Southeast Asia region to China's southern provinces through ports and railways is fast being realized in Hong Kong. Two of the latest major works finished – the Hong Kong-Macau-Zhuhai Bridge and the Hong Kong West Kowloon Railway Station at the end of the Hong Kong section of the Guangzhou-Shenzhen-Hong Kong rail link – both opened this year. The latter effectively links Kowloon (on the New Territories side of Hong Kong) to China's massive inter-city train network. This is a huge opportunity for Hong Kong as an arts and cultural hub because the train terminus is part of the arts/retail complex still partially under construction for the West Kowloon Cultural Hub, which also includes Museum +. It is also just across the harbour from the Hong Kong Convention Centre where key ICAFs are mainly held. Not many major cities have such good connectivity for the arts.

In terms of shipping art by rail, there are already some opportunities to transport goods via rail between China and Europe, which will increase once the rail link is fully operational. However, it could take many years before other impacts of the BRI are seen, particularly in terms of arts and culture. Many projects are still under construction, including commissioning public sculpture in 60 cities on the route in Western China, because the BRI is envisaged as open ended (Konings 2018; Sui 2018). Trade facilitation barriers between countries also need to be addressed, particularly in relation to art. While there are many opportunities hovering on the horizon because of this greater connectivity, there is still the challenge of devising an equitable import/export tax system that encourages art sales without being open to exploitation along the BRI.

Finally, in terms of cultural soft power, it remains to be seen whether China can successfully use Hong Kong ICAFs, particularly Art Basel HK, as signature events to polish its national brand. This can be a double-edged sword as could be seen with the way that the authoritarian government of Azerbaijan used the Eurovision Song Contest in 2012 and the unexpected consequences of that for its brand (Vuletic 2018). Branding associations with a major Western brand such as Basel could be much more slippery than BRI proponents could imagine. Donald Yung's approach to finesse the process or leave it entirely to specific event organisers (supported only as needed by Brand HK or BRI advocates) would be the best strategy in this case.

Challenges

One of the major challenges for art collectors, particularly those from mainland China, is that China's import tax/VAT on contemporary art is around 34 percent combined since changes made suddenly around 2012 (Dezan Shira and Associates 2016). Works older than 100 years old are subject to much less tax, which contemporary collectors find unfair. They are also upset that state museums do not pay tax on any of their purchases. It is not unexpected that some collectors have been finding ways around this challenge when bringing art into their home country. One such solution involves establishing art storage facilities or bonded warehouses within tax-free economic zones or "freeports" close to major airports in Beijing and Shanghai (Chow 2013). Some collectors have even been able to move art from their art warehouses to private museums "on loan" and then take it back again in order to enjoy it without tax (Geng 2014).

Hong Kong is also an example of an Asian freeport. It differs from other freeports because its entire territory is essentially a "freeport" in itself. In Hong Kong, art is not considered a dutiable good for export and import purposes and attracts neither sales nor capital gains tax. Thus, in Hong Kong, artwork can be stored in private settings, outside a warehouse, and still incur many of the benefits that traditional freeports and bonded warehouses offer. One of the newer Asian freeports is the Singapore freeport, located at Changi Airport (Wierbicki and Rottermund 2016). Singapore is also trying to challenge Hong Kong's status as an art hub by establishing more contemporary arts events and areas dedicated to private galleries (e.g. Gillman Barracks, which is a publicly sponsored arts precinct that has attracted a number of international art galleries recently).

Lessons to be learned

This example of art events' evolution and development in Hong Kong may provide lessons for other international destinations with major art fairs, auction houses and galleries. Although the case presented here comprises a complex destination portfolio for arts events, it is also one that is strongly linked to particular urban spaces in this city, and is clearly contributing to the identity of Hong Kong as an arts hub for the region. The destination profile of the place in relation to arts events is illustrated by the tacit buy in by the HKTB, expanding the Hong Kong Arts Week into the Hong Kong Arts Month.

Examining the process, it is clear that there are many players and many interests, although the influence of the international contemporary arts fairs, as well as the bundled arts events, is playing a key role in Hong Kong's place branding with

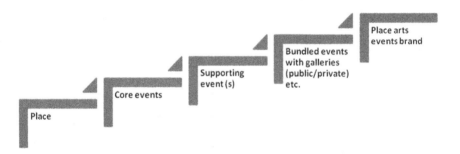

Figure 10.4 A model for place arts events branding
Source: Authors

a possible flow-on effect to the BRI's cultural soft power in future. A model for place arts events branding has been developed based on evidence from the Hong Kong case and is presented here (Figure 10.2).

Conclusion

There are several issues that this study has been able to find some resolution on and many that still remain opaque, probably because such a complex interdisciplinary inquiry really needs a more detailed long-term investigation. From the information gathered so far, it seems that the nature of the arts event portfolio examined is uniquely Hong Kong, with very little influence from China in regard to the BRI. However, in relation to China's interest in cultural soft power generated in association with the BRI, this could all change. As Rectanus (2002) observed, it does not always go the government's way, particularly in regard to how corporate sponsorship interacts with cultural soft power in the area of marketing. China's policy on anything has also been shown to change suddenly, as with the increase of tax on art imports. However, the market and private sector always find methods to deal with these challenges in Asia.

The actual arts events in terms of their programming and gallery mix have not been influenced much at all at this stage by BRI policy. This result will not change in the immediate future, unless market forces drag them in that direction (e.g. they show an increasing interest in showing artists and galleries from along the BRI). They would also prefer to show such artists and galleries only if they consider them to be as appealing and on the same level as current participants.

Meanwhile, it appears that HK art world entrepreneurs/ICAF organisers see themselves as leaders, not followers of the government, in developing Hong Kong's events portfolio and arts hub branding. This style of place-based market-ing still requires some emphasis on local Hong Kong artists and galleries in the mix, though the presence of international galleries is a major draw card. These aspects are there in both the programming and style of events. What has really opened up an interesting future research area is the scale of recent construction and conversion of buildings in Hong Kong to house private art galleries, with ICAFs benefitting from art collectors and tourists drawn to these new art spaces just opened and those that are about to open (and vice versa).

Hong Kong is being developed and branded through events as an arts hub by a number of actors that include those in the trade, investment and art communities against the backdrop and long-term agenda of China's BRI policy. Meanwhile, this place event branding through the arts is being more driven by the trade entities than the tourism authorities, although the local tourism board is in effect "on board" to promote arts events in Hong Kong to portray the city as a vibrant arts hub for visitors.

Notes

1 List of acronyms used in this chapter:
   BRI   Belt and Road Initiative
   HKTDC Hong Kong Tourism Development Council
   HKAGA Hong Kong Art Gallery Association
   HKTB   Hong Kong Tourist Board
   ICAF   International Contemporary Arts Festivals
   OBOR   One Belt One Road (term for BRI before 2016)
   WKCD   West Kowloon Cultural District
2 John Batten, Secretary of Hong Kong Art Gallery Association personal communication 2014.
3 Brett Free, Public Relation Officer, Brand HK, personal communication 2018.

References

Art Basel. (2018a). History. Available at: www.artbasel.com/about/history (Accessed 19 November 2018).

Art Basel. (2018b). Facts and Figures. Available at: https://d2u3kfwd92fzu7.cloudfront.net/asset/factfigures/Art_Basel_l_Facts_and_Figures_Art_Basel_in_Hong_Kong_1_2018-1.pdf (Accessed 15 January 2019).

Art Central. (2019). 29–31 March 2018. Available at: http://artcentralhongkong.com/wp-content/uploads/2018/06/ACHK2019_Application-Pack.pdf (Accessed 15 January 2019).

Artnet. (2018). Attention, Art Collectors: Here Is the Definitive Calendar of International Art Fairs for 2018. Available at: https://news.artnet.com/art-world/2018-fair-schedule-1191641 (Accessed 18 November 2018).

Asia Contemporary Art Fair. (2018a). About. Available at: www.asiacontemporaryart.com/home/main/en/ (Accessed 15 January 2019).

Asia Contemporary Art Fair. (2018b). Catalogue Fall Edition. Available at: www.asiacontemporaryart.com/home/main/en/ (Accessed 19 November 2018).

Beeton, S. (2005). The case study in tourism research: A multi-method case study approach. *Tourism Research Methods: Integrating Theory with Practice*, 37–48.

Berkowitz, P., Gjermano, G., Gomez, L., & Schafer, G. (2007). Brand China: Using the 2008 olympic games to enhance China's image. *Place Branding and Public Diplomacy*, 3(2), 164–178.

Bodet, G. S. P., & Lacassagne, M. F. (2012). International place branding through sporting events: A British perspective of the 2008. *Beijing Olympics, European Sport Management Quarterly*, 12(4), 357–374.

Brand HK. (2018). About. Available at: www.brandhk.gov.hk/html/en/BrandHongKong/
WhatIsBrandHongKong.html (Accessed 19 November 2018).

Brand HK. (2019). Art, Cultura Sports. Available at: https://www.brandhk.gov.hk/uploads/
brandhk/files/factsheets/Hong_Kong_Themes/Art_culture_sports_E_July%202019.pdf
(Accessed 10 August 2019).

Cai, P. (2017). Understanding the Belt and Road Initiative. Report to Lowry Institute. Available at: www.lowyinstitute.org/sites/default/files/documents/Understanding%20China's%
20Belt%20and%20Road%20Initiative_WEB_1.pdf (Accessed 11 November 2018).

Chow, J. (24 March 2013). Chinese create tax-free zone for art: Project aims to stoke global
interest in culture, entertainment. *Wall Street Journal*. Available at: www.wsj.com/articles/
SB10001424127887323854904578261171833355606 (Accessed 7 November 2018).

Chu, S. Y. (2010). Brand Hong Kong: Asia's world city as method? *Visual Anthropology*,
24(1–2), 46–58.

Cudny, W. (2016). Festivalisation of Urban Spaces: Factors, Processes and Effects. Cham:
Springer.

Dezan Shira and Associates 6 December 2016 Import-Export Taxes and Duties in China.
China Briefing. Available at:www.china-briefing.com/news/import-export-taxes-and-
duties-in-china/ (Accessed 7 November 2018).

du Cros, H. (2017). The evolving nature of commercial art fairs. In J. Laing and W. Frost
(eds). *Exhibitions, Trade Fairs and Industrial Events* (pp. 51–64). London: Routledge.

du Cros, H., & Jolliffe, L. (2014). *The Arts and Events*. Abingdon and London: Routledge,
(Taylor and Francis).

du Cros, H., & Leong, S. (2011). A New Approach to Arts Policy Formulation that directly
supports the Arts and Cultural Identity in Hong Kong". The Asian Conference on Arts
and Humanities, IAFOR, Osaka, Japan 27–30 May 2011. Available at: http://iafor.org/
acah_proceedings.html pp. 193–205. (Accessed 11 November 2018).

Geng, O. (28 July 2014). Artful Dodge: Why Chinese collectors are 'Borrowing' their
own pieces. *Wall Street Journal*. Available at: https://blogs.wsj.com/chinarealtime/2014/
07/28/artful-dodge-why-chinese-collectors-are-borrowing-their-own-pieces/ (Accessed
7 November 2018).

Gerritsen, D., & van Olderen, R. (2014). *Events as a Strategic Marketing Tool*. Oxfordshire, UK: CABI.

Getz, D. (2008). Event tourism: Definition, evolution, and research. *Tourism Management*,
29(3), 403–428.

Govers, R., & Cull, N. (9 November 2018). *Place Branding and Public Diplomacy: Overview*. Available at: www.palgrave.com/gp/journal/41254.

HKAGA. (2018). Art week. Available at: www.hk-aga.org/hong-kong-art-week-2018/
(Accessed 19 November 2018).

HKTB. (2018). Arts Month. Available at: www.discoverhongkong.com/au/see-do/events-
festivals/highlight-events/hong-kong-arts-month.jsp (Accessed 19 November 2018).

HKTB. (2019) Hong Kong Art Week. Available at: http://www.discoverhongkong.com/us/
see-do/events-festivals/events-calendar/details.jsp?id=74581 (Accessed 10 August 2019).

HKTDC. (25 June 2017). Art Hub for the Belt and Road. YouTube video. Available at:
www.youtube.com/watch?v=-eJDgOnyRVQ (Accessed 9 November 2018).

HKTDC. (2018). About us. Available at: https://aboutus.hktdc.com/en (Accessed 15
January 2019).

Konings, J. Trade (25 October 2018). Impacts of the Belt and Road Initiative. Belt and
Road Hong Kong. Available at: https://secure.beltandroad.hktdc.com/en/insights/trade-
impacts-belt-and-road-initiative (Accessed 7 November 2018).

Lau, J. (24 March 2016). Embracing the Spotlight. *International New York Times*, S1.

Manzenreiter, W. (2010). The Beijing games in the Western imagination of China: The weak power of soft power. *Journal of Sport & Social Issues*, 34(1), 29–48.

McDonald, J. (2018a). 29 September 2018. A tale of two fairs. Spectrum, *Sydney Morning Herald*: 10–11.

McDonald, J. (2018b). 7–8 April 2018. Art after a fashion. Spectrum, *Sydney Morning Herald*: 10–11.

Rectanus, M. W. (2002). *Culture Incorporated: Museums, Artists, and Corporate Sponsorships*. Minneapolis: University of Minnesota Press.

Richards, G., & Palmer, R. (2010). *Eventful Cities: Cultural Management and Urban Revitalisation*. London: BH/Elsevier.

Seno, A. (2013). Museums for the many is Hong Kong's new mantra. *The Art Newspaper* 25–26 May 2013: 4.

Shaw, C. (6 October 2017). Now Art Galleries in Hong Kong have a purpose-built alternative to cramped office buildings or remote industrial lofts. *South China Morning Post* Available at: www.scmp.com/lifestyle/article/2113985/now-art-galleries-hong-kong-have-purpose-built-alternative-cramped-office (Accessed 19 November 2018).

Sui, J. G. (5 November 2018). The Sculpture of Professor Sui Jianguo – Beijing. % November 2018, Sydney Sculpture Conference, Sydney Opera House, Sydney.

Sylvestor, C. (2016). *Art/Museums. International Relations Where We Least Expect It*. Abingdon and London: Routledge.

Vuletic, D. (2018). The Eurovision song contest in musical diplomacy of authoritarian states. In F. Ramel and C. Prévost-Thomas (eds). *International Relations, Music and Diplomacy Sounds and Voices on the International Stage* (pp. 213–234). London: Palgrave-Macmillan.

Wang, X. (2012). Editorial. 20 May 2012. *South China Morning Post*: 14.

Wierbicki, D., & Rottermund, A. (19 February 2016). Freeports for the Art World. Wealth Management.Com. Available at: www.wealthmanagement.com/art-auctions-antiques-report/freeports-art-world (Accessed 7 November 2018).

Yung, D., & Zuni. (28 September 2018). Hong Kong Belt-Road City-to-City Cultural Exchange Conference 2018 (Asian Strategy): Cultural Think Tanks. *South China Morning Post*. Available at: www.scmp.com/presented/lifestyle/topics/zuni-hkbr-conference-think-tank/article/2165761/hong-kong-belt-road-city (Accessed 9 November 2018).

11 Conclusions

Waldemar Cudny

This book is an edited volume dedicated to the issue of event marketing in relation to cities. The first chapter presents how to understand the concept of event marketing. On the one hand, event marketing can be treated as an issue strictly related to events, i.e. to the process of their proper organization and successful selling. Event marketing understood in this way derives from product marketing. In this case, the product is an event, and marketing consists of its proper construction, organization, promotion, and implementation so that the event reaches the intended goals, including attraction of many visitors including tourists (Hoyle 2002). In this sense, research on event marketing can be included in event studies and event management (Getz and Page 2016).

The second understanding of event marketing includes the situation in which an event is a tool for the promotion and creation of a brand of other products. These products are presented, used, and promoted during an event. Many companies use existing events (e.g. through sponsoring) and even organize their own events (Jaworowicz and Jaworowicz 2016; Raj et al. 2013; Wohlfeil and Whelan 2006) for the purposes of their marketing campaigns. In this case, we are dealing with event marketing as one of the means of promoting and creating a brand of companies and their products. In this sense, research on event marketing should be included in the field of marketing of companies and products (Kotler and Armstrong 2010).

However, one more approach to event marketing exists. It includes the situation in which the event is used to brand and promote a place or space (country, region, city). Organization of events becomes part of the cultural and entertainment or sports offering of the given place. In this way, the area is enriched with a new product which develops and creates its brand. Events are therefore an element of many socio-economic and branding strategies in various urban areas around the world (Ashworth 2009). Moreover, events are widely commented on in the media. Therefore, apart from the development function, they offer promotional benefits for host places (Cudny 2016). Research devoted to this understanding of event marketing (as related to places) should be included in place or city marketing, as well as city and place branding (see Hubbard and Hall 1998; Kavaratzis 2004; Kotler et al. 1999). This book considers case studies representing the latter understanding of event marketing.

In the first chapter, the notion of place event marketing in relation to cities was characterized. The issue was defined as activities aimed at enriching the product of a given city by offering its consumers a well-chosen, interesting, and diverse portfolio of events. This activity also includes the promotion of a city through the events. This, in turn, enables marketing communication with the recipients of urban products and shapes a positive image and brand of a city. Place event marketing is, therefore, a comprehensive group of activities related to city branding and city promotion and can be part of long-term urban development and promotional strategies. Place event marketing in cities includes planning, organizing, and promoting urban events, but its goal should be the realization of broadly defined host city development goals and the needs of the urban products' consumers.

This book includes case studies presenting the impact of events on the promotion and branding of cities in North America (Fredericton and Saint John in Canada), South America (Rio de Janeiro in Brasil), Europe (Umeå in Sweden, Lublin in Poland, Berga in Spain, Athens in Greece), Africa (Oudtshoorn in South Africa), and Asia (Macao and Hong Kong Special Administrative Regions in China). The broad portfolio of event types was presented through the case study chapters, including sports events through various festivals to events connected with the development of business projects.

In Chapter 2, Håkan Appelblad characterized how the organization of Umeå2014 – the European Capital of Culture (ECoC) in Umeå – affected the city's socio-economic situation, promotion, and brand. Appelblad's chapter proved that the city of Umeå (Sweden) gained several important benefits in terms of branding and promotion from the organization of Umeå2014. Among the advantages of hosting the event were the rich cultural yearlong programme, co-creation of cultural projects with international partners as well as with local and regional cultural operators, and large investments in cultural facilities. Organizing Umeå2014 strengthened the city's cultural sector and caused growth in the number of visitors. The event also strengthened the image of the city; however, some opinions presented by the members of the local community included concerns about a lack of inclusion and the promotion of mainstream culture instead of alternative forms of locally based culture.

Chapter 3, written by Alba Colombo and Natàlia Cantó-Milà, presented the relation between the promotion and branding of the city of Berga (Spain) through the La Patum event and its authenticity. La Patum in Berga is a traditional cultural event related to the Corpus Christi celebrations. The event was declared a UNESCO Intangible Cultural Heritage of Humanity in 2005 and is an important tourist asset of the city, drawing the attention of many tourists. The event has a significant impact on the increase in Berga's attractiveness to tourists. It attracts many visitors to the city and promotes it as a cultural and tourist destination. However, it should be remembered that what attracts visitors is the authenticity of the event and the strong relationships resulting from the experiences associated with participation in La Patum. The study, however, also revealed that there is some contra-reaction to rising event tourism. Some respondents taking part in the research mentioned that there are now too many people during La Patum as a result of the popularity of the event; therefore, some of them even advised that the city should limit access to the event instead of promoting it further. The study confirmed the importance of even small events for increasing the attractiveness and promotion of a city. However, on the other hand, it indicated the need for a reasonable approach to the use of events in city branding. If they are exploited too much, the authenticity may be lost, which is one of the most important threats to their attractiveness.

Chapter 4, written by Zafeirenia Brokalaki and Roberta Comunian, characterized how the participatory grassroots art events affected the perceptions, sentiments, and attitudes towards a place. The chapter focused on the case study of the Athens Fringe Festival (Greece). The results showed that participatory art festivals allow people to familiarise themselves with the city and experiment and interact with other spectators as well as to discover and control the surrounding urban space. Such festivals as the Athens Fringe Festival stimulate place attachment of event participants and create spatial experiences, perceptions, and sentiments towards the host city. This induces a sense of authenticity, security, possession, and post-event nostalgia in event participants and positively influences the city brand and visitors' loyalty.

The authors highlighted the importance of grassroots events in the creation of place attachment and brand development. They postulate that the creation of grassroots participatory cultural events may be a good strategy for city branding and promoting based on authenticity. This may well be used instead of the very popular copycat strategy of culture-led regeneration. The authors, moreover, proposed that similarly to Mould's (2015) subversive creativity idea, a new category of events may be created i.e. subversive participatory festivals. Such festivals have a high potential to question existing urban politics and develop urban creativity, social interaction, and spatial reconfiguration. However, in order to fulfil the aforementioned functions, such events must be authentic, independent, and based on grassroots activity.

Chapter 5, written by Aleksandra Kołtun aimed to analyze whether outdoor cultural festivals organized in the Polish city of Lublin improved the image and brand of their host city. Based on the multi-method approach (including observation, expert opinions, document analysis, and questionnaires), the chapter clearly proved that such festivals, when properly planned, organized and promoted, are a good offer for city users and an important part of city branding strategy based on culture-led regeneration. The four large festivals which were investigated brought a significant number of visitors to the city of Lublin. Moreover, they were an interesting cultural and socializing offer for city inhabitants. The festivals were an important generator of event tourism in Lublin. As the research showed, the events positively influenced the image of Lublin as a city. The positive branding impact of these festivals was confirmed in other investigations concerning Lublin's image. As the author of the chapter stated, in 2007 the city of Lublin did not evoke any particular associations. However, in 2015 Lublin (thanks to the festivals, among other things) could already be described as a "cultural melting pot", offering a wide range of attractive events and activities.

Chapter 6, written by Lee Jolliffe and Nancy Chesworth, focused on the case study of Fredericton and Saint John, located in New Brunswick, Canada. The authors investigated how different events (five organized in Fredericton and seven in Saint John), created with the help of destination management organizations (DMOs) co-created city brands. This is another chapter, along with the afore-mentioned case of Umeå, devoted to medium-scale cities. Presented events draw from host cities' tradition, history, and heritage. They are organized in historic city districts with the help of two small DMOs. The chapter's results demonstrated the importance of culture and arts events as part of destination branding initiatives. The mixture of distinctive historic spaces paired with interesting events proved to be a good path to city brand strengthening and the rebranding of the former industrial urban image. Social media and influencers (e.g. bloggers) supported by local DMOs were successfully used in the cities' brand creation.

Chapter 7, written by Anne-Marie Broudehoux, presented the issues of Rio de Janeiro's branding through events. The author discovered the top-down policies of urban image construction through the use of sporting mega-events. The chapter presented the example of Rio de Janeiro's hosting of the 2014 FIFA World Cup and the 2016 Olympic Games. According to the chapter, the endeavours lead-ing to the image reconstruction in Rio de Janeiro led to a fabricated, seductive, highly exclusive, and inauthentic place image. This image of a tropical paradise of excitement and leisure, consistently implemented by the city authorities, avoided certain problems such as violence, drug-related crime, and social inequalities. The chapter also showed that the top-down narrative was opposed by an insurgent rebranding movement. As stated in the chapter the results documented "various ingenious strategies to counter the event-spectacle, that allowed victims of its exclusive vision to regain a part of their dignity, of their right to representation as part of their city's image and of their right to participate in urban life". The chap-ter perfectly shows that in some cases copy-paste branding models don't work well and could be a source of social insurgency as well as bottom-up branding counter-narrations.

Chapter 8, written by Ronnie Donaldson and Henry Duckitt, used the example of the branding impacts of non-metropolitan music festivals in the Western Cape Province of South Africa. The authors presented a spatio-temporal analysis of three categories of music festivals (youth music festivals, classical music fes-tivals, and community music festivals) in the Western Cape province. On this basis, the authors investigated art festivals hosted by the town of Oudtshoorn. The municipality endeavours are to promote the town as an art and culture centre, creating economic and social opportunities through the arts and heritage. These endeavours aim to change the image of the town, which is currently strongly asso-ciated with the ostrich industry and the Cango Caves. Therefore, the well-known national art festival Klein Karoo Nasionale Kunstefees (the Little Karoo National Arts Festival) (KKNK), which is organized in Oudtshoorn, is strongly supported by the local authorities. Additionally, the town hosts a smaller art event called the

Klein Karoo Klassique (KKK), which is a classical music festival organized since 2009. As shown by the chapter, music festivals in the Western Cape province are an important element of localities' promotion and brand creation. Moreover, they also induce tourism to rural spaces, towns, and cities in the region. Regarding the town of Oudtshoorn, the KKNK festival receives maximum media exposure, induces tourism, and is an important element of the urban brand. Its younger brother, the KKK event, is branded as a classy winter event. It is presented mostly in regional media and is attended by fewer tourists; however, the festival has a group of devoted fans interested in classical music. These events are good examples of how art festivals could be used in renewing image and visitors' interest in smaller destinations.

Chapter 9 is authored by Xu Ye and characterizes the case study of Macao Special Administrative Region (China). As a major gambling destination, the city has a high position in the tourism market and the image of the world's gambling capital. However, in order to ensure long-term tourism development, the Macao SAR government exerted a lot of pressure to strengthen the destination image with the use of several branding pillars e.g. historic, leisure tourism and business events, gaming, and transport, indicating the significance of non-gaming entertainment. The chapter presents the case study of the Lusofonia cultural festival, based on Portuguese culture. Macao was once a Portuguese colony and still has a Portuguese-speaking community and Portuguese-style architecture. The festival is a good opportunity to show this multicultural heritage and is a very interesting leisure and cultural opportunity for inhabitants as well as tourists. As shown by the research conducted among the visitors in Macao, the festival is an important asset of the city. Thanks to such events as the Lusofonia Festival, visitors perceive Macao not only as a gaming centre but also as a colorful, multicultural destination. For tourists, the event is an important attraction while, for the city, it is part of its image, displaying the city's versatile culture, establishing the brand, and satisfying tourists' needs.

Chapter 10 is devoted to the role of Hong Kong art events in the branding of the city as an art hub for China's Belt and Road Initiative (BRI). The chapter, written by Hilary du Cros and Lee Jolliffe, proved that art events and art institutions may be used to brand metropolises, but they can simultaneously impact the image of large economic and infrastructural projects like BRI. As stated by the authors, the "Hong Kong art and event scene is being developed and branded through events as an arts hub by a number of actors that include those in the trade, investment, and art communities against the backdrop and long-term agenda of China's BRI policy". The development of the art scene in Hong Kong, including event sector, is a good opportunity for China's soft power creation, but the intensive use of art events in the city for BRI branding is rather an opportunity for the future.

The examples presented in this book are a good start for further analysis of the impacts of events on branding and the promotion of urban spaces as part of the place event marketing process. Event sectors are developing very dynamically and will be increasingly used for event marketing in cities. Further research should not only include other case studies but should also present diverse topics. Future research directions should include:

- Residents' and other urban products consumers' reactions (e.g. creative people, entrepreneurs) to event marketing. It should be remembered that city marketing is not only applied to tourists.
- Multidimensional impacts of place event marketing on place image.
- The reasons cities and other places decide to implement event marketing endeavours. It should be explained what they try to achieve and how it is correlated with their development strategies.
- The results of event marketing activities, including analysis of the media impact of event organization, should be analyzed.
- Negative impacts of event marketing on places.

In order to summarise the analysis in this book, a model was constructed (Figure 11.1). It presents factors that contribute to the development of place event marketing in cities. Then, the activities that make up the event marketing and their results for the broadly understood city branding and promotion are characterized. Among the factors, there is the desire to change an unfavourable city image (e.g. the image of an uninteresting post-industrial city) or to strengthen the existing image (even favourable) in order to gain new customers. The rise of place event marketing often results from the desire to expand the city offer by creating

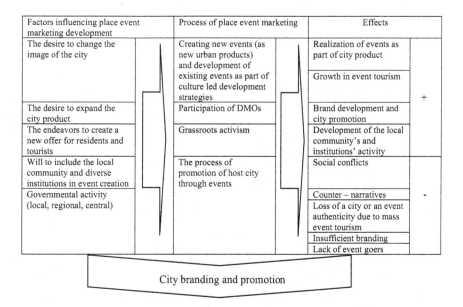

Figure 11.1 The structure of the place event marketing process

Source: Author elaboration

interesting urban experiences that can be used by residents or tourists. The analysis carried out through the book showed that it is favourable to implement event marketing activities based on grassroots activity and in cooperation with local destinations management organizations (DMOs). Of course, in many cases, the activity of local (as well as regional or central) governments is most important for the development of place event marketing in urban areas.

Place event marketing in cities involves the creation of new events and the development of those already existing as part of the urban product (Figure 11.1). This process involves DMOs and the local community (activists, artists). These activities are often an element of grassroots activism.

Place event marketing also includes promotional activities that shape the image of the city and its brand. The effects include urban product development, brand creation and city promotion, tourism development, and the inclusion of different institutions and people in the development of the city brand. As the examples presented in this book show, some events (if they are badly organized and carried out) may have a negative impact on cities and their brands. Negative impacts include social conflicts induced by event organization, counter-narrations, and loss of authenticity.

References

Ashworth, G. (2009). The instruments of place branding: How is it done? *European Spatial Research and Policy*, 16(1), 9–22.
Cudny, W. (2016). *Festivalisation of Urban Spaces: Factors, Processes and Effects*. Cham: Springer.
Getz, D., & Page, S. J. (2016). *Event Studies: Theory, Research and Policy for Planned Events*. London and New York: Routledge.
Hoyle, L. H. (2002). *Event Marketing: How to Successfully Promote Events, Festivals, Conventions, and Expositions*. New York: John Wiley & Sons.
Hubbard, P., & Hall, T. (1998). The entrepreneurial city and the new urban politics. In T. Hall and P. Hubbard (eds). *The Entrepreneurial City: Geographies of Politics, Regime and Representation* (pp. 1–23). Chichester: John Wiley & Sons.
Jaworowicz, M., & Jaworowicz, P. (2016). *Event marketing w zintegrowanej komunikacji marketingowej*. Warszawa, SA: Difin.
Kavaratzis, M. (2004). From city marketing to city branding: Towards a theoretical framework for developing city brands. *Place Branding*, 1(1), 58–73.
Kotler, P., & Armstrong, G. (2010). *Principles of Marketing*. Pearson: Prentice Hall.
Kotler, P., Asplund, C., Rein, I., & Heider, D. (1999). *Marketing Places Europe: Attracting Investments, Industries, Residents and Visitors to European Cities, Communities, Regions and Nations*. London: Pearson Education.
Mould, O. (2015). *Urban Subversion and the Creative City*. London: Routledge.
Raj, R., Walters, P., & Rashid, T. (2013). *Events Management: Principles and Practice*. London: Sage.
Wohlfeil, M., & Whelan, S. (2005). Consumer Motivations to Participate in Marketing Events: The Role of Predispositional Involvement, Association for Consumer Research, Duluth 2006- Available at: www.acrwebsite.org/volumes/eacr/vol7/EuropeanVolume7_16.pdf

Index

Note: Page numbers in *italics* indicate figures and in **bold** indicate tables on the corresponding pages.

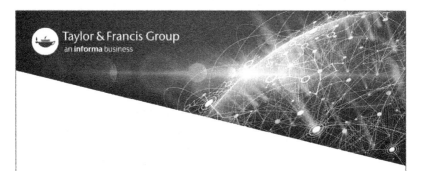